Georges Bataille

Titles in the series Critical Lives present the work of leading cultural figures of the modern period. Each book explores the life of the artist, writer, philosopher or architect in question and relates it to their major works.

In the same series

Michel Foucault
David Macey

Jean Genet
Stephen Barber

Pablo Picasso
Mary Ann Caws

Franz Kafka
Sander L. Gilman

Guy Debord
Andy Merrifield

Frank Lloyd Wright
Robert McCarter

James Joyce
Andrew Gibson

Noam Chomsky
Wolfgang B. Sperlich

Jorge Luis Borges
Jason Wilson

Erik Satie
Mary E. Davis

Georges Bataille

Stuart Kendall

REAKTION BOOKS

For Vanessa Corrêa

Published by Reaktion Books Ltd
33 Great Sutton Street
London EC1V ODX, UK

www.reaktionbooks.co.uk

First published 2007

Printed and bound in Great Britain
by Cromwell Press, Trowbridge, Wiltshire

British Library Cataloguing in Publication Data
Kendall, Stuart
Georges Bataille. – (Critical lives)
  1. Bataille, Georges, 1897–1962 2. Bataille, Georges,
  1897–1962 – Influence
  I. Title
  194

  ISBN–13: 978 1 86189 327 7
  ISBN–10: 1 86189 327 2

Contents

Introduction: *Ecce Homo*   7

1   Abandonment   13

2   An Attempt at Evasion   22

3   Violence and Sumptuosity   32

4   Underground Man   43

5   *Incipit Parodia*   52

6   Heterology   66

7   Excremental Philosopher   80

8   The Democratic Communist Circle   86

9   Crisis   104

10   Counter Attack   118

11   Acéphale   129

12   The College of Sociology   139

13   War   151

14   Beyond Poetry   159

15   Between Surrealism and Existentialism   174

16   *Summa*   184

17   Unfinished   198

References   211
Select Bibliography   229
Acknowledgements   231
Photo Acknowledgements   233

Georges Bataille in 1961.

Introduction: *Ecce Homo*

Opposition is true friendship.
William Blake

Shortly after the death of Georges Bataille in 1962 the French
Ministry of Culture banned his final book, *Les Larmes d'Eros*
(*The Tears of Eros*), as an outrage to morality. The book sketches a
history of desire from prehistory to the present, largely in images
from the tradition. The most shocking images – those of a Chinese
torture, the Leng Tch'e – were erotic only in a sadistic sense that
most readers would hardly embrace or even recognize. In Bataille's
argument, the images evidenced the proximity of opposites –
sex and death, horror and delight, religious deliverance and
the violation of communal law. In the proximity of opposites,
Bataille discerned a capacity for infinite reversal, a passage from
the 'most unspeakable to the most elevated', a deliverance from
the most acute agony to the highest ecstasy.[1]

Over a lifetime of writing – cut short by death – no other
book with Bataille's name on its cover had ever been banned.
For forty years he had secreted his identity behind pseudonyms
and published his most scandalous works in small, rather
sumptuous, limited editions. The many writings that he did sign –
essays, novels, poetry; studies in economics, anthropology and
aesthetic criticism – were scandalous only to careful and attentive
readers. As an employee of the Bibliothèque Nationale, Bataille

could not afford to be prosecuted: he would have lost his job. More interestingly however, the drama of pseudonymous publication – the play of identities, the revelatory masks – was itself central to Bataille's literary endeavour. Bataille did not write for recognition, far from it: He wrote to disrupt the assumptions and processes that might make recognition possible. He wrote to ruin words, to reveal the ultimate impossibility of complete communication and to open a sphere wherein the impossible – the heterogeneous, the different, the sacred – could be communicated. In keeping with this strategy, in *The Tears of Eros* Bataille spoke without speaking, through the arrangement of images: his final testament was largely a silent one. That his book was banned only testified to the virulence of its contagious power, doubling its silent allure.

A counter-movement was, however, already in motion. A fount of recognition had begun to flow; an effect of friendship and necessity. In 1963 *Critique* – the journal Bataille founded in 1946 – memorialized him in the first of its special issues.[2] The journal gathered the memorial voices of old friends – Alfred Métraux, Jean Bruno, Raymond Queneau, Pierre Klossowski, Michel Leiris, André Masson, Jean Piel, Jean Wahl and Maurice Blanchot – together with voices from a new generation of French intellectuals who found Bataille's work particularly necessary – Roland Barthes, Philippe Sollers and Michel Foucault. Foucault would go on to introduce Bataille's *Oeuvres complètes*: 'We know it today: Bataille is one of the most important writers of his century.'[3]

The post-structuralist trend in Western thought is in fact impossible to imagine without him. Roland Barthes, Jacques Derrida, Jean-François Lyotard, Julia Kristeva and Jean Baudrillard each wrote about Bataille – and under his influence – on numerous occasions. In 1972 the Tel Quel group organized a week-long conference on Bataille and Artaud. It would be the first of many such conferences held in the decades since Bataille's death. During the 1980s the art critics associated with the American journal

October devoted a special issue to Bataille, signalling the centrality of his work to their enterprise.[4]

New editions of Bataille's works and new books and anthologies about him continue to appear. The reasons for this ongoing fascination – a fascination which shows no signs of abating – are myriad, confusing, and conflicted. They are primal – Bataille was among the foremost writers of pornographic fiction in his era, he was a devotee of horror and atrocity; an extreme thinker for extreme times. And they are poignant – Bataille fashioned a method for the analysis of whole systems that may yet prove to be among the most essential critical developments of the twentieth century; he wrote with endless compassion for human frailty and devotion to human freedom. As a psychologist and philosopher of language, a novelist and a poet, a religious devotee and a mystic, he explored the uses and limits of knowledge and communication in human life more diversely, more thoroughly than anyone else in his century. No other writer contributed so substantially to so wide a range of fields.

Yet, like his progenitor, Friedrich Nietzsche, Georges Bataille lived a profoundly untimely life. Always on the margins, he was never at home in his time, and his life and work remain obscure to us even now.

Bataille wrote against – violently against – each of the main intellectual, artistic and political trends of his era. An atheist in a deeply Catholic country, he rejected Surrealism, Marxism and Existentialism in turn. To Bataille, Surrealism was an inconsequential idealism, a frenzy in art rather than in life; Marxism failed to found its materialism in the energies animating the material world and Sartrean Existentialism remained bound by a theory of consciousness that had been betrayed by the passage of time. In the structuralist era Bataille pushed structuralist methods to the point of paradox, of contradiction. He rejected both psychoanalysis and the French School of Sociology as incomplete, while retaining their essential insights, refashioned to his needs. Bataille was not simply an atheist: to borrow a phrase from *L'Expérience intérieure* (*Inner Experience*), he threw himself on the throat of his god, he sacrificed his own highest values, and the values of his time, in an act of creative destruction.

Bataille did not seek new knowledge. Rather, he sought experience, sovereign experience, which for him meant the experience of boundless freedom: freedom from language, discipline, utility, culture and identity; an impossible freedom. 'The issue' as Bataille wrote, was 'not that of the attainment of a goal, but rather of escape from those traps which goals represent.'[5]

To simply say that Bataille wrote against the major currents of thought in his time is to overlook his methods. He wrote against these currents by writing within them, by writing in response to them, in response to both the dead writers of the tradition and the living legacy – the disciples – of those writers. Most importantly, he wrote in the context of friendship.

When it is a question of the greatest influences on Bataille's life and work, one always encounters both a body of work, like that of Nietzsche, and a personal connection to that work, like the Russian émigré philosopher Lev Shestov, who schooled Bataille in Nietzsche's thought in the early 1920s. Alfred Métraux introduced Bataille to Durkheim and Mauss; Michel Leiris and André Masson brought him into contact with the Surrealist movement; Adrien Borel was his psychoanalyst and Alexandre Kojève tutored Bataille – and several other influential members of his generation – in the intricacies of Hegel's *Phenomenology*. Bataille then developed his thought in conversation with these individuals and in distinction from them. Public conversations – lectures – were essential to this man who published far more in timely but ephemeral journals than he did in 'lasting' books. Bataille's thought, his work, is inseparable from his life.

Bataille lived and wrote in friendship and betrayal, each word and gesture marking both the proximity of shared language and concern, and the distance of biological and intellectual distinction. Nietzsche observed: 'To understand one another, it is not enough that one use the same words; one also has to use the same words for the same species of inner experiences; in the end one has to have one's experiences in *common*.'[6]

Bataille's life and work were an exploration of this impossible commonality. They were ultimately a contagious evocation of what he termed the community of those who have no community, a phrase which recognizes the impossibility of recognition.[7] His closest friends – Michel Leiris, André Masson, Colette Peignot, Patrick Waldberg, Maurice Blanchot, René Char, Dionys Mascolo and Robert Antelme among them – shared the experience of this hopeless search, this openness to the impossible.

Has Bataille been understood? His pre-war writings were rescued from oblivion a generation ago, with the publication of his *Oeuvres complètes* beginning in 1970. These writings and his later books – even those published under pseudonyms – were gathered together along with thousands of pages of notes and drafts for books he never completed. New manuscripts continue to come to light, much to the delight of the thesis mill. This despite the fact that Bataille was a profoundly non-academic writer.

At this point all of his books have been translated into English, though some of them have passed, once more, from print. Many of his essays still remain to be gathered in translation and, unfortunately, many of his principle works are in desperate need of retranslation.[8] Nevertheless, the initial work of assimilation has been accomplished.

But the question remains: has Bataille been understood? The obvious answer – given the pages that follow – is that he has not. Contemporary literature has failed to fully ingest Bataille's lessons. Indeed, the novelistic tradition, after the experiments of the *nouveau roman* – now fifty years out of date – has returned to the comforts of representation, as if Bataille's work, and most of twentieth-century writing, never took place. Worse, philosophers still too often read Bataille as a philosopher; art historians read him as an art historian; novelists as a novelist. They select concepts from a corpus that only reluctantly yields discrete concepts. These strategies have proved fatal to a thought predicated on its resistance to specialization, its rejection of conceptual utility. Perhaps we will never escape the lure of the same: the same disciplines, institutions, limits. Yet, following Bataille, as Foucault does, we must observe that these limits offer us limitless fields for the expression of our freedom.

Critique – now under the direction of Philippe Roger – recently celebrated its sixtieth anniversary. This is one among several signs that in many ways Bataille's future has only just begun. This book hopes to relocate Bataille's words both in his time and in relation to his life, and to open the possibility of reading Bataille in the way that he wrote, which is to say, as a field of experience.

1

Abandonment

In 1913, when Georges Bataille was about fifteen, his father went mad.[1] Joseph-Aristide Bataille's syphilis was simply running its course. Contracted long ago, perhaps before he had abandoned his medical studies, certainly before he moved the family from Billom, in the volcanic Puy-du-Dôme, where Georges was born in 1897, to Reims where they now lived. Joseph-Aristide had been blind since before Georges' birth and paralysed for more than a decade. The unhappy conclusion of the disease was inevitable.

Confined to a chair, coursed by tabes, Joseph-Aristide lurched in agony. Decades later, Georges would remember his father's 'sunken eyes, his hungry bird's long nose, his screams of pain, soundless peals of laughter'.[2] And he would remember the degradation of the old man, despite his own attempts to help:

What upset me more was seeing my father shit a great number of times . . . It was very hard for him to get out of bed (I would help him) and settle on a chamber pot, in his nightshirt and, usually, a cotton nightcap (he had a pointed gray beard, ill kempt, a large eagle nose, and immense hollow eyes staring into space). At times, the 'lightning sharp pains' would make him howl like a beast, sticking out his bent leg, which he futilely hugged in his arms.[3]

This scatological primal scene was also reflected, echoed and extended for Georges in the way Joseph-Aristide 'looked while pissing':

> Since he could not see anything, his pupils very frequently pointed up into space . . . He had huge gaping eyes that flanked an eagle nose, and those huge eyes went almost entirely blank when he pissed, with a completely stupefying expression of abandon and aberration in a world that he alone could see and that aroused his vaguely sardonic and absent laugh.[4]

We can imagine the boy aiding the invalid in his agonies. As a youth, Georges loved his father, but as an adult, he found this love unnatural: most young boys loved their mothers, he thought in terms testifying to his recent psychoanalysis.[5] But Georges loved his father, at least early on, even in his father's degradation.

Georges was however, then and ever after, beset by terrifying and repeated dreams and memories associated with his father's 'pleasures' and with the cellar of the family home at 65c, rue du Faubourg-Cérès in Reims. (Reims, it might be remembered, is a city famous for its cellars: it is the capital of Champagne.) Bataille references the scene on several occasions but his notes are unclear: which part is a dream he experienced while young and which part a memory, whether of his youth, from his youth, or more recent. Over and over again in Bataille's life and writing, fiction folds over fact; definitive truth slips away.

> I remember having gone down into the cellar with my father, a candle in my hand. Dream of the bear with the candlestick. Terrors of childhood spiders, etc. linked to the memory of having my pants pulled down on my father's knees. A kind of ambivalence between the most horrible and the most magnificent. I see him spread his obscene hands over me

with a bitter and blind smile . . . I'm something like three years old, naked on my father's knees and my penis bloody like the sun . . . My father slaps me and I see the sun.[6]

Another note identifies his father with a bear dressed in bells and coloured ribbons, with a candle in his hand. The cellar stairs were apparently steep; the darkness and damp frightening; an abode of spiders and rats. Bataille associated the memory with the fireworks and festivities of 14 July – Bastille Day.[7]

But what really happened? Was Georges Bataille physically abused by his father? Once? Often? And if so, how did he react to this violation? What role did it come to play in his work? Throughout his life, Bataille would be fascinated equally by monstrous sexual criminals (like the paedophiliac Gilles de Rais) and by saints ravaged by God. Bataille's own erotic imagination – the imagination that produced *Histoire de l'oeil* (*Story of the Eye*), arguably the single greatest work of pornographic fiction written in the twentieth century – would eventually turn on the transgressive commingling of violation and ecstatic release. But the logic of submission inscribed within the narrative of abuse remains ambiguous. On one hand, the violator is clearly a monster, a monster who submits to his own most primal desire, and the violated youth is clearly abused. On the other, the violator is clearly pathetic and weak, and the youth overwhelmed by a pleasure that exceeds his capacity for understanding.

But again, what really happened? The evidence that remains is inconclusive, too fraught with fiction to convict Joseph-Aristide of a crime that may after all be nothing more than an appalling screen memory. In the 1940s, nearly forty years after the events in question, Bataille recognized that his father could only have negotiated the cellar stairs with great difficulty, if at all. Still another note recalls his father showing him 'the same affection' one day after returning from vacation.[8] Despite, or perhaps because of, the insistence and repetition of his recollections, Bataille shrouded the traumatic affection in the ambiguity of tragic fiction.

Bataille abruptly left school in December 1912. He was fifteen at the time and he'd never been a good student. His mind wandered easily. His classmates picked on him. Rather than do his assignments, he filled his notebooks with doodles; ceaselessly altering lines, shapes, comic profiles. Once he spent an entire class period colouring the shirt of a classmate with his pen.[9] When he was thirteen, he asked a fellow student who was laziest in their studies. He was. But of the whole school? Bataille again.[10] He claimed to have been 'almost expelled in January 1913'.[11] 'I lived for a long time as the martyr of indifference.'[12] (Much later, in the 1930s, he would doze off listening to Alexandre Kojève explicate Hegel's *Phenomenology*.[13])

He spent his days wandering in solitude, bicycling around the grape-laden, forested hills, and found that his previous affection for his father had slipped into 'a deep and unconscious hatred'.[14] Nowhere does he specify how or why.

That same spring, his father lost his mind. Georges' older brother Martial had already moved out of the family home, so Marie-Antoinette Bataille, Georges' mother, sent him to fetch a doctor. He returned quickly. The doctor undoubtedly did what little he could for the raving patient, but Georges' father was beyond help. When the physician stepped into the next room, Joseph-Aristide shouted after him, 'Doctor, let me know when you're done fucking my wife!'[15]

The inexplicable statement seared the son. Years later Georges wrote: 'For me, that utterance, which in a split second annihilated the demoralizing effects of a strict upbringing, left me with something like a steady obligation, unconscious and unwilled: the necessity of finding an equivalent to that sentence in any situation I happen to be in.'[16] The statement carries the contagious taint of

Bataille's entire thought and style: it contrasts a split second and a steady and lasting obligation; an unconscious, unwilled or chance event and a necessity and, most importantly, it functions by means of extreme reversals of logic and perspective (what is demoralizing about a strict upbringing?). Everything follows from here.

Joseph-Aristide's mad accusation ripped the mask off Georges' youth, off propriety, off his parents' and the doctor's faces; the respected, beloved faces of order and authority. The odious utterance opened a world of infinite freedom. Forever after, Bataille's obligation, his necessity, would be to find an equivalent of that phrase in every situation throughout his life: not only in every story and erotic encounter but in every action, every experience, every word, every thought. That which previously had been held on high would be brought low, that which was low would be raised on high. This slippage would characterize every experience. He would submit all of life to a similar trespass, debasement and inversion: an endless irregularity, ceaseless turning and overturning; an endless repetition of the rule of lawlessness.

Years later Bataille would remember his adolescent realization that his purpose would be to formulate a philosophy of paradox and to commit that philosophy to writing.[17] This purpose is Dostoevskian – Dostoevsky's 'underground man' had been a 'paradoxalist'[18] – and therefore perhaps anachronistic, for Bataille discovered Dostoevsky only later, but it finds its root in the words of his father. Ruminating on his father's blind suffering, his soundless laughter and screams of pain, Bataille admits: 'I think I'd like to be like him! How can I avoid questioning that tangible gloom?'[19] The young man who hated his once beloved father found a way to identify with him again, even in his degradation.

Georges returned to school the following October, this time as a boarder at a boy's school in Épernay on the Marne, 26 km south of Reims. Within a year he had completed the first part of his *baccalauréat*, passing in Romance languages without distinction.

A new friend from school, Paul Leclerc, seems to have awakened Georges' interest in Catholicism. Neither of Georges' parents believed: his father was irreligious, his mother indifferent.[20] Paul Leclerc was not only a 'fervent Christian', he was also close to Cardinal Luçon at Notre Dame de Reims.[21]

That summer, the summer of 1914, Georges attended morning mass at the cathedral. It was no ordinary summer. What would be the bloodiest war in history was an inevitability looming on the horizon. Georges' brother, Martial, was mobilized in July. Cardinal Luçon's morning mass was conducted for a cathedral full of soldiers come there to 'prepare themselves to die well'.[22] Georges would later claim to have accepted the sacrament of baptism in August 1914, the month the war began.[23]

Reims quickly became a city under siege: 'It was like being on the eve of a martyrdom.'[24] The phrase comes from Bataille's first publication, a pamphlet composed at the request of a friend in honour of the cathedral and sharing its name, *Notre Dame de Rheims*, but the notion will last, in his work, as an equation for understanding life during wartime.[25] In *Le Coupable* (*Guilty*), written twenty-four years later and during a different war, at a moment when the German invasion of Paris has forced him to flee to safety in the region where he was born, Bataille again speaks of 'saint's lives'.[26] War, for Bataille, portends apocalypse and unimaginable human suffering: along with revolution and religious ecstasy, he claims it provides the strongest of stimulants for the human imagination.[27]

During the week of 5–12 September German shelling destroyed much of the city and nearly destroyed the cathedral. Most of its windows were blown out, its masonry pitted and torn into crumbling shards of stone. The city overrun, the Germans set the cathedral on fire, but it remained standing. 'Today, she rises in desolation, mutilated,' Bataille wrote in 1918.[28]

Bataille and his mother fled with most of the city's inhabitants. He described the scene as one of 'convoys of people in flight driven

ahead of the invasion in distress as dire as human wretchedness; carts came one after the other crammed with furniture and families perched on top; along the roads there were burdened, pathetic people, letting all their destitution show like those for whom all hope is lost'.[29] Joseph-Aristide Bataille was too sick to be moved, the refugees left him with the housekeeper.

Living out of harm's way with Georges' maternal grandparents Antoine and Anne Tournadre in the tiny medieval mountain village of Riom-ès-Montagnes, south of Pascal's city, Clermont-Ferrand, mother and son received occasional letters from Joseph-Aristide, who was raving in his death throes within the year. The son wanted to return to his ailing father. He implored his mother to go back to Reims, but she refused. Even after the Germans had been forced out of the city she resolutely refused to return. Georges' piety deepened. He passed long hours praying in the cramped and brutally archaic gray stone church of St Georges in Riom-ès-Montagnes and wandering the countryside and surrounding villages. He considered pursuing a religious vocation, becoming a monk.

Bataille's mother, for her part, had fallen into a state of suicidal depression in 1915 that lasted for months. Having abandoned her blind and paralysed husband to almost certain death in a war ravaged city, thoughts of damnation and catastrophe haunted her. Georges had taken to twisting her wrists violently in an attempt to beat sense into her. Their relationship became so strained that he removed a pair of heavy candlesticks from his room, thinking she might attempt to murder him in his sleep. Once when she wandered off, they found her hanging in the attic, strangling on a rope that was not tight enough to kill her. One night, she tried to drown herself in a creek, but the water wasn't deep enough. Georges found his mother 'drenched up to her belt, her skirt *pissing* creek water'.[30]

Come autumn, through treatment by Jules Delteil, a local doctor and family friend, Marie had regained her senses enough to grant her son's wish to return to his father. When the family received news that Joseph-Aristide was unmistakably near death, Marie agreed to return to her husband. By then however it was too late. Joseph-Aristide Bataille died in Reims on 6 November 1915, in the company of his housekeeper, which is to say effectively alone. He even refused to see a priest. In Bataille's mind his blind, paralysed, syphilitic and obviously suffering father died alone but not merely alone; abandoned by his wife and son in his hour of greatest need. They arrived in time to bury him.

Solitude and abandonment: such is the truth of life for Georges Bataille, and the truth of death. For Bataille, human beings are not thrown into the world, they are abandoned into it. And this solitude is indistinguishable from the agony of war. Years later, in *Guilty*, Bataille ruminates on his own isolation: 'A wounded cry! I'm deaf in the depths of my solitude, its chaos surpasses that of war. Even cries of agony seem empty to me. My solitude is an empire in a struggle for possession: it is the forgotten star – alcohol and knowledge.'[31] Despite the passage of time, one might hear in that wounded cry the cry of Bataille's dying father, calling for help, the unanswered cry of an abandoned man dying in isolation. But the empire of solitude is also Pascal's empire: that of a man whose wretchedness is rooted in his inability to be alone, and his flight into the diversions of knowledge and alcohol.[32] Bataille's entire life is characterized by his flight from solitude, both from the solitude of his isolation from others – his flight into their groups, communities, arms – and his flight from the solitude of the creature alone in the crowd, the ontological isolation of the insufficient being, man. Bataille's corpus is the record of a man who understands the limits of community and that of a man who cannot be alone with himself. The dilemma of a paradoxicalist.

2

An Attempt at Evasion

Following his father's death, Georges sought a still deeper refuge in faith. Years later, he claimed: 'My piety was merely an attempt at evasion: I wanted to escape my destiny at any price, I was abandoning my father. Today, I know I am "blind", immeasurable, I am a man "abandoned" on the globe like my father.'[1]

As the war dragged on, and in the years immediately following it, Bataille's life was consumed by religious practice and by a longing for a religious vocation. Above all, Bataille longed to experience a call to the cloister; a call that never came. He hoped to be called to the monastery rather than to the offices of the priesthood. The life of a priest would be a public life, a life in the community of the church, while the life of a monk would be one of solitude, isolation and escape.[2]

In January 1916, and in ironic counterpoint to these hopes, Bataille was drafted for service in the 154th infantry regiment. Like his brother before him, he did his basic training in Rennes. Almost immediately he contracted a pulmonary illness and spent most of his time languishing in a hospital sickbed. He never made it to the front. This period was doubly portentous. Bataille would never again be healthy: ever after this his life would be physically tenuous, a delirious struggle for breath. Again and again Bataille would become intimately acquainted with a very Nietzschean gratitude, that of the convalescent, intoxicated by the recovery of his health.[3] Prolonged and recurrent illness serves as a reminder that human beings are frail, physical animals. A life of illness is a life lived on the fringes of participation, and hence of social utility. It is hardly surprising that Bataille would later characterize his existence as one of 'unemployed negativity'.[4]

Effectively sitting out the First World War, while nevertheless being trapped in a military hospital, also framed Bataille's future reflections on war. In such a scene, thoughts of war easily consumed the whole horizon of experience. High-minded ideals and political or social motivations seem empty; only the life of the individual combatant matters.

> My life and that of the soldiers among whom I lived, seemed to be enclosed in a kind of apocalypse, distant but nevertheless present among the hospital beds. In this vision, where rights and justice were inert words, WAR alone reigned, heavy, blind, itself, war alone, demanding blood, like Caesar seated in the tiers. In the shadows of that time, I search and searched: I found only a dead night, a human absence crying with anguish.[5]

Bataille kept a notebook for his reflections on the war, titling it *Ave Caesar*.

A wasted year later, he was discharged and returned to his life of piety in Riom-ès-Montagnes. Georges Delteil, the son of the doctor who treated Bataille's mother two years previously and a close friend of these and later years, wrote of the careful attention Bataille paid to his mother and of his religiosity: 'At 20 years old, in our Auvergne mountains, he lived the life of a saint, imposing a schedule of work and meditation on himself.'[6] One evening Bataille's prayers were so fervent that he failed to hear the sacristan lock the heavy doors of the tiny church.

The 'imposing schedule of work' mentioned by Delteil undoubtedly references Bataille's renewed academic studies. With the help of tutors from the nearby seminary at Saint-Flour, Jean Chastang in philosophy and Georges Rouchy in history and

German, Bataille passed his second *baccalauréat* exam, this one in philosophy, again without academic distinction. Bataille's real education in philosophy would not begin until he met Lev Shestov in Paris in 1923. For now, he 'picked up the essentials, on the go, from a textbook bound in green cloth'.[7] He apparently read some extracts from Nietzsche's *Zarathustra*, but they didn't make much of an impression.

He also returned to his 'old mania': writing. Before his military service Bataille had drafted a poem in free verse about Notre Dame des Rheims. Now he began a new poem about Jerusalem. It was to be an inspirational poem on the subject of the crusades. 'Nothing is real for me but Christian life,' he wrote to a friend, Jean-Gabriel Vacheron.[8] Later in the year, Vacheron encouraged Bataille to write a prose piece on Notre Dame Des Rheims, a patriotic inspirational pamphlet printed in St Flour for the 'youth of the Haute-Auvergne'.[9] Only the last of these early writings survives.

Bataille's letters to Vacheron reveal a young man torn by conflicting desires. On 10 January 1918, he confessed:

> I would like to realize a warm ideal family life – Christian of course – but still full of earthly joys, typical and honest. On the other hand, it is no less certain that I want to serve God not through actions that are as frequent and sincere as they should be but by offering my whole life – my entire will . . . I now see that if God asked me to, I would abandon everything, but I don't know how to make this decision on my own . . . There is in me a bliss that surpasses me and shatters me – and it is joyously that I am ready to sacrifice everything to God.[10]

The 'warm ideal family life' that Bataille evoked was not some vague or abstract desire. He had someone specific in mind: Marie Delteil, the sister of his friend Georges, the daughter of the doctor who had treated Bataille's mother. Marie apparently shared both

Georges's emotional longings and his religious aspirations: she wanted to become a nun. In a previous letter to Vacheron, Bataille admitted that he 'continues to dream' about Marie, and alluded to an activity he characterized as an 'old weakness', suggesting self-abuse.[11] Their courtship would continue until the end of 1919, caught in the limbo of uncertain faith.

Yet, above all, Bataille longed to experience a religious calling. He had converted in 1914 and had been confirmed in the private chapel of Monsigneur Lecoeur at St Flour in 1917, but he still longed for greater clarity of religious sentiment and purpose. He proposed entering into the seminary but put it off, claiming, perhaps honestly, that he could not leave his mother. (He had already abandoned his father, and could not bear abandoning both of his parents.)

Through Vacheron he met Jules Saliège, a canon at St Flour, future archbishop of Toulouse, and Eugène Théron, another canon at the principle seminary at St Flour. In June 1918, on the advice of Saliège, Bataille devoted a week to Christian meditation in La Barde, a Jesuit monastery in the Dordogne. To Vacheron, he reported: 'I lived five hurried, overheated, violent days at La Barde: I left with the conviction that there is no vocation for me and with real peace.'[12] This was not the end of his religiosity, of his longing for a vocation, or of his practice of meditation, but it did encourage him to redirect his energies and to find another career.

Raised without religious practice, Bataille had initially turned to it, as he would turn to all of his later intellectual and personal enthusiasms, with the encouragement of a close friend. The period of Bataille's most fervent piety coincided with that of the war and also with that of the greatest suffering of his parents: his father's descent into madness and abandonment and his mother's violent depression. Most importantly perhaps, Bataille's Christianity was a faith in waiting rather than in fulfilment; a faith longing for vocation rather than one firmly established in a Christian thought or practice; the faith, in short, of someone who wants to believe rather than that of someone who, with calm certainty, believes. Finally, this was a violent longing, a longing that more or less consumed Bataille's life during these years, that drove him to spend time in a monastery, and one that informed his budding literary vocation. Bataille's Christianity, however abortive, established many of the most basic figures and terms that he would later use to understand the human condition: infinite power and its absence, the abandonment of humanity in a world of suffering, the truth of desire and its relationship to the physical world.

Having failed to find a religious vocation within himself, Bataille shifted his focus away from the living church toward the study of its history and of the history of the era of its greatest dominance, the Middle Ages. In November 1918 Bataille entered the École des Chartes in Paris to become a medieval palaeographer and librarian. Once a disinterested and mediocre student, now he devoted himself to his work and was regularly near or at the top of his class.

For the first year he lived just off the Place St Sulpice in a small student apartment at 65 rue de Bonaparte. In his second year his mother and brother joined him in Paris, renting a larger apartment nearby at 85 rue de Rennes, where he would live, on and off, until his marriage eight years later.

Bataille's studies were not purely academic. They were an extension of his Christian thoughts and practices, and of his reflections on the social, moral and political forces shaping human conduct, particularly in extreme circumstances like war and romance. These circumstances were summarized for the medievalist by the term 'chivalry'. For his thesis project, inspired by Léon Gautier's *La Chevalerie*, Bataille prepared an edition of *L'Ordre de chevalerie*, an anonymous thirteenth-century didactic poem on the proper conduct of Christian knights. The poem regards knighthood as an extra-ecclesiastic equivalent to the priesthood, ordered by the same vocation and moral structure. For Bataille, the life of a knight could be – and in his estimation was – comparable to the life of a saint.[13]

The project animated him for several years, even taking him to London in 1920 for research purposes, and it is easy to see why. The poem offers a historical statement of many of the theological and moral problems that Bataille had recently been working through in both his writing and his life. Lacking a vocation, Bataille continued his Christian conduct outside the church. Chivalry provided a model for that conduct.

Thirty years later, Bataille returned to these materials in a long review essay published in *Critique*.[14] Having lost his faith in the intervening years, he could approach the topic without reserve. Chivalry, he argued, imposed a moral order on a band of essentially Germanic warriors whose physical passion opened a realm of unrestrained martial and sexual violence within an increasingly ordered world. The laws of chivalry, extending the laws of the church, sanctified that violence by restricting its social form, function and appearance. Chivalry thus embodied a clash of several cultures: military and religious, Germanic and Mediterranean, and, most importantly, that of the Dark Ages and that of an emergent post-medieval Europe. In Bataille's argument and in his corpus the career and crimes of Gilles de Rais represent the final flowering of this dark enterprise: a creature of excess, the last true knight errant. The appearance of a new knight – he of the sorrowful countenance – marks, with parody, the definitive end of the era and the birth of a new form of (unhappy) consciousness and expression, the modern novel.

Written forty years after his thesis and at the very end of his life, Bataille's edition of *Le Procés de Gilles de Rais* (*The Trial of Gilles de Rais*) can be read as the dark double of his early work, a horrific inversion of his original impetus. It celebrates, point for point, the inversion of his original concerns. This is not to say that the young man was not already grappling with the threat or even the demands of passionate frenzy. Indeed, such thoughts cannot have been far from his mind.

In a memorial piece written after Bataille's death, André Masson, a fellow student from the school and Bataille's neighbour (not the painter), mentions that Bataille's night-table book in 1919 was Remy de Gourmont's *Le Latin mystique*: a thousand-year history of ecclesiastic poetry in Latin, stretching in excerpts and de Gourmont's summaries from the end of Rome to the end of the Middle Ages. The collection demonstrates the diversity of this writing, its constant metamorphosis, as well as its consistency of theme and substance, primarily the obsession of the medieval mind with the burdens and eventual putrefaction of the flesh.

Bataille's chaste romance with Marie Delteil reached its terminus in August 1919. He had been away at school for a year and had apparently fallen in love with another woman. He nevertheless approached Marie's father, the doctor Jules Delteil, to ask for Marie's hand in marriage, fulfilling what seemed to be his obligation to her and her family. Having treated Bataille's mother and therefore understanding the medical details of Bataille's family history, the doctor refused. The son of a syphilitic madman had a 'greater chance than others of having an unhealthy child', as Bataille put it in a letter to his cousin, Marie-Louise. The letter reports these events in a tone of intense hopelessness. Bataille says that he is ready to die. Being a devout and proper young man, he will not pursue Marie without her family's blessing.[15]

Writing about his father in *Story of the Eye*, Bataille claims, 'so much horror makes you predestined'.[16] Dr Delteil's refusal certainly fulfils at least part of that destiny. His father's illness had determined this crucial turn in the life of the son. One can easily imagine the sense of physical malady and self-disgust, of powerlessness and potent exile from normal life that Bataille undoubtedly must have experienced in this moment. Three years later, in a letter to a friend, he says only that he 'lived certain hours . . .', passing over his suffering in silence.[17] Toward the end of his life he told his nephew Michel Bataille that Marie Delteil was the only woman he ever dreamt about.

Following this disappointment, Bataille's longing for escape inspired him to travel. The impulse was not so very different from the one that drove him into the cloisters of La Barde in 1918, and in fact his first trip was to another monastery, Quarr Abbey on the Isle of Wight. Other trips were planned or at least anticipated (to the Far East for example), and would continue to be for the next several years.

Quarr Abbey, where Bataille spent three days in October 1920, had only recently been established as a refuge for the monks of the abbey at Solesmes. In 1901 laws permitting cloistered communities in France changed drastically, forcing Benedictines like those from Solesmes to flee the country if they wished to continue living in seclusion from the surrounding secular society. Though the site boasted a rich monastic history dating to the Middle Ages, Quarr Abbey was re-established in 1901 by the French Benedictines, who initially leased several buildings and eventually, over the next two decades, built a new abbey. In 1922, two years after Bataille's visit, the French laws changed again, permitting the community to return to France. For a young man like Bataille, struggling with the depths of his faith, Quarr Abbey presented a vision and experience of the cloister as a site of religious refuge and escape: outside secular society, under the aura of persecution.

Years later, writing about his stay at the Abbey, Bataille remembered a

house surrounded by pines, beneath a moonlit softness, at the seashore; the moonlight linked to the medieval beauty of the service – everything which made me hostile toward a monastic life disappeared – in this place I only experienced the exclusion of the rest of the world. I imagined myself within the walls of the cloister, removed from agitation, for an instant imagining myself a monk, saved from jagged, discursive life.[18]

Despite the warmth of this memory, in the autobiographical note Bataille prepared for his publishers in the late 1950s he claimed that he 'brusquely lost his faith' after his visit to Quarr Abbey 'because his Catholicism caused a woman he loved to cry'.[19] Who was this woman? Marie Delteil, still lingering in his dreams? Some new love? We don't know.

Moreover, the notion that Georges Bataille lost his faith abruptly at this moment hardly coincides with his usual habits of thought. Bataille was not a romantic, and would have been unlikely to change his own thought in response to feelings of a woman. And his faith had, since its onset, been unstable. Its very violence testifies to this. His yearning for a religious vocation had gone unanswered for several years, despite his devotion and, in many ways, even his later atheism would be a violent response to that unanswered call. This is not to say that he was not thorough in his understanding and denunciation of faith, hardly.

Bataille visited Quarr Abbey on his way to London on a research trip connected with his thesis. While in London, Bataille met the then well-known French philosopher Henri Bergson at the house of some mutual friends. In preparation for the meeting, he read the only book by Bergson that he could find, *Le Rire* (*Laughter*). As Bataille would later write, both the book and the man disappointed him. In Bergson's description laughter is a human, carefree and shared phenomenon. Laughter doesn't occur in nature, it precludes emotional involvement and it presupposes a community of shared opinion. For Bataille, on the other hand, laughter interrupts commonality, shatters the rational indifference of the mind and negates the humanist ideal. Laughter is always 'intermingled with a pleasant sensuality'. Bergson's laughter is lighthearted comedy; Bataille's is convulsive and overwhelming. Recounting the meeting, he distinguishes himself from the philosopher by admitting that, even at that point in his life, he 'had an extreme mind'.[20]

Despite Bataille's disappointment with the philosopher and his work, the meeting proved momentous. Laughter unexpectedly presented itself as the 'key question'. 'In the beginning, I laughed, my life, emerging from a long Christian piety with a springlike bad faith, dissolved in laughter.'[21] 'Laughing at the universe liberated my life,' he says in *Guilty*.[22] In 'Nonknowledge, Laughter, and Tears', a lecture from 1953, he said: 'Insofar as I am doing philosophical work, my philosophy is a philosophy of laughter . . . It is a philosophy that doesn't concern itself with problems other than those that have been given to me in this precise experience.'[23]

Bataille's insistence on the *experience* of laughter should be noted, but it should not lead us to confine his entire thought or experience to the realm of laughter, even in its foundational impulse. Laughter epitomizes the experience of reversal: as when his father shouted 'Doctor, let me know when you're done fucking my wife!' In such moments dignity slips away. What was once held on high has been brought low.

Nietzsche too had announced his own loss of faith – and indeed the death of god – in a book of laughter, his *gaya scienza*. But Nietzsche's laughter bespeaks the Mediterranean brightness of a sunny, grateful disposition; his work echoes Horace's dictum to speak serious truths while laughing. Bataille, on the other hand, rediscovers his own laughter in the mouth of Nietzsche's madman, a madman reminiscent in his way of Bataille's father, whose screams of pain alternated with 'soundless peals of laughter'.[24] A clear case of misrecognition, of mistaken identity, perhaps even counter-memory. Such are the vicissitudes of genealogy.

3

Violence and Sumptuosity

Having successfully defended his thesis at the end of January 1922, and done well enough to be second in his class, Bataille was awarded the honour of continuing his archival work at L'École des Hautes Études hispaniques de Madrid, a French centre for advanced scientific and cultural research in Spain.

During the six months Bataille spent there in 1922 he catalogued six new medieval manuscripts; travelled from Madrid to Miranda, Valladolid, Granada, Toledo and Seville; developed a rather complex method of meditation; wrote at least part of a novel and witnessed the spectacular death of the bullfighter Manuel Granero. He chronicled his activities in letters to his cousin Marie-Louise and continued to reflect on them, directly or indirectly, in many of his most important writings over the course of his life.

To Marie-Louise he wrote that he sensed 'a Spain full of violence and sumptuosity, a very pleasant presentiment'.[1] Sumptuosity can be heard in a remark Bataille made about a dancer, 'who seemed like a panther with a thin, small, nervous and violent body'. He comments that 'a little animal of this breed seems suitable to put a fire in a bed in a more devastating way than any other creature'.[2] The chaste Catholic of previous years seems to have crossed into a new territory of desire. The violence of Spain most certainly refers, among other things, to bullfights, which became a lifelong and abiding passion for Bataille.

On 17 May 1922 Manuel Granero – a 20-year-old bullfighter widely regarded as the best of his generation – was thrown against the wall of the ring and gored three times by a bull. The third blow tore through his right eye, into his skull. In one of Bataille's descriptions of this event, this one written twenty-four years afterward, 'the vast crowd got to its feet, a stunned silence fell; this theatrical entrance of death, at the festival's height, in sunlight, was somehow obvious, expected, and intolerable'.[3] Granero's eye dangled from its socket as they carried his corpse from the field.

Bataille witnessed the incident from across the ring but newspaper stories and photographs clarified its details. This was to be one of the decisive events of his life. From that moment, Bataille tells us he 'began to understand that malaise is often the secret of the greatest pleasures'.[4] He wrote about the goring twice, in nearly identical terms, in *Story of the Eye* and nearly twenty years later in an article on Ernest Hemingway's *For Whom the Bell Tolls*. The 'eye' in *Story of the Eye* is Granero's eye. But the event also informed his fascination with bulls and with their sacrificial slaughter, as in the Mithraic cult, and by extension his understanding of sacrifice and the sacred in general. 'Modern bullfights,' he wrote in an article on the sacred, 'owing to their ritual enactment and their tragic character, represent a form close to ancient sacred games.'[5]

That spring Bataille began writing a novel in the style of Marcel Proust. 'I don't really see how to write otherwise,' he wrote to his cousin.[6] Only the first four volumes of Proust's *Recherche* had been published at that time. In an essay on Beckett's *Molloy* that he published in *Critique* in 1951 Bataille made passing reference to a novel he began writing as a young man about the murder of a vagabond.[7] Perhaps this was that novel, perhaps not. The text, in any case, has been lost.

This was hardly Bataille's first attempt at writing. Religiously inspired poetry and prose had been the 'mania' of his adolescence;

Notre Dame de Rheims being an example. Three short stories –
'La Châtelaine gentiane', 'Ralph Webb' and 'Évariste' – also survive
from the early 1920s.[8] Each of them is derivative of either his
reading, his experience or both. None of these writings suggest
the depth or complexity of Bataille's later contribution to
French literature, so it is not surprising that he never mentioned
them again.

The duration and the apparent wilfulness of Bataille's literary
and intellectual apprenticeship is significant. Fourteen years
separate his earliest literary inclinations from *Story of the Eye*.
During these years he produced poems and short prose pieces,
began several novels, prepared a significant scholarly edition
of a chivalric poem, translated, as we shall see, a philosophical
work by Lev Shestov, and wrote scholarly articles and reviews in
numismatics. Despite the accomplishment, they remained works
of apprenticeship.

In June 1922 the Bibliothèque Nationale de France cut Bataille's
Spanish sojourn short with the offer of a job in its department of
printed materials. The following month he returned to Paris and
to the apartment he shared with his mother and brother at 85 rue
de Rennes. His experiences in Spain had changed him, but he
nevertheless renewed several relationships initiated prior to his
departure, one with Colette Renié, another with Alfred Métraux,
both fellow students at the École des Chartes.

Bataille's letters to Colette Renié cast her in the role of a
pleasant and encouraging moral paragon while they characterize
Bataille himself as both depressive and – increasingly and for
the first time – debauched. The brief exchange – it lasted only
a few months in the late summer and autumn of 1922 – charts
the vicissitudes of the relationship, Bataille's emerging character
and his budding literary and intellectual style.

The letters are notable for their wilful exaggerations and quick
reversals of temper and purpose. 'Suddenly, I had your letter on

the table. But I remained trembling with emotion for five minutes (this is perhaps not physically exact, but a similarly strong expression is required) before opening it.'[9] Such hyperbolic exaggeration will be an essential feature of his later provocative and polemical style of writing and thought.

Bataille wrote to Colette ostensibly in need of encouragement and a connection to a Christian moral universe. At the outset and throughout, he tells her he is 'very sad', 'very tired and tired of myself too'.[10] 'Life has withdrawn entirely outside of me,' he says, 'I can no longer bear my anguish.'[11] He is considering suicide. He does not really say why. In a hopeful moment, he says: 'I have entirely regained the courage that one must have so as to begin a life that is not pleasant.'[12] The unpleasant life he was about to begin might refer to his new job at the Bibliothèque nationale or perhaps to a staid and chaste life in Christian society.

Despite his depression, he also admits to being 'egotistical' and 'brutal'.[13] 'I may appear mad to you but, believe me, too bad, I wouldn't change myself or moderate myself for anything in the world.'[14] His emotions and self-evaluations are extreme and prone to quick reversals. Depressed in one letter, he is angry in the next. She soothes him.

Her friendship is 'good, like beautiful sunlight'.[15] 'I am happy at the moment but only because of you,' he says, 'because your letter was infinitely kind to me.'[16] She encourages him but she also apparently makes light of his concerns, politely dismisses him as 'impossible', as an 'awkward child', as 'mad' or foolish.[17] He accepts these terms and admits, 'I attach a lot of importance to nothing.'[18] She brightens his spirit, but he remains discouraged, distant, and enigmatic. 'Life will still remain very difficult for me,' he says.[19]

Brightly, he writes:

It is true that I am in general very happy and certainly taken with fantasy but I do not think that this should be so serious, if that is what you wanted to say. In any case, I absolutely do not understand 'sometimes', since if I am (which I do not deny), I am crazy all the time.[20]

Later, he reverses himself on this overstated and cavalier self-evaluation: 'I am enraged when someone attributes (or I imagine that someone attributes) my exuberances or my extravagance to madness.'[21]

Following this, Bataille admits that he has had a personal experience of 'real' madness in the madness of both his father and his mother. In the version of the story that he recounts to her, he attributes his father's madness to the 'morphine they were making him take' rather than to syphilis. He nevertheless also goes on to recount the rejection of his proposal by Marie Delteil's father and the pain that that rejection caused him. The rejection, of course, would not have taken place without Joseph-Aristide Bataille's syphilis. Speaking of his parents and of human frailty in general, he says flatly: 'Sometimes a chain of events occur that are so lamentable that half of the people could sink into madness.'[22] The letter is by turns fiery and calm, accurate, empathetic and pathetic.

As the letters progress, Bataille's relationship with Colette Renié changes dramatically. Initially depressed and hungry for encouragement, later he bristles at her potential and implied condemnation of him. 'It seems to me that we are speaking a different language and that, as far I can see, this is a world that you would prefer not to enter.'[23] Over the course of the correspondence, he alternately implores her for support and rejects her world view as confining. Unsurprisingly, sexuality emerges as the central concern.

In a later letter, Bataille begins by asking Colette for a favour: that she encourage him not to break his promise never to visit a 'certain woman' again. This promise should be easy to keep as he has visited her but once. (Once! and he is effectively writing to confess his sin.) The woman is, of course, a prostitute, though this goes unsaid. She 'is absolutely monstrous and at the same time I feel no kind of disgust because there is something rather magnificent about this monstrosity, and of course, to me, this woman is absolutely beautiful. Perhaps you think I have an abominable life?'[24] He hopes that Colette's knowledge of this encounter will keep him from repeating it.

But his argument is hardly straightforward. 'What reason do I effectively have to live chastely?' he wonders.[25] 'There are no evil pleasures' in his estimation, and he thinks of 'a bunch of very immoral things'. Nevertheless, the pleasure offered by this woman presents a problem because it 'exaggeratedly surpasses [his] faculties of assimilation.' He neither sought it nor avoided it, and he 'tasted it with a perfect serenity of mind'. But then he recognized that he must absolutely not do it again.[26]

Commingling malaise and pleasure – as in the death of Granero – the prostitute is both monstrous *and* beautiful, and Bataille experiences the pleasure itself with both a serenity of mind and the certainty that he should never partake of it again. The letter itself also serves as both a confession of his sin and an argument made in support of it. Bataille's reader, Colette Renié, functions as a potentially judgemental Christian conscience to which the rebellious and impossible child confesses his transgression, but she has been dressed for this part by Bataille himself. Throughout the correspondence, he appeals to her in this precise role and in no other. This is not to say she did not play her part. (Lacking her side of the correspondence it is also possible to view her as someone simply responding reasonably to an unreasonable interlocutor.) Bataille however was entering a new world, beyond chastity, a world in which no confessor could help him.

Bataille met Alfred Métraux one autumn afternoon at the École des Chartes, prior to his graduation. Bataille was then looking forward to his upcoming trip to Spain and Métraux had just returned from Andalusia. An uncanny physical resemblance provided the ground for their familiarity and conversation ensued. Forty years later Métraux remembered Bataille's concentration on the banal facts that Métraux reported. The scholarly purposes of Bataille's trip seemed secondary to his interest in the Moorish influence on Spanish culture and in bullfights.[27]

Upon Bataille's return the two deepened their friendship, and it would endure for the rest of their lives. Métraux by then had quit the École des Chartes to pursue studies in ethnology under Marcel Mauss. He would eventually enjoy a celebrated career studying Latin American cultures: the Inca, Easter Island, the religious practices of indigenous populations and Haitian voodoo, in which he became an initiate. In the preface to *Eroticism*, published in 1957, Bataille credits Métraux with introducing him to the fields of anthropology and the history of religions, saying Métraux's 'uncontested authority permitted me to feel firmly assured when speaking on the decisive question of taboo and transgression'.[28] *The Tears of Eros* includes photos from Métraux's book on Haitian voodoo: a 'beautiful book' by 'one of the finest ethnographers of our time', according to Bataille.[29]

Métraux introduced Bataille to anthropology and the history of religions by introducing him to the work of Marcel Mauss.[30] Mauss's influence on Bataille's work equals that of Hegel, Sade and Freud; though all were bested by Nietzsche. Mauss stands behind Bataille's thought on social organization, on structures of exchange and communication, transgression and sacrifice. (We will come to these concepts as they arise in Bataille's work.[31])

When Métraux began following his lectures Mauss was studying archaic structures of exchange; the material that would become *The Gift*. His writings on sacrifice, magic and primitive classification were already classics in a field fundamentally oriented by Émile Durkheim's *The Elementary Forms of Religious Life*. (Durkheim was Mauss's uncle and teacher.) Métraux and Bataille spent hours walking the rue de Rennes, where Bataille was then living, and the Champs Elysees, talking about Mauss, Nietzsche, Gide, Freud and Dostoevsky, all recent discoveries for Bataille. As was the case in his discoveries of Christianity and laughter, and as would be the case with his introduction to the reading of Hegel in Alexandre Kojève's seminars, Bataille acquired his fundamental understanding of the anthropological thought of Marcel Mauss not in quiet independent study but in conversation with a friend.

Bataille also discovered Nietzsche in 1922. He had read portions of *Zarathustra* in 1917 but then being under the cloud of his Catholicism he had resisted Nietzsche's message. On 12 August 1922, however, shortly after his return from Spain, he borrowed *Untimely Meditations* and *Beyond Good and Evil* from the Bibliothèque nationale. This time the books had a 'decisive' effect. It is in fact difficult to imagine the depth and scope of the impact these books had on him. Reading Nietzsche, Bataille experienced a shock of recognition: 'Why continue to think, why envision writing, since my thought – all of my thought – had been so completely, so admirably expressed?'[32] The assertion proves a paradox: whether Nietzsche truly expressed Bataille's thought or Bataille wilfully sought to express a thought held in common with Nietzsche.[33]

In *Guilty*, Bataille admits: 'To me, nothing is more alien than personal modes of thought . . . If I utter a word, I bring into play the thought of *other people*.'[34] This will often be Nietzsche's thought, but it is rarely Nietzsche's thought alone. Sade and Dostoevsky, Hegel and Freud, Frazer and Mauss often hide behind Bataille's Nietzschean mask. Like the Greek tragedians, who rewrote myths familiar to their viewers, Bataille rewrites ideas in order to provoke an experience. He relies on and repeats the language of 'authorities' whose work he writes through, challenges and carries into unexpected territories, to unexpected uses and conclusions. He writes for, with and against, in simultaneous repetition and betrayal, acknowledgement and sacrifice of his authorities.

In November 1923, returning to his conviction that life was elsewhere, Bataille formulated new travel plans. While working at the Bibliothèque nationale he enrolled in language courses at the École des Langues orientales and checked out armloads of books on Chinese and Russian language and culture. He wanted to go to Tibet. A year previously he had attempted to be assigned to a post in Cairo, before that, to one in America. Almost nothing came of any of these plans. While Bataille did not manage to make his escape, he did meet someone who helped free his mind, the Russian émigré Lev Shestov.

A generation older than the twenty-six-year-old Bataille, Shestov was a well-known and well-published philosophical essayist writing in the vein of Dostoevsky and Nietzsche. Though he supported the Russian revolution, his upper-class background made life in the new Soviet Union uncomfortable, so he fled to Paris, courting an international reputation. D. H. Lawrence prefaced a translation of one of his books in 1920.

The Shestov that Bataille began to frequent for long evenings of philosophical conversation had published several books on Nietzsche, Dostoevsky, Tolstoy and Pascal. For Shestov, following Dostoevsky, human life proposes a tragic dilemma and requires an impossible faith. All of life, in his vision, can be summarized in the suffering of a Job whom no God deigns to address. Death is the compelling fact of life and idealistic thought – including rationalism in science and in theologically inspired moral systems – only a vague and delusional evasion of that fact. The thinker's first task was to destroy idealistic illusions and thereby restore both man and God to their respective and rightfully distinctive dominions. His second task was to seek to understand those dominions. Prey of an inaccessible, unknowable, and omnipotent deity, how might human beings seek both a moral life and an experience of that deity? Shestov is both anti-idealistic – and hence anti-systematic and anti-rational – and visionary. His thought reveals both God and man in their respective and mutual states of omnipotence, impotence and abandonment. His work embodies a profound and impossible yearning for a groundless faith. It does not preach rationalistic atheism.

Shestov discovered a kindred spirit in Nietzsche but his was a profound though selective reading of the philosopher of the death of God; a reading as dependent upon Pascal as it was on Nietzsche himself. To Bataille, who had only just begun to read Nietzsche and whose Christianity could be characterized as an unanswered yearning for the comfort of faith, the voice of the older man must have been particularly compelling. They spoke of Nietzsche and Dostoevsky, of Pascal, Plato and the purpose of philosophy. Years later, Bataille noted: 'I owe the foundation of my philosophical knowledge to Shestov . . . what he knew to say to me about Plato was what I needed to hear.'[35] Looking back, Bataille admired Shestov's patience with the difficult young man that he had been. A 'fundamental violence' affected him during those years, he said. He expressed himself only with a kind of 'sad delirium'.[36] Shestov of course was his guide in violent thinking. From him Bataille learned that 'the violence of human thought is nothing if it is not the fulfilment of that thought'.[37]

In 1924, Bataille co-translated Shestov's book *The Good in the Teaching of Tolstoy and Nietzsche* with the author's daughter, Teresa Beresovski-Shestov, and anticipated writing a study of Shestov's works.[38] The translation was published by Éditions du Siècle in 1925, but the proposed study never materialized.[39] In a post-humously published note, written thirty years after the fact, Bataille claims he drifted away from the philosopher when he drifted toward Marxism.[40] Intentionally or not, the claim is disingenuous. Bataille abandoned his relationship with Shestov during the mid 1920s but didn't drift toward Marxism until the early 1930s. Yet, in a lifetime of writing about Nietzsche, writing *through* Shestov's reading of Nietzsche, Bataille never mentioned Shestov's influence in print. Perhaps the anxiety of influence was simply too conflicted to bear. A perspective, like Bataille's, predicated on the mutual and violent abandonment of man and god, in which a madman hurls himself on the throat of that which embodies his highest value, cannot confess the patient and nurturing tutelage that engendered it. To speak of Shestov's influence would have been to speak of his former and conflicted faith: the author of *Inner Experience* preferred to pass over it in silence.

4

Underground Man

Sometime in October 1924 Georges Bataille met Michel Leiris at the Café Marigny, near the Elysée Palace. Jacques Lavaud, a colleague of Bataille's from the Bibliothèque Nationale and a long-standing friend of Leiris, made the introduction. Afterward, Lavaud told Leiris that he had arranged the meeting to see 'what strange precipitate might result'.[1]

Possessed by immediate mutual admiration – mutual intimidation even – the two quickly became friends. Their memoirs provide images of one another at this turning point in their lives. Leiris was twenty-three, Bataille twenty-seven. According to Leiris, Bataille dressed with an 'elegance that went very deep and that manifested itself without any vain ostentation in his clothing'. He was non-conformist, with a sarcastic laugh betraying his dark sense of humour.[2] Of himself, Bataille says, 'despite a certain extravagance of thought, I had a rather bourgeois appearance: an umbrella with a bamboo handle'.[3] Leiris too was extremely elegant (he even powdered his face), but he was nervous and bit his fingernails to the quick. He tended toward detachment.[4]

Bataille encouraged Leiris to read Dostoevsky's *Notes from Underground*, a book he had undoubtedly discussed with Shestov. And Leiris found its pages to contain a portrait on which Bataille seemed to have modelled himself. Dostoevsky's degraded and desperate everyman figure inhabited a world of drunken gamblers and prostitutes, sick souls at war with themselves. The underground man sought to live fully, not simply within the bounds of reason, but, in Pascalian paradox, he could not find calm satisfaction within himself. Rather, he experienced his most definitive sense of self in the eyes – and in the sufferings – of others. Yet even these experiences struck him as shallow and clichéd. He couldn't speak except as if speaking someone else's language, as if from a book. Boastful and vain, consumed by empty agitation, the underground man carried to an extreme what others 'have not dared to carry even half way'.[5]

With Leiris and Lavaud, Bataille spoke of founding a new literary movement and a magazine. In contrast to the No-saying childishness of Dada, which was then sputtering in inconsequence, Bataille wanted to found a 'Yes' movement, requiring a 'perpetual acquiescence to all things'.[6] Dada wasn't 'idiotic' enough, according to Bataille; it didn't go far enough, failed to transcend itself into a larger vision of life.[7] The magazine would use the address of a charmingly sordid and decrepit brothel near the Porte Saint-Denis, the girls would contribute.[8]

The proposed movement is significant not only as a mark of its moment, when café – or in this case brothel – conversations gave rise to magazines and movements. It is also significant as a measure of Bataille's emergent thought, indeed of his fundamental position, and of his intellectual inheritance. Nietzsche too had formulated an ethic of acquiescence, one that embraced and celebrated the world in all of its sensual offerings rather than rejecting it as Christianity did.

The fact that this movement was to have its headquarters in a brothel also signals a definitive shift in the character of Georges Bataille. It had been a mere two years since Bataille had written to Colette Renié asking for her help in curbing his desire for the pleasures of a certain monstrous woman, a woman he claimed to have visited only once. By the following year he and Alfred

Métraux were habitués of such women.[9] Now, with Leiris, he was a caricature of ill repute: a gambler, an aggressive and excessive drinker, a devotee of debauchery. For the rest of his days, only illness would prevent his pursuit of pleasure. As he put it in *Guilty*, 'My true church is a whorehouse – the only one that gives me true satisfaction.'[10]

Nothing came of the proposed movement. In October 1924 André Breton published the first Surrealist Manifesto. A month or so later, Michel Leiris joined the group. Bataille felt betrayed by, and a little worried about, his new friend. But nothing could be done. The friendship continued to grow, if a bit warily.

As with Métraux and Mauss, Shestov and Nietzsche, Leiris mediated Bataille's relationship with Surrealist thought and with the Surrealists; at least initially. First, he took Bataille to meet the painter André Masson at Masson's somewhat shabby studio at 45 rue Blomet. Joan Miró had a studio next door and Bataille felt immediately at home with the group of writers and painters who frequented Masson's studio as if it were a salon. Georges Limbour, Roland Tual, Jean Dubuffet and Antonin Artaud were regulars in the group, as was Max Jacob, though he was a little older than the others. The Surrealists of the rue Blomet loved Dostoevsky and Nietzsche, and, in their company, Bataille discovered the then only recently published works of the Marquis de Sade. Among the artists and writers of the rue Blomet the sensual and intellectual excesses of Dostoevsky, Nietzsche and Sade were indistinct from the excesses of their own lives. They drank too much and weren't opposed to smoking opium. They visited brothels and gave themselves freely to the passions of the flesh.

At this moment and over the years Bataille became particularly close to Théodore Fraenkel and André Masson, both of whom would eventually be his brothers-in-law. Fraenkel had known André Breton since 1906 and had gone to medical school with him. An early animator of the Dada movement in its French incarnation,

Fraenkel made his living as a doctor rather than a writer or artist, but Bataille found him to be a 'very quiet night bird with a sort of nocturnal sadness, but ridiculous deep down'.[11] Later in life Fraenkel became Bataille's doctor.

André Masson painted erotically charged images with an automatic or unconsciously motivated line. More so than the other members of the rue Blomet group, he and Bataille understood one another intuitively and were united by shared interests. Masson would play an enormous role in Bataille's life over the coming years, illustrating several of his books and creating the image that would motivate *Acéphale*, the journal and secret society Bataille founded in 1936.

Masson's style of automatic painting was central to the Surrealist aesthetic, but the rue Blomet group was not the central tendency within the Surrealist initiative. André Breton lived on the rue Fontaine and gathered another group of writers and artists around him there: Louis Aragon, Paul Éluard, Philippe Soupault, Benjamin Péret, René Crevel, Max Ernst and later Salvador Dalí. Rue Fontaine was the original and true home of Surrealism.

Leiris introduced Bataille to Louis Aragon at Zelli's, 'perhaps the most charming nightclub of all', in Bataille's opinion.[12] Bataille found Aragon to be confident in both his thought and his personality, but neither stupid nor particularly intelligent; rather naïve but also very serious, seductive and ambitious. Aragon struck him as someone 'playing the great man' and this would be his principle complaint about the rue Fontaine Surrealists during these years. They took themselves far too seriously; they acted as though they had answers to social ills. Bataille, for his part, though extreme in thought and in action, was too shy and self-effacing to confront the Surrealists in their moment of youthful and supreme confidence. He sat in silence and let them talk. He also read their books, or some of them anyway: Breton's *Manifesto*, *Mont de piété*, and *Poisson soluble*, Aragon's *Anicet ou le Panorama* and *Le Paysan de*

Paris, several collections of Éluard's poems. He found the *Manifesto* 'unreadable'.[13]

Leiris also facilitated a meeting with André Breton, this time on the terrace of Cyrano, a café on the Place Blanche. Bataille delivered some translations he had done of thirteenth-century nonsense poetry – Fatrasies – that were to be published in *La Révolution surréaliste*. Breton published the poems the following year but disliked Bataille immediately and intensely. The feeling was mutual. Where Breton was rigid and moralizing, above the fray, Bataille was unstable and compromised, caught in the midst of life. Breton found Bataille obsessive; Bataille found Breton suffocating.[14]

With Masson, Leiris, and Nikolay Bakhtin (Mikhail's brother), Bataille thought about forming another group, a secret society of Nietzschean orientation and orphic intent. Leiris suggested that they call it Judas, but once again nothing came of it.

Bataille did however keep writing. He attempted to publish his edition of *L'Ordre de chevalerie* in 1925 through the Société des anciens textes français, but they turned it down. He proposed an edition of *Bérinus*, a fourteenth-century prose narrative, but the Société rejected that as well. In 1926 he began publishing scholarly articles and reviews in *Aréthuse*, a journal of art and archaeology directed by Pierre d'Espezel and Jean Babelon, two colleagues from the Bibliothèque Nationale.

He also continued to write fiction, drafting a novel entitled *W.C.*, 'in violent opposition to any form of dignity', as he later claimed.[15] He also claimed that he burned the manuscript.[16] According to Michel Leiris, however, the introduction to *Le Bleu de ciel* (*Blue of Noon*) actually constitutes the beginning of *W.C.*, or a version of it.[17] Bataille published this same text as 'Dirty' in 1945. Why did he claim to have destroyed the manuscript?

The narrative begins in a cellar; in French this is a '*sous-sol*', an underground space, and *W.C.* is the story of another underground man. As the narrator observes, the scene is 'worthy of Dostoevsky'.[18]

The narrator, Henri Tropmann, takes his name from Jean-Baptiste Troppmann, who murdered a family of eight in 1869 and was guillotined for his trouble. In a French–English pun, Tropmann can be read as meaning 'too much man'. 'Henri' might reference one of Troppmann's victims, Henri Kinck. Rimbaud includes the names of the murderer and his victims in the list of names in 'Paris', a poem he contributed to the *Album Zutique*.

At the Savoy Hotel in London, during a drunken revel, the main female character – Dirty – recounts a childhood visit to the hotel. During that visit, her dignified mother tripped when exiting an elevator and revealed herself to be drunk, thereby inverting Dirty's view of her mother both physically (because she was upside down) and morally (because she was drunk and degraded). This shift in perspective is complicated by the presence of an animalistic elevator operator, whose presence triggers the memory, and a maidservant, to whom Dirty tells the tale. By telling the story, Dirty degrades herself before the maidservant in the same way her mother degraded herself before Dirty. Thereafter the story proceeds through further degradations among fishmongers in Belgium. The book, in short, pursues the gesture of reversal Bataille first experienced when he heard his father exclaim: 'Doctor, let me know when you're done fucking my wife!'

For Bataille, the book constituted a 'shriek of horror . . . at myself, not for my debauchery, but for the philosopher's head in which, since then . . . how sad it is!'[19] Debauchery he could accept, but rationalism, justification, ideas, the stock in trade of a philosopher, he could not. The novel concerned an underground man, and it seemed to have been written by one. Yet author violently rejected his violent text, at least in part. He retained the first chapter and published it twice in two different versions. And he retained a residue of the title in the pseudonym he adopted for his next fiction, Lord Auch.

Bataille showed *W.C.* to Leiris and other friends. He may also have shared other writings, perhaps even an early version of *Story of the Eye*. Dr Camille Dausse was among those friends and was so disturbed by the 'virulently obsessive' nature of the writing – and undoubtedly by Bataille's personal habits, his drinking and gambling – that he suggested the author undergo psychoanalysis with Dr Adrien Borel, one of the founders, that year, of the Société psychanalytique de Paris.[20] A connoisseur and an aesthete, Dr Borel was sympathetic to artists and interested in the workings of the imagination. Over the next decade, in Bataille's immediate circle, Dr Borel would also treat Raymond Queneau, Michel Leiris, Colette Peignot and perhaps also her brother Charles.

According to Bataille, his analysis was not very orthodox, lasting only a year, but it was effective, transforming him from someone who was 'unhealthy' into someone who was 'relatively viable'. He spoke of it in terms of a 'deliverance'.[21] It put an end to a series of 'dreary mishaps and failures in which he had been floundering, but not to his state of intellectual intensity'.[22] The indecisive young man who could not speak when confronted with the certainty of the Surrealists was unleashed.

The precise process of Dr Borel's cure in this case remains obscure. Bataille may have prepared a short text recounting the dream of his father abusing him in a cellar.[23] He also read passages of *Story of the Eye* to the doctor as he was writing them and Dr Borel commented on them. He corrected an anatomical misunderstanding on Bataille's part: a bull's testicles are white rather than red and therefore roughly similar to both eggs and eyes.[24] Beyond this nothing is certain.

Whether as part of the analysis or simply during its course, Borel gave Bataille a photograph of a Chinese man being cut into pieces, reproduced from Georges Dumas's *Traité de psychologie* (1923). In 1905 Fou Tchou Li murdered Prince Ao Han Ouan. He was sentenced to be burned alive but the Emperor felt this method of execution was too cruel. Instead, the Emperor ordered that the criminal be subjected to the *Leng Tch'e*: that he be cut into one

The execution of Fou-Tchou-Li by *leng tch'e*, China, 1925, reproduced in
The Tears of Eros (1961).

hundred pieces. Whether to numb or to prolong the pain, Fou
Tchou Li was given opium. He was suspended by his arms amid a
crowd of onlookers, his shoulders undoubtedly broken by the
weight of his body. Strips of flesh were cut from his chest, his sex
removed, his body dismembered piece by piece. In the photo Borel
gave Bataille, Fou Tchou Li's eyes appear to have rolled back into
his potentially ecstatic head: an unsettling echo of Bataille's father's
tortured and inverted eyes. The image would play an essential role
in Bataille's method of meditation. Bataille imaged himself in the
flesh of that tortured figure, torn apart, and he was ecstatic: his
body cast his mind out of itself, beyond the limits of consciousness.

Bataille had begun reading Freud in 1923 with the *Introductory
Lectures on Psychoanalysis*, published in France the previous year.[25]
After his analysis he read *Totem and Taboo* repeatedly in 1927 and,
in 1931, he considered co-translating Freud's essay on Dostoevsky
with Simone Breton (André's soon-to-be ex-wife). He did not read

The Interpretation of Dreams until 1932.[26] Thus his knowledge of psychoanalysis prior to undergoing treatment was literally introductory and Dr Borel might be understood as the intermediary who initiated Bataille in his study of this approach to anthropological analysis. For Bataille, *Totem and Taboo* would remain the fundamental text of psychoanalysis. His interest in psychoanalysis would be as a means of cultural or anthropological analysis rather than one of personal analysis. No matter: Bataille's analytic experience resulted in 'deliverance'.

5

Incipit Parodia

Georges Bataille turned thirty in 1927. His closest friends were members of a movement he did not join. His profession did not entirely fulfil his intellectual agendas. And, a decade after his rejection by Marie Delteil's family, his romantic life had slipped into debauchery. His faith had been an evasion, and he had abandoned it, first for a historian's approach to its contents and, later, with virulent insistence.

In January 1927 Bataille began writing 'The Solar Anus', an exercise in mythological anthropology. The text is both unclassifiable and confident in its originality. The Galérie Simon – Daniel-Henry Kahnweiler's gallery – published it four years later with illustrations by André Masson. It is the earliest text that Bataille published under his own name and continued to recognize throughout his life.[1]

'It is clear that the world is purely parodic,' he begins, 'that each thing seen is the parody of another, or is the same thing in a deceptive form.'[2] Where Bataille's previous literary and intellectual endeavours were derivative – his translations and critical editions being only the most obvious examples of this – those that followed would be parodic and utterly original. A derivative work merely copies a respected original; a parody degrades that original with mocking mimicry, assaults its absent and abandoned authority, while nevertheless remaining indebted to it. Parody is the literary equivalent of transgression, upholding as it undermines. As an analytic principle, parody is a form of denigration through distillation, of recognition through reduction, indeed a *reductio ad absurdum*. A provocation to laughter, parody also appears in Bataille's writing and thought as dramatization, mimicry and betrayal: a textual eternal return of the same in which repetition is the sole means of articulating difference.

Parody is the precise opposite of allegory, the medieval theological and literary trope par excellence. Bataille's own *Notre Dame de Rheims* typifies the allegorical gesture: The specific cathedral in Reims stands in not only for all churches but also for the Madonna whose namesake it is and for the love and salvation she bestows upon all Christians. A real object in this profane world is seen as suffused with holy purpose. But where allegory inverts and elevates, parody inverts and degrades. Allegory reifies theological certainties, parody ruins the very notion of truth: as Bataille put it in *Inner Experience*, 'Thought ruins'.[3] This is also a favourite strategy of Nietzsche's. In the preface to *The Gay Science*, Nietzsche inverted the book's conclusion: *incipit tragoedia* became *incipit parodia*; the parody begins.

'The Solar Anus' is an exercise in what Bataille calls mythological anthropology: a style of provocative thought embracing both rational and irrational forces at work in the world and in the observer simultaneously. Scientific anthropology, like that of Marcel Mauss, proceeds by means of rationally defensible hypotheses grounded in observational evidence. Psychoanalysis, too, masks its reliance on mythic structures behind a scientific veneer. Mythological anthropology, on the other hand, provokes by means of potentially irrational hypotheses: it hopes to reveal a myth. In the late 1930s this agenda will return in the secret society and journal *Acéphale*. A decade later still, in *The Accursed Share*, Bataille will write: 'The ebullition that I consider, which animates the globe, is also *my* ebullition. The object of my research cannot be distinguished *from the subject at its boiling point*.'[4]

'The Solar Anus' proposes parody as a key to understanding the relationships between diverse objects in the universe: animals, plants, the sea, the sun, locomotives, umbrellas, etc. Thereafter it explores these relationships and then situates its narrating consciousness within them: 'I am the *Jesuve*, the filthy parody of the torrid and blinding sun.'[5] In French, Jesuve combines '*je*' or I, Vesuve or Vesuvius (the volcano), and Jésus. Bataille used the neologism in several unpublished writings, many of which also articulate the myth of a pineal eye, an eye at the top of the human head, hungry for direct sight of the sun. With minor stylistic differences all of these texts pursue the same mythic agenda.

'The Solar Anus' concentrates on the parodic structure of the world, where each thing reflects or reverses the identity of another thing. Sunlight pours down to the earth below. Flowers rise to meet the sun. Unable to rise fully, terrestrial beings – plants and animals, human beings – and forces – like the sea – struggle against their limitations, they reach beyond themselves. Two axes of motion organize this struggle: vertical motion down from the sun and up toward it, and horizontal motion, caused by the near-vertical rising and falling of energies reaching up and falling back as the earth turns. The motion of the sea epitomizes this horizontal activity. Animals too participate in the horizontal world: they rise from the earth but direct their attention to the objects of the world around them rather than to things above them. Human beings alone among the animals contemplate the heavens. We are torn between the two axes.

Bataille's thought here is not substantially different from that of Heraclitus and Hesiod.[6] As Bataille puts it, filtering his classical vision through psychoanalytic terminology, 'The great coitus with the celestial atmosphere is regulated by the terrestrial rotation around the sun . . . Polymorphous coitus is a function of uniform terrestrial rotation.'[7] As in Freud, Eros is the arbiter of all relationships. 'The Solar Anus' articulates a myth of general economy, a vision of the circulation of *all* energies not only around the globe but within the cosmos.

Parody figures in this vision through the play of opposites. As an analytic strategy this thought motivates an imaginative search for contrasts and an attempt to think their impossible unity: the opposite of pure solar energy is terrestrial filth, excrement; the myth of the solar anus proposes the unity of these forces.

Parody also appears here through a misunderstanding of scissiparity, i.e. reproduction via cellular division. Cellular division creates difference through the repetition of identity rather than through a parodic mirroring of identity, as Bataille would have it. Fascinated by this problem, Bataille will address it directly at the Collège de sociologie, in 'La Scissiparité', and in *Eroticism*.[8] Metaphysical and psychological concepts like identity are useless in the world of nature. Bataille's thought here is valuable, however, as an attempt to relocate the actions of human beings within the natural order: it presents a fantasy of desire in which human desire manifests cosmic energies.

In Bataille's vision, predicated on expenditure, human desire expresses itself most profoundly in a desire for self-loss, self-forgetting or self-sacrifice, whether in sex or in some other form. 'In bed next to a girl he loves, a man forgets that he does not know why he is himself instead of the body he touches.'[9] The myths proposed by these texts – the solar anus, the pineal eye and the Jesuve – each reflect and repeat this desire for self-loss.

In 'The Solar Anus', the anus presents the night side of the human flesh. A solar anus is of course an impossible commingling: that which is most high brought together with the lowest part of the body. Here, 'the Sun exclusively loves the Night and directs its luminous violence, its ignoble shaft, toward the earth, but it finds itself incapable of reaching the gaze or the night, even though the nocturnal terrestrial expanses head continuously toward the indecency of the solar ray.'[10] In this vision, cosmic coitus replicates sodomy; functionally useless anal intercourse, pure expenditure.

'The Pineal Eye' proposes an 'eye, at the summit of the skull, opening on the incandescent sun in order to contemplate it in a sinister solitude . . . not a product of the understanding, but instead an immediate existence; it opens and blinds itself like a conflagration . . . This great burning head is the image and the disagreeable light of the *notion of expenditure*.'[11] 'The pineal eye fantasy is an excremental fantasy.'[12] Vision and identity burn from the top of the tortured skull. Understanding is thrown out, cranial disjecta.

The figure of the Jesuve weds man and volcano, I and Vesuvius with the name of the Saviour. 'The Pineal Eye' elaborates the myth of the Jesuve most explicitly. During July 1927 Bataille visited the London Zoological Gardens while in the English capital doing research. He was struck by the shocking brightness of a gibbon's protuberant rear. Schoolgirls nearby were laughing uncomfortably at the beast. As a marker of identity and a sign of sexual arousal, the gibbon's rear makes a mockery, in Bataille's thought, of the human face. Bataille imagined a ritual scene in which men dig a hole and bury a gibbon in it, leaving its posterior raised above the recovered earth. In his vision, a blonde Englishwoman prostrates herself on the animal after a ritual orgy.

> All the stupefied glances are fixed on the filthy, beautifully blood-covered solar prominence, sticking out of the earth and ridiculously shuddering with convulsions of agony. Then the Englishwoman with her charming rear end stretches her long nude body on the filled pit: the mucous-flesh of this bald false skull, a little soiled with shit at the radiate flower of its summit, is even more upsetting to see when touched by pretty white fingers . . . Contracted by strangulation, and even by death, the beautiful boil of red flesh is set ablaze with stinking brown flames.[13]

The underground animal sacrifices its life with a volcanic excremental explosion, soiling the dignity of a pale, blonde woman. This is the Jesuve: a subterranean sacrifice of animal identity straining for the sky. 'The fecal eye of the sun has also torn itself from these volcanic entrails, and the pain of a man who tears out his own eyes with his fingers is no more absurd than this anal maternity of the sun.'[14]

These solar and excremental myths of reciprocal catastrophic expenditure reformulate and extend Freud's writings on thanatos and anality; Mauss's thought on social facts, potlatch and sacrifice; Nietzsche's thought on expenditure – the will to power is first and foremost a theory of expenditure – and his vision of humanity as a form that must be overcome; and Sade's understanding of animality, self-destructive desire, and sodomy, the practice of non-productive desire. Unpublished save for 'The Solar Anus' they constitute the ur-text of his entire corpus, the generative originary myths.

Story of the Eye extends the parodic agenda of 'The Solar Anus'. It also betrays several antecedents: psychoanalytic literature and methods, Gothic novels like Matthew Lewis's *The Monk*, beloved of the Surrealists and, of course, pornographic writings like those of the Marquis de Sade.[15] Psychoanalysis is often present in the narrative situations and sexual games of the characters (chapter six neatly negotiates the oral, anal and genital stages of pleasure and character development, for example). The Gothic tradition is perhaps most visible when Marcelle is confined in a sanatorium which takes on the aura of a haunted castle.

Story also parodies ideas and specific scenic elements from Maurice Barrès' *Du Sang, de la volupté, et de la mort*. Barrès was a right-wing political agitator and novelist famous for promoting the 'cult of the self'. A generation older than Bataille, the Catholic nationalist died in 1923 but his works set the intellectual stage for the rise of fascism in France. Barrès therefore constituted a figure of dark fascination for the Catholic Bataille and a perfect foil for his parody. *Story of the Eye* is also a parody of language itself, of stories and story-telling in general, of representation and the process of signification. *Story of the Eye* is not really a story and it is not really about an eye, at least these two things are not its primary points of interest. The story, such as it is, is an excuse for the tableaux and linguistic effects explored in each chapter and the eye is less a singular eye, whose peregrinations we follow, than a series of eyes and other related objects which collapse into one another across the text. The only singular eye that remains consistent throughout the text is the eye of the implied reader, whose mind's-eye imagines the represented tableau and whose actual eyes scan the surface of the text. If the reader reads the story as a more or less straight-forward story, suspends his or her disbelief and enjoys the representation, he or she fails to see the text at its most basic level, as words on a page. In *Story of the Eye* this oversight causes the reader to miss the linguistic games that motivate the text.

The work consists of two parts: a narrative and a short analytic piece explaining the biographical origins of selected images and ideas in the 'partly imaginary' narrative.[16] *Story* isn't much of a story. The adolescent narrator meets a girl of his own age, Simone, to whom he is distantly related. Innocent at first, the two experiment with masturbation together. They scandalize Simone's mother and corrupt an innocent girl, Marcelle. Marcelle is mentally broken by her experiences and interned in an asylum. Simone and the narrator break Marcelle out of the asylum only to discover that she has truly gone mad. (But what is madness in this story?) Marcelle eventually realizes that her rescuers are the same individuals whose behaviour troubled her in the first place and she kills herself. Effectively murderers now, Simone and the narrator flee to Spain where they attend a bullfight with Sir Edmond, a wealthy and debauched Englishman. At the bullfight, Simone obtains the testicles of the first bull as a trophy. She eats one and inserts the other into her vagina at the precise moment that the bullfighter Granero is gored through his eye. The trio travel to Seville and visit the church where Don Juan is buried. There Simone masturbates while making her confession. Unsatisfied, the three attack the priest. They tie him up, rape him, violate the vehicles of the Eucharist, and eventually murder the priest, who believes he is being martyred. They tear out one of his eyes; Simone inserts it into her vagina. They flee the crime. Simone makes superficial changes to her appearance every day so that she can be violated afresh by the narrator. At the end of the book, Sir Edmond buys a yacht in Gibraltar and they set sail for further adventures.

'Coincidences' ostensibly 'explains' several elements of the narrative. The narrative voice in this section is no longer necessarily that of the adolescent narrator. The present voice is that of the 'author', identified as Lord Auch. 'Auch' puns on the words 'aux chiottes' ('to the shithouse'), a phrase Bataille borrowed from Theodore Fraenkel. Lord is an English word for divinity. Lord Auch is thus 'God relieving himself', according to Bataille, a reminder of *W.C.*[17]

Lord Auch explains that the image of the sheet flapping in the night at the sanatorium might derive from a moment in his own adolescence when his brother wore a similar sheet near a similar castle while acting like a ghost. The scene in which Granero is gored is of course historically accurate, though the narrator claims he did not think to connect eyes and testicles until his doctor made the connection for him. Lord Auch observes the difference between two levels of information in his mind: elementary images and completely obscene, scandalous images, images upon which consciousness floats but in response to which consciousness explodes. Deep in his mind, he believes these different regimes of images and information coincide: the everyday becomes explosive. Lord Auch's father was syphilitic, blind and paralysed at the time of his birth. The father lost his mind and shouted at a doctor who was trying to help him: 'Doctor, let me know when you are done fucking my wife.' The everyday world exploded. Lord Auch's mother provided him with one model for the character of the young innocent, Marcelle. There were other models, but Lord Auch saw his mother as a woman shattered by her experience. Lord Auch tells us that he writes to restore his memories to life by transforming them, making them unrecognizable: 'During that deformation they acquired the lewdest of meanings.'[18]

'Coincidences' thus provides clues as to the origins of various tableaux and sentiments found in the narrative, but it hardly explains their meaning or relationship to the other elements of the text. Knowing that Granero's death references a real incident hardly suggests that the rest of the text, or even the rest of that scene, has any basis in fact. Making a point of this, as Lord Auch does, merely casts this problem more clearly before the reader's eyes. What, after all, is real? Similarly, the autobiographical details that Lord Auch supplies only seem to clarify the psychoanalytic primal scene at the bottom of the mind that gave birth to the narrative. If nothing else, 'Coincidences' testifies to a psychoanalytically informed methodology at work: images and tableaux have been and are being transformed – condensed and displaced – in the text. The ostensible plot moves, in other words, by means of displacement from object to object rather than according to the psychological motivations of the characters. Psychoanalytic in methodology, the narrative is not psychological. In this way, *Story of the Eye* parodies psychoanalytic insights and the psychological novel, hence the entire novelistic tradition. Whatever source or original meaning the objects and incidents may have had remains inaccessible. Unlike a traditional narrative, written to be interpreted, *Story* cannot be recuperated so easily by any single interpretative key. As in 'The Solar Anus', the world of *Story of the Eye* is parodic and lacks an interpretation.[19]

Using the same analytic and imaginative strategy of opposition and reversal he used in 'The Solar Anus', *Story of the Eye* proceeds through a series of increasingly complex transgressive acts. In the beginning, the narrator and his accomplice, Simone, are innocent: they soon violate that innocence. Thereafter they violate someone else's innocence (Marcelle's), the family structure (in the person of Simone's mother), and eventually religion (in the person of Don Aminado, the sacerdotal pig).

Another form of transgression is operative more directly in the descriptions and actions of the characters. If bourgeois society forbids nudity, nudity is here revealed. If society respects the dead, the dead (corpses) are here disrespected. Transgressive reversals and contrasts such as these generate textual ideas and structure the text. If Simone is a brunette, Marcelle must be blonde (in keeping with her innocence). If Simone sits in white milk, she must be wearing a black pinafore. If Simone is going to piss on her mother (on 'family'), she must do so from above (equating piss and sunlight), and therefore must be climbing in a room where the rafters open onto the space below her.

Transgression violates a social or moral norm. Contrasts and reversals generate action and also contribute to the bewildering chaos of the text and textual universe as a whole. When the narrator locks Marcelle in a wardrobe, he is wearing a red cap in the Jacobin style. Marcelle, in her incipient madness, mistakes him for a Cardinal, but also conflates the two figures: a priest and a murderer of priests.[20] In Seville the final action takes place in a church founded, after his eventual remorseful redemption, by the historical Don Juan, Miguel Mañara. Simone pisses on his grave. While Don Juan is dead and redeemed, the current erotic criminals are motivated to violate that redemption and that death. Again and again, the indifferent gaze, the empty eyes of the dead, spurs these characters to life: Theirs is an eroticism beyond the pleasure principle. As the narrator reports early on, at their first sight of a corpse: 'The horror and despair at so much bloody flesh, nauseating in part, and in part very beautiful, was fairly equivalent to our usual impression upon seeing one another.'[21]

The most startlingly original aspect of *Story* occurs, in several ways, on its surface. As the story proceeds it becomes clear that it concerns a series of similarly shaped objects more so than anything that those objects might represent: a round saucer of milk, an egg, an eye, the sun, a circular urine stain on a white sheet, a bull's testicles. Simone sits in the saucer of milk; she crushes eggs with her buttocks and pisses on them; she places the Priest's eye and the bull's testicles in her vagina. Pale round objects circulate both around Simone's body – anus, vagina, mouth – and throughout the text.

Another series of objects are not solid objects at all but liquids or other kinds of flowing substances: milk, saliva, semen, urine, sunlight. In 'The Solar Anus', Bataille equates the sun baked sea – as generative source of all life – with the female sex organ that 'liquefies under the excitation of the penis'.[22] The explicitly pornographic *Story of the Eye* forces a similar liquefaction at every level of the world it describes and of the language that is used to describe that world. The coincidence of Simone's ingestion of a bull's testicle into her vagina and Granero's eye being gored by the bull is linked, for example, to a 'urinary liquefaction of the sky'.[23] Every transgression, every transformation, every contrast or reversal is predicated upon a similarly fluid metamorphosis.

On its surface Bataille's language utilizes a series of puns and linguistic coincidences to further flatten and liquefy the text. On the first page, Simone observes that *assiettes* (plates) are for *s'asseoir* (sitting), before promptly sitting in the cat's saucer of milk. Later, when the narrator asks her what the word *uriner* (urinate) means to her she replies *buriner* (to engrave or carve), a purely orthographic connection, utterly without depth. The two central figures in the text, *oeils* (eyes) and *oeufs* (eggs), enjoy a similar affiliation; one that links the shape of the first letter with the shape of the object in question.

Surrealist automatic writing deploys psychoanalytic insights into slips of the tongue in search of an unconsciously motivated literature, a deeper truth. Bataille's writing, on the other hand, like that of the Comte de Lautréamont or Raymond Roussel, explores the hidden relationships between but on the surface of the words themselves. Nothing about this writing is automatic. It is in fact over-determined: objects are related by contrasts of every kind, by similarities of shape, for example, by everything, in short, but deeper meaning. For Bataille, to write is to revel in a language that reveals nothing.

Pascal Pia designed the book, illustrated with eight unsigned lithographs by André Masson. René Bonnel published an edition of 134 copies in 1928 without revealing the name of the publisher. That year Bonnel also published Louis Aragon's similarly pseudonymous *Irène*. These were by no means the only pornographic or soft core titles that circulated by subscription or were sold under the counter at the time. Books like these also circulated within an economy of luxurious, illustrated volumes and artist's books that sold to collectors. Pseudonymous or not, books published in so small an edition and within such circles were hardly anonymous. This is not to say that every potential reader of the text knew Bataille well or even personally. Pseudonymity protected Bataille – and Bonnel and Masson – from prosecution and it gave publishing the allure of what it in fact was, a criminal act. Further, as an employee of the Bibliothèque Nationale, Bataille would have lost his job had he been convicted of such a crime. Pseudonymous or not, *Story of the Eye* helped establish Bataille as a startlingly original and darkly disturbing writer.

Sometime in 1927, perhaps at Raymond Queneau's studio in the square Desnouettes near the porte de Versailles, Bataille met Sylvia Maklès. He was thirty, she was nineteen. Sylvia had three sisters, Bianca, Simone and Rose, and a brother, Charles. Her oldest sister, Bianca, went to medical school and met André Breton, Théodore Fraenkel and Louis Aragon there. In 1922 Bianca married Fraenkel and gave up her medical studies to become an actress, an aspiration Sylvia shared. After the wedding Sylvia moved in with the young couple. Things seemed fine, as Sylvia adored her older sister, but Fraenkel fell in love with Sylvia. He made several passes at her, creating trauma enough to end the ménage. Whether to escape the situation or as testament to genuine affection, Sylvia married Georges Bataille on 20 March 1928. Michel Leiris and Sylvia's sister Simone witnessed the wedding in Courbevoie, a suburb of Paris. (In a jealous rage, Fraenkel got a gun and went to the Bibliothèque Nationale in search of Bataille. Luckily, Bataille wasn't there that day, giving Fraenkel a chance to cool off.) Simone eventually married Jean Piel and the fourth sister, Rose, André Masson, in 1934, further cementing the friendships of everyone involved.[24]

After the wedding Bataille moved out of the apartment he shared with his mother at 85 rue de Rennes. He and Sylvia were itinerant for a year or two, moving from apartment to apartment, but they eventually settled at 3 rue Claude Matrat in the Parisian suburb of Issy-les-Moulineaux.

All the while, Georges continued to indulge in his dissolute nightlife: drinking to excess, gambling, frequenting brothels. We know nothing of his erotic life with Sylvia (beyond the evidence

Bataille's first wife, Sylvia Bataille, in Jean Renoir's 1936 film *Partie de Campagne*.

Bataille (far right) as one of the seminarians in *Partie de Campagne*.

supplied by the life of their daughter, Laurence). In 1934 when their marriage collapsed, both Georges and Sylvia admitted in their letters that they had failed one another. But this does not necessarily mean that either party failed the other's expectations in a traditional sense (i.e. monogamy). When evaluating the life of Georges Bataille and his companions it is best to set such traditional expectations at least partially aside. Transgression requires the law, but the law need not be so rigid or rigidly enforced as traditional expectations would allow. Nor too should we underestimate the allure, imagination or independence of Bataille's companions, Sylvia among them.

6

Heterology

While writing 'The Solar Anus' and *Story of the Eye* by night, Bataille worked with Pierre D'Espezel and Jean Babelon in the Cadinet des Médailles at the Bibliothèque Nationale by day. D'Espezel and Babelon directed *Aréthuse*, a journal of art and archaeology published three times a year, and in 1926 they invited their younger colleague to contribute reviews and articles in his then field of professional specialization, numismatics: the study of monies and medals no longer in circulation. Cast between archaeology and ethnography, economics and aesthetics, these writings evidence concerns that Bataille would maintain throughout his career, but they do not yet evidence his characteristic style of either language or thought. That language would only begin to be heard publicly in 1928, in a short article entitled 'Extinct America': Bataille's contribution to a volume of the *Cahiers de la république des letters, des sciences et des arts* commemorating the first major European exhibition of pre-Columbian artefacts. As with *Aréthuse*, Pierre D'Espezel directed the *Cahiers* and solicited Bataille's article.

Bataille's friend and former schoolmate Alfred Métraux, by then a specialist in the ethnography of Latin America, also contributed to the volume and to the organization of the show itself. Bataille knew a little about pre-Columbian culture and Métraux recommended a few additional references, which the librarian borrowed from the Bibliothèque Nationale in March and April 1928. Foremost among them were W. H. Prescott's classics

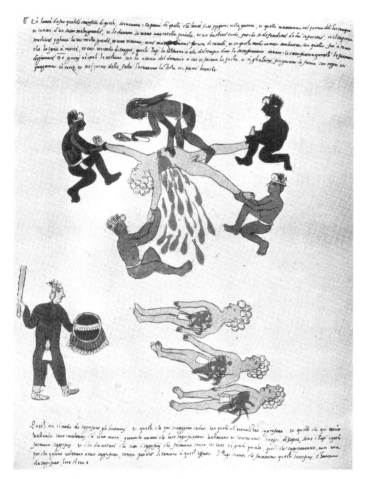

An Aztec sacrifice image reproduced in *The Tears of Eros* (1961).

The History of the Conquest of Mexico and *The History of the Conquest of Peru* and Bernardino de Sahagún's *General History of the Things of New Spain*; eight books borrowed in total, some primary sources, some general histories; some popular, others technical: hardly an exhaustive reading list on this topic even in 1928. What Bataille did with this limited amount of information was, however, both extraordinary and foundational. According to Métraux, Bataille anticipated future developments in ethnography by evaluating the cultures in question based on their hierarchies of social values.[1] This gesture was, of course, Nietzschean.

Bataille also discovered in that vanished world a field of phantasms identical to his own and thereby put history in the service of his life, again in Nietzschean fashion. Before faulting his obsessiveness, his interpretive zeal or his inaccuracies, we should remember that Bataille was neither a historian nor an ethnographer; nor again a philosopher or a clinical psychologist. His work melds Mauss and Freud, Hegel, Nietzsche and Sade to forge new ways of thinking about culture. He does not seek to propose new facts, only new interpretations, and thereby new experiences for himself and for his reader.

In 'Extinct America', Bataille contrasts the essentially bureau-cratic culture of the Inca State – a culture incandescent with gold – with the monstrous excesses of the Aztecs. The orderly Inca, in his estimation, produced almost nothing of artistic brilliance. The Aztecs, on the other hand and following Prescott, created hypnotic and horrifying sculptures of their grotesque and malefic deities. In Bataille's tragic vision the Aztecs worshipped and enjoyed life to the extent that they worshipped and respected death. Their gods and the objects and ceremonies that represent and placate those gods possess an ambiguous and equivocal power, a power that is the essence of the sacred, according to Durkheim and Mauss. These authorities are never mentioned, despite Bataille's obvious debt to them. His only explicit historical references are to Prescott and Sahagún. He does however mention the decadent writer Octave Mirbeau and the Marquis de Sade. 'Continual crimes committed in broad daylight solely for the satisfaction of deified nightmares, terrifying phantasms! More than an historical incident, the priests' cannibal meals – the corpse ceremonies flowing with blood – evoke the blinding debauchery described by the illustrious Marquis de Sade.'[2] Bataille's interpretive imagination pushes fact into the realm of fiction: his language challenges his topic in its excess. Hyperbole, for Bataille, is both a strategy and a vice (again and again he will be faulted for this hermeneutic excess). The Aztecs did not simply lose this contest of wills, he suggests, they were crushed in a spectacle of fantastic, theatrical characters. And yet, 'death for the Aztecs was nothing'.[3]

The Aztecs will haunt Bataille's imagination throughout his career. They reappear in *Documents* (second year, no. 4) and a decade later in his article 'The Sacred'; they furnish the central and most compelling example in *La Part Maudite* (*The Accursed Share*) and, along with photographs of the Leng Tch'e, close his final work, *The Tears of Eros*. Their importance to him cannot be overemphasized and yet, historically speaking, they stand out as an utter anomaly.

Bataille's writings in *Aréthuse* and on the Aztecs proved an apprenticeship adequate to convince Georges Wildenstein, the publisher of the prestigious *Gazette des Beaux-Arts* and a dealer in art works by old masters, to finance a new publication under Bataille's editorial control. Pierre D'Espezel again facilitated the project, which he undoubtedly viewed as a continuation and extension of *Aréthuse*. Bataille proposed an innocuous title for the new publication: *Documents*.[4]

Subtitled 'Doctrines, Archaeology, Fine Arts, Ethnography' in the first year, the replacement of 'Doctrines' with 'Varieties' in the second signalled a substantial shift in the journal's agenda. The masthead listed Bataille as 'General Secretary', but he served as de facto editor. The well-known art historian Carl Einstein received editorial credit and was a major contributor, but Bataille's vision guided the publication.

Documents cast itself between several fields, each of which was undergoing a crisis of methodology and legitimacy in the late 1920s. It challenged the Fine Art tradition with ethnography and

DOCUMENTS

ARCHÉOLOGIE
BEAUX-ARTS
ETHNOGRAPHIE
VARIÉTÉS

6

Magazine illustré
paraissant dix fois par an

Carl EINSTEIN. Tableaux récents de Georges Braque. — Georges BATAILLE. Le gros orteil. — Dʳ Henri MARTIN. L'art solutréen dans la vallée du Roc (Charente). — Dessins inédits d'Ingres. — Marcel GRIAULE. Totémisme abyssin. — Le trésor de Nagy-Szent-Miklosz. — Alejo CARPENTIER. La musique cubaine.
Chronique par Jean Babelon, Jacques Baron, Georges Bataille, A. Eichhorn, Carl Einstein, Marcel Griaule, Michel Leiris.
Photographies de Jacques-André Boiffard et Eli Lotar.

PARIS,   106, Bᵈ Saint-Germain (VIᵉ)

ethnography with art history. Where ethnography flattens the field of cultural objects, endowing every artefact with equal value, art history elevates some objects and practices above others. Where the aesthetic trend in art criticism isolates objects from their world – by concentrating on the purely formal characteristics of those objects – ethnography insists that objects possess value only within the cultural context of their use: formalism is useless to the ethnographer. *Documents* brings the two methods together. It documents every aspect of life, says yes to everything.

Contributors included an array of luminaries from the fields in question, some already renowned, others soon to be: Jean Babelon and Pierre D'Espezel, Georges Henri Rivière and Paul Rivet, Marcel Griaule, André Schaeffner and, in one issue, a young Claude Lévi Strauss (writing as G. Monnet). Gradually, another group of writers and photographers began to appear in its pages with increasing frequency: dissident Surrealists for the most part, many of whom had been excluded from the Surrealist group and attacked in the Second Surrealist Manifesto of 1929. Like Pierre D'Espezel and Jean Babelon, these were also Bataille's friends, but they were friends from an entirely different world, André Masson's rue Blomet studio: Michel Leiris, Georges Limbour, Jacques André Boiffard, Roger Vitrac, Robert Desnos. *Documents* brought together the disparate worlds of Bataille's days and his nights.

The contents of the journal ranged even more widely than its various sub-titles promised: exercises in art history from the painted caves to the present; methodological meditations in ethnography and art history; forays into as yet critically unexplored territory, like jazz music; as well as the increasingly unclassifiable pieces for which the journal is famous. The inter-disciplinary agenda of the journal is summarized in the title of Carl Einstein's article, 'André Masson, an ethnographic study' (in no. 2). Masson too is exemplary of the contemporary artists considered in the journal's pages and plates: Giacometti, Léger, Miro, Dali, Arp, Gris, de Chirico, Lipchitz, Braque are among the others. In its second year, *Documents* devoted an entire issue to Picasso (no. 3). Established art, like that of Delacroix, was considered alongside unfashionable but classic works, like those of the all but forgotten mannerist Antoine Caron, and objects of material culture, including numismatic studies.

In *Documents*, however briefly, Bataille brought together an impossible community of radicals and reactionaries, respected elders and impertinent youths, from a range of disciplines that were actually hostile to one other in terms of their basic methods and orientation. Almost from the first issue tensions between these two groups and over Bataille's vision threatened to tear the publication apart. Scheduled to appear ten times per year, only fifteen issues were published before Wildenstein, at D'Espezel's exasperated suggestion, stopped footing the bill. As unlikely as the venture was in its day, such an interdisciplinary exercise is unthinkable in our own.

Our knowledge of Bataille's editorial control remains phantasmic. Editing is authorship by other means, as Bataille was well aware. His interests are visible in texts and images on almost every page of the journal. Though idiosyncratic, these interests were also both very specific and very wide-ranging. Bataille solicited articles from particular contributors who brought their own style, expertise and interests to the journal. At any given moment *Documents* betrays several overlapping and intersecting agendas. Its very instability, however, is itself an effect that Bataille undoubtedly intended to achieve. Leiris commented: 'Under Bataille's direction, items that were irritating, incongruous, even troubling, soon ceased to be mere objects of study and became inherent features of the publication itself.'[5]

Documents no. 2 initiated a 'Critical Dictionary' written by various contributors, though primarily by Bataille and Leiris.[6] Leiris had already undertaken a similar project, publishing 'Glossary: My Glosses' Ossuary', in *La Révolution Surréaliste* no. 1 in 1925: it consisted of Leiris's personal and poetic interpretations of seventy-five words.[7] As Bataille put it in his definition for the word 'formless', 'a dictionary begins when it no longer gives the meaning of words, but their tasks'.[8] The 'Critical Dictionary', then, proposes an essentially ethnographic inquiry into language. And it does so on the linguistic model Bataille exploited in *Story of the Eye*, where words can slip from their definitions through proximity to other similarly spelled words (*oeils* and *oeufs* for example) or through their denotation of similar objects (like circular ones). Bataille in particular extended this problematic into longer articles as well: an article on the 'The Big Toe' and his contribution to the special issue on Picasso, 'Rotten Sun'. The 'Critical Dictionary' did not appear in alphabetic order nor did it appear with any regularity. Rather it appeared in an idiosyncratic order in keeping with its principles: an assault on order, it was itself disordered.[9]

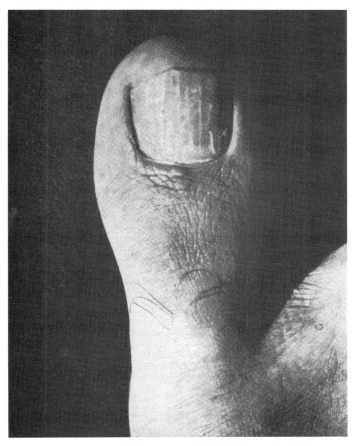

A human big toe, photographed by Jacques André Boiffard, reproduced in *Document* issue 6 (1929).

Documents also makes startling use of images. Many are simply illustrations for the articles in question: ethnographic images, material culture, paintings from the tradition. When an article treats a modern artist, it is generally accompanied by a substantial selection of photo plates illustrating their work. Many of Bataille's own contributions depend upon their illustrations. His article 'Base

Materialism and Gnosticism' is ostensibly an exercise in numismatics, commenting on representations of Gnostic gods on ancient medals and coins. When Bataille illustrated 'The Language of Flowers' (no. 3) with photographs by Karl Blossfeldt, the powerful images took on a life of their own. Similarly, in 'The Big Toe' (no. 6), Jacques André Boiffard's close-up photographs of big toes seem to sever the digits from the bodies to which they are undoubtedly attached. A few pages later, photographs from the slaughterhouses of La Villette feature a neat row of severed hoofs. All of these images anticipate, in their way, Bataille's article 'Sacrificial Automutilation and the Severed Ear of Vincent Van Gogh' (no. 8).

On 17 February 1930 Bataille audited Russian filmmaker Sergei Eisenstein's lecture at the Sorbonne. In Eisenstein's argument, concrete images provoke abstract thought by affecting the viewer both compositionally, within a given frame, and through montage.[10] Bataille referenced the lecture in 'The Deviations of Nature' (second year, no. 2) and reprinted images from Eisenstein's work. For Bataille, 'the expression of the philosophical dialectic through forms [as in Eisenstein] may take on the value of a revelation and determine the most elementary and thus consequential human relations'.[11] In *Documents*, as in Eisenstein, images *make* an argument through forms. They also make an argument through their relationship to texts. *Documents* disrupts the evidentiary or documentary function of images, without doing away with it entirely, by setting them in startling juxtaposition to one another. No text or image exists in isolation, though every text and image seems to push and pull away from the others, to put meaning and reference in question through montage.

Bataille's contributions to *Documents* coalesce around two main themes: materialism and a critique of ideal forms, particularly that of human beings. In his arguments materialist thought, Marxist or otherwise, has thus far been insufficiently materialist and the uniqueness of each human being requires us to reject any notion of an ideal form of humanity. Both of these themes are again Nietzschean, though Bataille's particular inflection of them owes a great deal to his reading of the Marquis de Sade.

His 'Critical Dictionary' article, 'Materialism', begins:

> Most materialists, even though they may have wanted to do away with all spiritual entities, ended up positing an order of things whose hierarchical relations mark it as specifically idealist. They situated dead matter at the summit of a conventional hierarchy of diverse facts, without perceiving that in this way they gave in to an obsession with the *ideal* form of matter, with a form that was closer than another other to what matter *should be*. Dead matter, the pure idea, and God in fact answer a question in the same way . . . a question that can only be posed by philosophers, the question of the essence of things, precisely of the *idea* by which things become intelligible.[12]

Materialism, in other words, finds its ideal in matter and this discovery obscures the nature of matter, which of necessity eludes thought. 'Materialism', for Bataille, 'is above all the obstinate negation of all idealism, which amounts to saying, finally, of the basis of all philosophy.'[13] Bataille, once again, is not a philosopher and does not seek to be. Philosophers are men and women of knowledge, while Bataille is a man of the world. For his part, Bataille proposes base materialism, a notion of base matter 'external and foreign to ideal human aspirations'. Base matter 'refuses to allow itself to be reduced to the great ontological machines resulting from these aspirations'.[14] In 'Base Materialism and Gnosticism' he says, 'I submit entirely to what must be called matter, since that exists outside of myself and the idea.'[15] Base materialism is a corrosive sense of matter, one in which form ruins. 'Matter', he writes, 'can only be defined as the *nonlogical difference* that represents in relation to the *economy* of the universe what *crime* represents in relation to the law.'[16] 'The universe,' he says, 'resembles nothing and is only *formless*.'[17]

Bataille's notion of base matter owes a great deal to the materialism of the Marquis de Sade, whose works depict a vast and vastly indifferent Nature within which human beings are prey to physical desires. Human beings are in nature but not of it. Animal desires are of course unique, situated as they are in unique moments in time and space. Sade's Enlightened sense of the uniqueness of each being is the foundation for his ethics, even though it tears humanistic thought up by its roots. Here again Bataille follows Sade. 'The Deviations of Nature' – illustrated by eighteenth-century studies in teratology – rejects any notion of an ideal human form, whether discovered through composite photography or through mathematical formulations, because 'each individual form escapes the common measure and is, to a certain degree, a monster'.[18] 'The Human Face' analyses old wedding photographs with a mocking laugh. Unlike Greek sculpture, for example, old photographs figure particular individuals, often in stilted and distinct clothing and poses. Looking at old photographs does not engender a sense of the continuity of the human race, quite the opposite. While we understand that the individuals captured in the photographs are in fact human beings and we may even be related to them, we cannot fully identify with them, with their habits of dress and behaviour. Old photographs, in this interpretation, capture the comportment and clothing, the aberrant forms and deviant figures of atavistic monsters.[19] Bataille does not simply reject humanism, he celebrates uniqueness, which is to say monstrosity.

Among the Gnostics, and in continuation of these themes, Bataille discovered his tutelary spirit, an acephalic or headless god, often depicted with the head of an ass or another animal. The ass, in Bataille's reading, is the 'most hideously comic animal' and at the same time 'the most humanly virile'; the Gnostic god, the solar ass, is an animal whose 'comic and desperate braying would be the signal for a shameless revolt against idealism in power'.[20] The braying ass can be heard in all of Bataille's work, most directly in the secret society Acéphale.

Alongside *Documents*, Bataille pursued several other projects. He continued working through his essays and drafts on solar mythology – 'The Solar Anus', 'The Jesuve' and 'The Pineal Eye' – none of which had been published yet. Several articles published in *Documents* grew out of drafts of 'The Pineal Eye' and vice versa. 'The Solar Anus' itself would finally be published, in an edition of 112 copies, in 1931, after *Documents* had ceased publication.

Another project was linked, in its way, to the *Story of the Eye*. Pascal Pia, who had been instrumental in publishing *Story*, agreed to help Bataille publish an *Erotic Almanac*. André Masson, who had illustrated *Story*, contributed some illustrations for the Marquis de Sade's *Justine*. Maurice Heine, himself almost single-handedly responsible for bringing Sade back into print in the 1920s and 1930s, gave Bataille an unpublished piece by Sade for use in the *Almanac*. Georges Limbour wrote a short story and Michel Leiris wrote an autobiographical text, which became the germinal seed of his book *L'Age d'homme* (*Manhood*). (Leiris dedicated *Manhood* to Bataille in thanks.) Bataille himself wrote a programme piece entitled 'The Use Value of the Marquis de Sade'. Plans for the *Almanac* collapsed with the trade in luxury books when the world economic crisis spread to France in 1930.[21] The project would however return in several forms at the very end of Bataille's life.

'The Use Value of the Marquis de Sade' brings together Durkheim and Mauss, Freud and Rudolf Otto, Marx and Hegel, Nietzsche and Sade in a startlingly original way. It stands as a summary of Bataille's influences up to 1930 and lays the foundation for his later work. Written as an 'open letter', the essay reproduces the dynamics of the solar mythology explored in 'The Solar Anus', 'The Jesuve' and 'The Pineal Eye' while simultaneously proposing a method of social and even cosmic analysis, a field of study he calls Heterology.

The essay proposes a binary division of material and epistemological forms and processes: interpenetrating ideas and things. Beings, including human beings, find materials to be either similar or dissimilar, homogeneous or heterogeneous to themselves (categories borrowed from Durkheim). The homogeneous world is familiar to us, recognizable, the potential object of knowledge. Its objects are useful. They are nutrients in our diet, tools in our toolbox, words in our language. Heterogeneous objects, on the other hand, are unknown to us, incomprehensible and useless. In process, these domains are dynamic; they open onto one another. The homogeneous system requires energy or information to maintain its form: it seeks to incorporate or synthesize the objects of the heterogeneous realm. But some things cannot be synthesized, they resist incorporation: just as some foods cannot be digested and must be excreted from the body, some things must be excreted from the system. Other things are too complex or too fearful for us to attempt to incorporate them. Instead we cherish them at a distance, we recognize their absolute difference from us, and see ourselves in the limits revealed by this distance. The homogeneous realm is thus bordered by two heterogeneous realms: one awe-inspiringly high, the other revoltingly low.

Human beings are thus caught in a world divided between known and unknown realms. Our bodily needs drive us into that world for food and information. Philosophers and scientists appropriate that world for use, they make it sensible and make the tools that we need to tame it. Workers ply those tools. Farmers till fields. Poets, in this argument, make sense of the world by proposing linguistic homogeneities: discourses of sense, ways of talking about things. They are philosophers of language. But the world itself – matter – remains beyond sense, beyond recuperation, beyond homogenization. The referent always exceeds the word. Matter always occurs in excess of meaning. The dialectic of forms is a negative dialectic in which forms ultimately do not cohere.

'The Use Value of the Marquis de Sade' proposes a field of study that will grapple with this elusive matter. Heterology, the study of heterogeneous materials, desires, words, ideas, does not seek to recuperate the objects of its study. Rather it studies their effects, it follows their course through the universe. Heterology is thus as opposed to philosophical system building as it is to the balanced harmonies sought by poetics. Heterology culminates in a form of 'intellectual scatology', a 'burst of laughter' that expels reductive explanations from philosophical speculation. It speaks only in order to reveal the limits of words. Heterology also forms the basis of a politics: one in which the realm of useful activity is separated from that of revolutionary desire, religious destruction or the squandering of wealth.

The essay's title is profoundly ironic. In Bataille's argument, Sade's work has no use value, it cannot be homogenized. It cannot be enjoyed as a literary representation of the homogeneous realm and it does not function as a workable philosophical world view. Philosophically, as an unlimited affirmation of materialist energy – of desire, of Nature, Sade's vision subordinates life itself to matter, creating a world in which self and social destruction are natural and common occurrences: a fantasy of pure thanatos. This reading of Sade is of course in sharp contrast to the Surrealist reading of the Divine Marquis. For the Surrealists, Sade is the ultimate avatar of freedom in all its forms. Bataille alone seems to have understood what that truly portends, and Bataille has incorporated that heterogeneous object – Sade – into the life of his thought, rendering his own work similarly useless. In *Blue of Noon*, written five years later, Bataille's narrator tells a literary dilettante, Xenie, that 'people who admire de Sade are con artists'.[22] He undoubtedly has the Surrealists in mind.

7

Excremental Philosopher

On 15 December 1929, in *La Révolution surréaliste* no. 12, André Breton published his Second Surrealist Manifesto.[1] It had been five years since the publication of the First Manifesto and the movement was simultaneously at its height and in tatters. In the previous two years Breton, Éluard and Aragon had each published books that secured their reputations: Breton's *Nadja* and *Surrealism and Painting*, Éluard's *Capital of Pain* and *Love, Poetry*, Aragon's *Paris Peasant*. They had also joined the Communist party, a move that at once galvanized the group and tore it apart. Members who had once been at its centre were now ostracized, publicly and violently. Philippe Soupault, Robert Desnos, Georges Limbour, Antonin Artaud, Roger Vitrac, Max Ernst and Joan Miró were all ousted. The Second Surrealist Manifesto served as a means of taking stock of all of these expulsions and as a means of reorienting the newly politicized group. Astonishingly, in a Manifesto of mostly *ad hominem* attacks, Breton's most sustained assault was against Georges Bataille. It closes the Manifesto with a profound and profoundly negative statement of principles offered in contrast to Bataille's work.

This is most surprising because Bataille had never been a member of the group. He had never even been tempted to join, even though most of his closest friends were members. It is also surprising in that Bataille had published so little at this point – a few articles in *Documents* and *Story of the Eye* (which Breton does not reference). Breton's attack is, however, not surprising in that, as he observes, several former members of the Surrealist group were now working with Bataille on *Documents*. By attacking Bataille, Breton could strike out at Leiris and Masson, Limbour and Desnos, and others as well. Breton identified Bataille as the leader of a splinter group even though such a group did not exist and Bataille had yet to become a leader. Finally, as the substance of Breton's attack concerned Bataille's materialism, attacking Bataille was a means of ingratiating Surrealism to the Communists on the basis of materialist philosophy.

Bataille's materialism, in Breton's reading, failed to complete the process of Hegelian synthesis: it recognized the opposed ideal and material realms but failed to see the ideal in material form and thereby to negate the negation. Breton himself, of course, failed to understand Bataille's critique of materialist philosophy. Breton recalled Bataille's image of the Marquis de Sade plucking petals from a rose – an image of material transformation – only to claim that a rose remains a rose with or without its petals: evidencing Breton's own failure to understand Bataille's critique of words and definitions. Breton finds Bataille's work 'philosophically vague', 'Pascalian', and 'poetically empty', characterized by a 'delirious abuse of adjectives'. For Breton, Bataille failed to grant reason its due by admitting that any attack on reason requires the tools of reason and that any attack on communication is itself an attempt at communication. In the end, Breton dismisses Bataille by diagnosing him with morbid psychasthenia: proclaiming him an 'excremental philosopher', obsessed with degradation and decay.

Bataille responded to Breton's aggression in several ways, one direct and immediate, others no less direct but much less immediate, over years and even decades. In the short term, Bataille responded with a few very pointed, occasionally polemic, essays. Over the long term, he would continue to write about – and against – Surrealism for the rest of his life. Much of Bataille's work can in fact be read as a complex riposte to the Surrealist exigency. He routinely reviewed new Surrealist publications and many of his major works – *Blue of Noon*, *Inner Experience* and *The Tears of Eros* – explicitly engage with Surrealism. André Breton would be, along with Jean-Paul Sartre after the Second World War, a privileged *other* for Bataille.[2]

More directly however, Bataille was instrumental in arranging the publication of a pamphlet denouncing Breton. Entitled 'A Corpse', the piece parodied a Surrealist pamphlet of the same title denouncing Anatole France in 1924. Robert Desnos came up with the idea while he and Bataille were sitting outside at the Deux-Magots. Bataille solicited additional contributions and got Georges-Henri Rivière to pay for it. By the time it was arranged, Desnos had cold feet, fearing that a reprisal might strengthen Breton's prestige. But it was too late. Jacques André Boiffard prepared a photo-collage of Breton with a crown of thorns. Michel Leiris, Georges Ribemont-Dessaignes, Roger Vitrac, Jacques Prévert, Max Morisse, Georges Limbour, Raymond Queneau, Alejo Carpentier and Desnos (after all), wrote pieces castigating Breton. Bataille's contribution referred to Breton as a 'castrated lion', an 'ox', an 'old aesthete and false revolutionary with the head of Christ', a 'pope'. He ultimately regretted it.[3]

Bataille also responded with another kind of writing which was less direct but only slightly less polemic, essays like 'The "Old Mole" and the Prefix *Sur* in the Words *Surhomme* [Superman] and Surrealist', 'The Use Value of the Marquis de Sade', and 'The Critique of the Foundations of the Hegelian Dialectic'. These pieces take up the dialogue with Surrealism by opening it to other discourses and debates: those around Nietzsche, Sade and Hegel. Bataille's attack is oblique; his language often double, a strategy borrowed from Greek tragedy; the enemy of his enemy is his friend.

In 'The "Old Mole" and the Prefix *Sur*', written in late 1930 for publication in *Bifur*, Bataille endorses a Marxist base materialism

('Decay is the laboratory of life', he quotes from Marx) against Surrealism ('a childhood disease of base materialism', he calls it).[4] Written alongside 'Sacrificial Automutilation and the Severed Ear of Vincent Van Gogh', and borrowing several of its terms, Bataille contrasts a materialist dialectic, yearning to steal fire from the sky in Promethean revolution, with an idealist – read Surrealist – dialectic, floating in detached irrelevance above the world. Surrealism lives for literature, for inconsequential and dreamy poetic language. Bataille sides with Nietzsche, who Breton loathes, praising the revolutionary laughter that follows the death of god, a laughter that sweeps social and linguistic hierarchies away.

Bifur ceased publication before the piece appeared in print and Bataille withheld it thereafter, perhaps already realizing that historical materialism itself failed to accommodate base materialism. A year later, the materialist ground of historical materialism became the topic of Bataille's first contribution to *La Critique Sociale*, 'The Critique of the Foundations of Hegelian Dialectic' (co-written with Raymond Queneau). In it he and Queneau observe that the famous Hegelian (and Marxist) 'negation of the negation' does not in fact apply to natural processes; the physically *material* processes in dialectical materialism. Engels struggled with the problem for years, understanding how deeply it cuts into the core of Marxist thought. Bataille and Queneau's article presents a profound challenge to that thought, but it also undermines the basis of Breton's criticism against him.

On 15 January 1930 Marie-Antoinette Bataille – Georges' mother – died. The son held vigil over her body. His wife was asleep in the next room. Sylvia was pregnant with Bataille's first child (his daughter Laurence would be born on 10 June). Writing about that night in *Le Petit* (*The Little One*), following an excursus on remorse, the narrator, Louis Trente, reports: 'I jerked off naked, at night, by my mother's corpse.'[5] Immediately thereafter he insists on the factual accuracy of the statement. Two years prior to her death, his mother away for the night, Bataille had held an orgy in her apartment, in her bed, on his birthday. Watching over her corpse, memories of the orgy kindled his desire. But the pallor and immobility of the dead woman in the gleam of the candles froze him in stupefaction. Agitated but unable to satisfy himself, he went into the kitchen to finish. Shortly thereafter he prepared a brief note on the topic.[6] The text does not mention that his pregnant wife was sleeping nearby.

In *Blue of Noon*, the narrator reports a nearly identical event on two separate occasions. He tells Lazare and Xénie, apparently testing their friendship but also clearly prostrating himself before their inevitable disgust. In his first version of the story, he omits the identity of the corpse: she is simply a shrivelled old woman.[7] In the second version, the corpse is that of his mother and he is aroused but also frightened, in a kind of trance.[8] Neither version admits that the narrator's real life alter ego could not satisfy his desire, nor do they locate the origin of that desire in memories of an orgy rather than in the body and state of the corpse. Both versions emphasize the ambiguous nature of the act, the narrator's simultaneous attraction to and repulsion from it. Both versions emphasize the simultaneous monstrosity and allure of the corpse. The novel, in short, clarifies its descriptions of the event for literary purposes.

Necrophilia, of course, appears as a central theme in *Story of the Eye* and, even more broadly than these two versions of the tale indicate, in *Blue of Noon*. All eroticism is ultimately beyond the pleasure principle: it transports its practitioner into self-loss, the 'little death'. Necrophilia carries eroticism to an extreme by presenting the indifferent body of a corpse as a field of identification for an erotic partner intent on passing beyond the limited pleasures of this world. Short of suicide, identification with the dead is the closest one may come to embodying the self-loss demanded by the death drive.

Bataille read about necrophilia in Sade's *La Nouvelle Justine* and in 1931 – and therefore after the fact – in Krafft-Ebing's *Psychopathia sexualis*.[9] And he would continue to discuss it in many, if not most, of his writings on eroticism. But mixing, as this incident did, memory and desire, can we speak of Bataille's actions in this case as true necrophilia? The narrator of *Blue of Noon* classifies himself as a necrophiliac, but we cannot make the same claim for Bataille himself on the basis of a unique incident in a lifetime of erotic excess. The event does however testify to Bataille's willingness to explore eroticism in all of its forms and to accept his desires – no matter how horrifying – whenever they overtake him. It also testifies to the degree to which such practices marked him: if it had not he would not have written about it so insistently nor hidden it in the ways that he did.

A month later, in February 1930, the Bibliothèque Nationale transferred Bataille out of the Cabinet des Médailles. He took the transfer as an affront. It certainly signalled the end of his proximity to Pierre D'Espezel, who had once been his staunch supporter. *Documents* ceased publication before the year was out.

8

The Democratic Communist Circle

Documents lost its funding in January 1931. Bataille's letters from that year betray his depressed and restless spirit. He didn't have much to say to old friends like Michel Leiris and he was simply too physically and morally depressed to write to newer ones like Raymond Queneau. At the same time, he embarked on a wide range of new projects and involvements.[1]

With Marcel Duhamel, a former Surrealist, and Jacques Klein, a journalist and playwright, Bataille attempted to found a weekly magazine devoted to universal history. They hoped to enlist former Dadaist Max Morise in the project as an illustrator but nothing came of it. The idea of universal history stayed with Bataille, however, becoming one of his primary ambitions during the 1950s.

In November 1931 Bataille began attending the presentation of patients at the Saint-Anne asylum. This may have been part of a short-lived effort to pursue a certificate in pathological psychology or he may simply have sought to ground his psychological and psychoanalytic readings in actual practice (beyond his own experience in analysis). Around this time, Bataille read *The Interpretation of Dreams* and gave some thought to translating a book of psychoanalytic essays on Dostoevsky by Freud and Theodor Reik. He also reviewed Krafft-Ebing's *Psychopathia sexualis* and Stefan Zweig's biographical essay on Freud in *La Critique Sociale*.[2]

Published in October 1931, Bataille's review of *Psychopathia Sexualis* was his first contribution to *La Critique Sociale*, a bi-monthly journal of books and ideas that would replace *Documents* as Bataille's primary venue of publication for the next three years. Edited by Boris Souvarine, *La Critique Sociale* was affiliated with the Democratic Communist Circle, a group which met in a café on Thursday nights to discuss politics and Marxist theory (for example on 30 March 1933 at the Café Augé they talked about 'Italian Fascism and German National Socialism').[3] As later with Acéphale, membership of the Circle did not require or imply participation in the journal. Bataille joined the Circle along with Raymond Queneau, Michel Leiris, Jacques Baron, Jean Piel and Dr Dausse, and there made the acquaintance of several people who would play an enormous role in his life over the next few years: Colette Peignot (known by her middle name, Laure), Simone Weil, Pierre Kaan, Jean Bernier, Patrick Waldberg, Georges Ambrosino and others: the core group of his collaborators in Counter Attack, Acéphale and beyond.

Boris Souvarine, the primary animator of both the Democratic Communist Circle and *La Critique Sociale*, was born Boris Lifschitz in Kiev in 1895 but raised in Paris from the age of two. His family was working class and he developed anarcho-syndicalist sympathies while still an adolescent. He began writing for a socialist journal while serving as a soldier in the First World War and wrote to Lenin shortly after the war. Lenin wrote back on the eve of the Russian revolution, establishing Souvarine, as he already called himself, as a well-informed and connected link between the worker's parties of France and Russia. In 1920 Souvarine spent ten months in jail for his role in an attempted general strike called for by railway workers, dock workers, steelworkers, miners and builders. While in jail he was elected to the managing committee of the nascent French Communist Party and began editing a theoretical journal, the *Bulletin Communiste*. Upon his release he left Paris for Moscow where he served on three committees within the Comintern: the presidium, the secretariat and the executive committee. In 1924 Souvarine stood up for Trotsky at the Bolshevik party Congress on moral and theoretical grounds and thereby compromised his own role within the party and in the Soviet Union. His return to Paris was as inevitable as was his excommunication.

After his return, the *Bulletin* became a vehicle for anti-Stalinist criticism, though without following Trotsky. Souvarine's adherence was to Marxist philosophy rather than to one or another contemporary embodiment of that philosophy. His ambition was to rejuvenate Marxist thought and political action by simultaneously returning to the classical texts and supplementing Marxism with the insights of French sociology, psychoanalysis, contemporary economic theory and historical studies. In 1926 he organized a discussion group for this purpose called the Marx-Lenin Communist Circle. Souvarine signalled further distance from Stalin's communism and even stronger adherence to his own independent thought when he changed the name of the group to the Democratic Communist Circle in 1930. He then devoted five years to writing a harshly critical biography of Stalin.

The Surrealists approached Souvarine en masse in 1927, viewing him incorrectly as a Trotskyist, but they joined the French Communist Party shortly thereafter. Later they would support Trotsky during his exile and last days in Mexico. This in mind, and aside from other personal or intellectual motives, it is easy to see why Souvarine's group may have seemed welcoming to ex-Surrealists like Jacques Baron and Michel Leiris.

Souvarine rarely had funds to publish his *Bulletin*. In early 1931 he met Laure through her former lover Jean Bernier, himself a committed Communist and a member of the Democratic Communist Circle. Laure had only recently returned from an extremely traumatic trip to the Soviet Union. A series of failed romances and political aspirations – beginning with her relationship with Bernier – had left her at a particularly low point. Souvarine set about saving her, providing a channel for her tremendous energy. And she saved Souvarine by funding *La Critique Sociale* with her inheritance. Boris was the nominal editor of the journal but he and Laure shared the production duties. Pierre Kaan helped organize the reviews.

In keeping with Souvarine's general project, the journal was intended to be a forum for the rejuvenation of Marxist thought through encounters with other fields: sociology, psychoanalysis, philosophy, economics and history. The project itself, and several of the fields of study it embraced, was forbidden by Stalinist orthodoxy. The contents of *La Critique Sociale* included long essays, archival materials and a substantial number of reviews of books and other journals. Contributors included, along with Souravine and Bataille, Pierre Kaan, Jean Bernier, Michel Leiris, Raymond Queneau, Julius Dickmann, Lucien Laurat, Franz Mehring, Pierre Pascal, Simone Weil and Laure writing under the pseudonym Claude Araxe for the occasional book review. *La Critique Sociale* thus had much in common with *Documents*, several shared contributors to be sure, but more importantly a willingness to rethink the very basis of any given field, to take all sciences and modes of thought seriously. Where *Documents* brought ethnography and aesthetics into encounters with one another and with psychoanalysis, *La Critique Sociale* set about revitalizing Marxism through very similar encounters. For Souvarine and his contributors, the challenge was to think the whole of society without denying themselves the insights offered by any useful set of tools.

Significantly, the Democratic Communist Circle was not the only discussion group Bataille frequented during the early 1930s. L'Ordre nouveau was, in Michel Surya's summary, 'an anti-Bolshevik, anti-Capitalist, anti-parliamentarian, corporative, pro-worker . . . federalist group' created by Arnaud Dandieu and Robert Aron. Alexandre Marc, Jean Jardin, Claude Chevally, Daniel-Rops, Jacques Naville and Gabriel Marcel were members.[4]

Dandieu worked with Bataille at the Bibliothèque Nationale. The group published a manifesto in 1930 and a journal after 1933. Bataille did not contribute to either, but he did frequent the group to some extent and perhaps even provided written comments on at least one chapter of Dandieu and Aron's book *La Révolution nécessaire* in 1933.

Masses was another such group, this one organized by René Lefeuvre. Here again Bataille did not contribute to the group's eponymous journal but did frequent the group to some extent. The photographer Dora Maar was a member of *Masses* and it was in this context that her relationship with Bataille began, in either the autumn of 1933 or the spring of 1934. They would be lovers on and off over the next two years, until she began her relationship with Picasso.

Beginning in 1931, simultaneously with his participation in the Democratic Communist Circle, Bataille began attending Alexandre Koyré's Monday night course at the École Practique des Hautes Études on the infinite and 'learned ignorance' in the thought of Nicholas of Cusa. As in the Circle, Raymond Queneau was his companion in the course. In 1932 Koyré lectured on the religious philosophy of Hegel while Bataille and Queneau co-wrote their 'Critique of the Foundations of the Hegelian Dialectic'. After Koyré's lectures, the speaker and his auditors retired to the Café d'Harcourt at the corner of the Place de la Sorbonne and the boulevard Saint-Michel to continue their discussion. Alexandre Kojève, Henry Corbin and Fritz Heinemann were among the auditors. In 1933 Koyré, Corbin and Henri Charles Puech founded *Recherches Philosophiques*, an annual that would publish Bataille's 'The Labyrinth' in 1936 and several of Pierre Klossowski's essays on the Marquis de Sade.

Despite Koyré's brilliance and philosophical reach, his influence on this generation of thinkers was far less than that of his successor, Alexandre Kojève. Born to bourgeois parents in Moscow in 1902,

Alexandre Kojevnikov lost his father in the Russo-Japanese war in Manchuria in 1905 and, twelve years later, saw his stepfather murdered by a gang of looters at the family country house. In 1918 Kojevnikov was imprisoned by the Bolsheviks for dealing goods on the black market. He converted to Communism in prison but his bourgeois background prevented him from continuing his studies after his release. Convinced that he was living through a monumental moment in history, he emigrated first to Poland and then to Germany, to Heidelberg University, where he studied philosophy with Karl Jaspers and several languages: Chinese, Sanskrit, Tibetan. (Bataille was himself studying these languages during these same years.) By 1928 Kojevnikov had moved on to Paris (his French and German were both perfect), where he continued his studies and eventually became friends with fellow Russian exile Alexandre Koyré. (Kojève, as he was now known, had an affair with Koyré's brother's wife, and his friendship with the philosopher was born of it.)

Koyré asked Kojève to take over his lectures at the École Pratique des Hautes Études in 1933 and Kojève reread Hegel's *Phenomenology of Spirit* in preparation. Though he'd read it on several previous occasions, reading the book in 1933 as Stalin consolidated his power, as the Nazis tightened their grip on Germany, as the rest of world stood watching, overwhelmed him. He felt he understood it with perfect clarity. Hegel's book wasn't abstract in the slightest, it was concrete, mistaken in a few particulars, but concrete, the drama of consciousness struggling against the horizon of death. Kojève's Hegel is a Hegel of the end of history: when thought and action have exhausted their possibilities and all that remains is repetition; an anthropocentric Hegel, whose God is a projection of man himself and whose man is a rejection of man's own animality; a Communist Hegel whose slaves are workers struggling for recognition and rights.

On Mondays at 5.30 Kojève explicated Hegel's *Phenomenology*. Like Ferdinand de Saussure before him and Jacques Lacan in his direct wake, Kojève's real legacy was in his lectures. The *Phenomenology* was not yet available in French (Jean Hyppolite's translation would not appear until 1939), so Kojève translated it for his listeners and explained it, clarifying its obscurities with contemporary examples. His words fell on the ears of a generation of French intellectuals: Jacques Lacan, Raymond Aron, Roger Caillois, Maurice Merleau-Ponty, Eric Weil and occasionally André Breton among others. Raymond Queneau kept such assiduous notes that they could be published in 1947 under Kojève's name.[5] Bataille registered for three of the six years Kojève held the seminar (1934–5, 1935–6 and 1937–8), though he undoubtedly attended during the other years as well. Speaking plainly, he later claimed that Kojève's reading was 'equal to the book' itself, that he was 'suffocated, transfixed' by it: 'Kojève's course exhausted me, crushed me, killed me ten times.'[6] Queneau, for his part, said that Bataille sometimes fell asleep in class.[7]

Kojève's lectures were hardly Bataille's first encounter with Hegel. He had borrowed Hegel's *Logic*, *Lectures on the Philosophy of History*, and even the *Phenomenology* from the Bibliothèque Nationale on repeated occasions beginning in 1925. He had attended Koyré's lectures on Hegel's philosophy of religion during the previous academic year. And he had already written, with Raymond Queneau, his 'Critique of the Foundations of the Hegelian Dialectic'. But Kojève's presentation of Hegel's thought was nevertheless decisive. In the same way that Alfred Métraux mediated Bataille's reading of Durkheim and Mauss, Lev Shestov mediated his reading of Nietzsche and Dostoevsky and Adrian Borel mediated his reading of Freud, Alexandre Kojève mediated his reading of Hegel.

After Kojève's lectures, Hegel became Bataille's favourite foe, the privileged enemy against whom he constantly fought. For Bataille Hegelian philosophy was the 'only philosophy that lives', but his *Phenomenology* was nevertheless a 'decisive failure'; a thought which acquired its power through its insistence on completeness but which was itself incomplete and susceptible to ruin.[8] Hegel's thought proposed itself as an absolute, as utterly homogeneous, while Bataille proposed himself as the living negation of that thought, as utterly heterogeneous to it. Where Hegel's philosophy was useful, meaningful, serious work, Bataille's 'work' was useless play; the tremor of chance in the realm of absolute necessity; laughter in the library. Writing against Hegel, too, was a way for Bataille to write against many of his other foes, Breton and later Sartre. Despite these differences, Kojève himself became and remained a good friend and collaborator. He lectured on Hegel at the Collège de Sociologie and continued to respond to Bataille's writing until the end of its author's life.

Bataille never published his heterological programme piece 'The Use Value of the Marquis de Sade'. Rather, he refined and expanded its ideas in the series of remarkable essays that he published in *La Critique Sociale* between 1932 and 1934: 'The Critique of the Foundations of the Hegelian Dialectic', 'The Notion of Expenditure', 'The Problem of the State' and 'The Psychological Structure of Fascism'. Alongside these articles, Bataille also wrote book reviews for the journal, which was structured primarily as a review of current publications across the disciplines. His topics ranged widely, from Céline's *Journey to the End of the Night* and Malraux's *Man's Fate*, to books on Hegel, Freud and Christianity. He also continued his polemic against the Surrealists in a series of short reviews of their latest books and of the journal *Minotaure*. (Swiss publisher Albert Skira had initially enlisted Bataille himself, along with André Masson, to direct the fledgling journal in the spirit of *Documents*. Then the Surrealists quickly took over the rather sumptuous review, which didn't interest Bataille very much. From its early issues, he praised only its reproductions of recent works by Picasso and Masson, and writings by Jacques Lacan and the Marquis de Sade.[9])

Bataille's longer articles testify to his primary and at this point primarily political concerns. They deepen and clarify many of the themes and ideas that he had been thinking through in his unpublished essays over the previous five years and they also explicitly propose a programme of additional reflection and elaboration. 'The Notion of Expenditure' was preceded by a note from Boris Souvarine, speaking as the editor of *La Critique Sociale*. The note was ostensibly there to mark a space of distance between Bataille's 'notion' and Souvarine's own social thought, but it also announced Bataille's essay as being part of a forthcoming and much larger book, suggesting that perhaps Bataille's position would become acceptable were it elaborated more thoroughly.[10] 'The Psychological Structure of Fascism' was preceded by a similar note, this time by Bataille himself. The note again located the essay within a much larger whole. It also made excuses for its author's failure to explain his methodology more clearly. 'This is obviously the principle shortcoming of an essay that will not fail to astonish and shock those who are unfamiliar with French Sociology, modern German philosophy (phenomenology), and psychoanalysis.'[11]

It would take Bataille another seventeen years to complete the first volume of the whole proposed by these notes – *The Accursed Share* – and even that book would announce additional elaborations and developments of its central thought. *L'Erotisme* (*Eroticism*) (1957) is one such elaboration; Bataille did not live long enough to complete the others. Of course, these later works cannot be subsumed beneath the initial impetus or the essays that germinated them. The whole proposed by the essays in *La Critique Sociale* was certainly not the whole found in or proposed by Bataille's works in the 1940s or 1950s. This is significant in a corpus devoted to the drift of meaning, the slippage of truth from fact to fancy and back. Over and over again Bataille will conceive or announce an enormous project and complete only a part of it or, conversely, he will complete a small essay or fiction only to claim that the completed piece is in fact a fragment of a much larger whole, which itself will remain unfinished.

Bataille's notes from the early 1930s suggest that the larger project he intended to write at that time was a book about fascism in France. His essays from *La Critique Sociale* speak directly to this issue as do a great many pages of notes, which nevertheless do not constitute a book. The book that he did complete in 1935 was not a sociological or historical study of fascism at all but rather a novel about it, *Blue of Noon*; a novel he did not publish until the late 1950s.

These complexities in mind, one may observe that Bataille's corpus often seems to present an enormous, labyrinthine hall of mirrors, where unpublished mythological speculation informs published essays in aesthetics and ethnography, where essays in psychology and sociology influence fictions, and the facts of language explored in fictional worlds inform economic theories elaborated across historical examples. The corpus is at once utterly and obsessively coherent and utterly incoherent and disrupted. In *Theory of Religion*, he explains:

> What is offered the reader, in fact, cannot be an element, but must be the ensemble in which it is inserted: it is the whole human assemblage and edifice, which must be, not just a pile of scraps, but rather a self-consciousness. In a sense the unlimited assemblage is the impossible.[12]

In Bataille, facts, falsehoods, and fantasies compete with, complete, and displace one another, the insights of various disciplines are used to complement and to undermine one other, and the whole is proposed as a means to *experience* the travails of consciousness grappling with its situation.

Bataille's single most significant essay, 'The Notion of Expenditure', inverts the classical – and hence also the Marxist – economic model by insisting that consumption rather than production determines the nature and goals of culture. In short, societies can and should be measured and understood based on the way they consume resources rather than on relations of production. Thorstein Veblen made a similar claim in *Theory of the Leisure Class* but from the opposite perspective. Where Veblen condemned consumption, particularly in its conspicuous form, Bataille accepted consumption and, following Freud, believed that human life would improve were human beings able to find appropriate channels for it. This is the central and often overlooked purpose of his work. Thirty years later, in *The Tears of Eros*, he restated this purpose plainly: 'Unless we consider the various possibilities for consumption which are opposed to war, and for which erotic pleasure – the instant consumption of energy – is the model, we will never discover an outlet founded on reason.'[13]

Accepting consumption, according to Bataille, means accepting the entirety of human experience: the useless, the wasteful, the irrational and the negative as well as the productive, the positive, the rational and the useful. A central fantasy of Western civilization has been that the entirety of the world and of human experience can be made useful and can be explained rationally. Bataille writes to reveal the madness of this fantasy, the blindness of this vision to the facts and mechanisms of consumption. Dramatizing this dilemma in 'The Notion of Expenditure', Bataille proposes the story of a father who is blind to the excesses of his son. The father cannot accept, or even *see*, the son's pursuit of pleasure, though the father himself also indulges in his own wasteful extravagances. The father will only speak of useful things with his son, will only support the son's entrance into the homogeneous world of responsibility, of respectability. This father is obviously a stand-in for our civilization, for all of our directors of conscience, but it is first and primarily a stand-in for Bataille's own father, a man who was literally blind to his own excesses. In Bataille's argument, it is incumbent upon the son to accept the truth of life in its entirety, to accept both utility and uselessness, to find a place for waste in society.

Consumption falls into two types: one in which resources are consumed in order to maintain the basic needs of a body or society and another in which resources are simply squandered. The first type of consumption is essentially part of the production process. Examples of the second type of consumption, on the other hand, are generally considered to be a waste of either money or time or both. These include our fascination with unreasonably expensive jewellery and other luxury objects; the ways in which earlier cultures squandered human and animal life through ritual sacrifice; the entire realm of sport in contemporary culture – not only our stadiums and the inordinate salaries of our athletes but also the money that we lose in gambling, the time we spend studying facts and figures related to sports, and the money we spend on products related to our teams. Finally, consumption characterizes the entire realm of the arts, which represents both real and symbolic types of expenditure. Architecture, opera and film are spheres in which vast sums are spent in creating spectacles for our amusement. Literature and visual culture squander language, signs and the structures that create and sustain communication in our culture. Activities too can be understood under the heading of this kind of consumption: laughter, eroticism (i.e. sexuality enjoyed for its own sake rather than for the purpose of procreation), dancing and the like. But these are only a few examples of the pervasive phenomenon of consumption. The essential aspect of this second type of consumption is of course that it involves profitless, useless or senseless expenditure. None of these activities can be justified by reasonable argument. Other than in the case of the ancient practice of sacrifice, these activities do not evoke or reveal a holy or transcendent realm. They are, quite simply and in their purest form, waste.

Once upon a time, however, consumption did serve a social function. It served to recirculate wealth in society through the practice of gift giving, it established power relations by establishing the symbolic structures of glory and prestige and it permitted individuals to reaffirm their identities as individuals within a social system based on the structures of glory and prestige. In such systems the social value of an individual was measured not by earnings (discussed in hushed tones, if at all) but rather by prestige, a factor related to an individual's ability to squander wealth. The most powerful individual was inevitably the individual with the power to lose the most, a power revealed only through the activation of that loss. Kings built castles, for example, congregations cathedrals, families mansions. These buildings were both symbolic and very real examples of wasted wealth. Those who could not make such social offerings or displays were nevertheless reciprocally affirmed in their obvious difference from those who could.

Among the Tlingit, the Haida, the Tsimshian and the Kwakiutl peoples of the northwest coast of North America, the practice of ritual potlatch – the ritualized squandering of wealth – assumed a central place in society. As Marcel Mauss described these rituals in *The Gift*, potlatch festivals – and all festivals inherently exemplify potlatch – were held at turning points in the life of an individual or community: birth, marriage and death were celebrated with ritual gifts. These gifts entailed a reciprocal obligation, the necessity of responding in kind once one had received a gift. Thus the entire society – and not only these societies – was structured around the giving and receiving of gifts, not for one's own use, but to continue a cycle of reciprocity and hence the recirculation of wealth. Property or wealth acquired as a gift did not become one's own private property, rather it became property that one must necessarily give away in one's turn, fulfilling one's obligations within the circuit of exchange. Under extreme conditions these structures of mutual obligation were challenged by the size or scope of gifts. Prestige was established by giving gifts so large that they could not be returned. Wealth in these cases might also simply be wasted: slaves' throats cut in honour of a neighbour, copper bars smashed and thrown into the sea as a means of securing prestige.

In potlatch, consumption is indistinct from the practice of sacrifice, as Marcel Mauss and Henri Hubert defined it in their classic treatise on the subject.[14] Sacrifice, as a religious practice, establishes a connection between two separate spheres of experience, the homogeneous profane sphere of everyday life and the heterogeneous sacred sphere of timeless and infinite value, the realm of the gods. In sacrifice an offering is effectively thrown out of everyday life, cast beyond utility into a realm beyond our comprehension. Bataille's notion of expenditure wilfully conflates sacrificial consumption and raw waste, the high and the low, religion and popular culture. The religious practice of blood sacrifice has of course disappeared from modern culture, as have the gods who demanded it. We no longer slaughter the firstborn of our animals or children, nor do we build cathedrals to the glory of our gods. But the structure and the social and psychological necessities of sacrifice have not disappeared, they persist in consumption. Consumption is, in short, a means by which individuals negotiate their identities through expenditure.

Bataille pushed this thought to its limits in 'Sacrifices', an essay in ontology that he wrote during July 1933.[15] He had become gravely ill during the summer. Bedridden one sunny afternoon, a visitor's painful departure sent him into an ecstasy of pain. He does not say who departed.[16] In agony, he envisioned a type of catastrophic subjectivity, a 'self that dies', a subject whose existence is a mere tremor in the void that is this world. The self that dies recognizes the tenuousness of its existences, the uniqueness of its being in the world – that a man and a woman came together to produce a unique child, a child nurtured by unique circumstances on a unique path through a persistently hostile physical, material world. The self is not of the world, it is heterogeneous to it, though it is in it. The self that dies recognizes its unique dilemma, its simultaneous isolation and openness, and it lives through laceration; by opening itself to its opposite, to discontinuity and death, the not 'I' accessed through expenditure. The self that dies pursues its own demise through intoxicated delirium, laughter, eroticism, meditation and a thousand other means. It gains access to the world beyond the self by eradicating, however briefly, self-consciousness. These gestures of personal expenditure repeat the gestures of social expenditure outlined in 'The Notion of Expenditure'. The paradox of sacrifice is the paradox of the prestige that follows from sacrifice. André Masson's illustrations of ancient gods in their death agonies, ancient sacrifices of ancient subjects, would illustrate the essay. But Bataille struggled to publish it for the next three years.

The piece failed to find a publisher at least in part because its message was and is unacceptable to bourgeois culture. In bourgeois culture, as Bataille put it, 'everything that was generous, orgiastic, and excessive has disappeared . . . wealth is now displayed behind closed doors, in accordance with depressing and boring conventions.'[17] The wealthy no longer squander their wealth in spectacles for civic enjoyment nor to establish the by-product of that enjoyment, prestige. In bourgeois culture, social relations and hence also individual identities are, in fact, no longer structured by prestige, rather they are determined by social contract, law and, ultimately, the power of the state. On the individual level sacrifice persists, but it remains unspeakable.

In the absence of prestige, social relations become unmoored, society becomes unhinged, identities become fluid: who is rich? who poor? who is responsible for whom? in what way and why? By withholding the social spectacle of wealth, the wealthy effectively withhold an essential element of social structure, and not just of social structure. The poor receive neither the direct fruits of their labour nor the spectacle of wealth provided by the wealthy in previous cultures. The very humanity of the poor becomes an object of denial and suppression on the part of the rich, whose wealth also no longer circulates as it once did. In the eyes of the rich, the poor constitute a heterogeneous mass, outside the world of society.

The poor, in Bataille's argument, have three ways out, each predicated on the opposed psychological necessities of identification and sacrifice. In the first option, Christianity offers them a mental spectacle which associates 'social ignominy and the cadaverous degradation of the torture victim with divine splendor . . . a mental agonistic orgy practiced at the expense of the real struggle'.[18] The saviour is both like the poor, because lowly, yet unlike them, because divine. He is at once homogeneous and heterogeneous to their experience and therefore presents a psychologically satisfying object of devoted contemplation.

In the second solution, the poor participate in the 'revolutionary destruction' of the dominating wealthy class, a 'bloody and in no way limited social expenditure'.[19] For Bataille the class struggle culminates in a potlatch in which the wealthy are the sacrificial victims. In this vision, the poor, who lack wealth of their own, have nothing else to consume but the very people who dominate and control their existence. Such a revolution would also of necessity consume all of the symbols of the previous social relation. Revolution in this vision is thus catastrophic, consuming the entirety of the socius (society) in a conflagration of wills that destroys every distinct class and individual identity. For Bataille revolution entails the convulsive release of repressed energies in an orgy of bloodshed. This revolutionary programme proposes a festival rather than a future for society.

Fascism offers a third way out. Bataille studies it length in 'The Psychological Structure of Fascism', an essay that melds Durkheim and Mauss with Freud's insights into mass psychology and the Marquis de Sade's vision of sovereignty. In fascism, the fascist leader plays the role of a sovereign with whom both rich and poor may, each in their own way, identify. The fascist leader is as exalted and powerful as the Christian saviour is degraded and dispossessed.

Both figures, however, one high, one low, are utterly heterogeneous to the poor. Through their identification with a figure who is so different from themselves, the psychological need for sacrificial consumption – the need to mentally escape the confines of one's own limited identity – is satisfied. For the poor, even the leader's excesses serve to reinforce the fundamental illusion on which the power of the leader depends: physical violence is secondary to the psychological violence, the self-renunciation that is the essence of the psychological structure of fascism. Fascism also functionally unifies the sovereignty of the leader and that of the state, in different ways under different circumstances, relieving fascist states of the threat of revolution by integrating the homogeneous and heterogeneous elements of society in mutual identification with the sovereign.

Even in the pages of *La Critique Sociale*, an essentially Marxist publication, the perspective evidenced in these articles offered slim hope for a proletarian revolution. Of the options Bataille saw as being available to the working class, revolutionary destruction seemed the least likely, while fascism seemed far from unlikely. Bataille understood and stated the appeal of fascism so clearly that he would later be misunderstood as embracing it.

Within the Democratic Communist Circle, and therefore among the other contributors to *La Critique Sociale*, Bataille's position occasioned profound misgivings. Boris Souvarine, as we have seen, distanced himself from Bataille with a note prefacing 'The Notion of Expenditure'. Simone Weil, at this time a fellow traveller in the Circle, wrote a letter which crystallized the stalemate she and undoubtedly many others in the Circle faced when confronting Bataille's thought.

> The revolution is for [Bataille] the triumph of the irrational, for me of the rational; for him a catastrophe, for me a methodical action in which one must strive to limit the damage; for him the

liberation of the instincts, and notably those that are generally considered pathological, for me a superior morality. What is there in common? . . . How is it possible to coexist in the same revolutionary organization when on one side and the other one understands by revolution two contrary things?[20]

The first half of 'The Psychological Structure of Fascism' was published in November 1933. Three months later, before the second half had a chance to appear, the political landscape in France, and indeed in Europe, changed utterly, and so did the personal ties that bound the central members of the Circle together.

9

Crisis

However hyperbolic it may seem to us now, Bataille's vision of political revolution as a catastrophic upsurge of unconscious and irrational emotion – a view captured in the phrase 'revolutionary destruction' – was not particularly extreme in its day. Hitler had been in power for a year and he had solidified that power, purging the German state of communists and other undesirables. In the Soviet Union Stalin continued his own purges (Trotsky arrived in France in 1933). Conditions of economic depression were at their peak. Alexandre Kojève took over Koyré's lectures on Hegel in January 1934: during their course he would announce the end of history. Bataille wrote: 'It seems that today, as in 1848, a revolutionary contagion is showing itself across Europe.'[1]

Also in January 1934, on the 8th, Alexandre Stavisky – a businessman, loan-shark caught laundering bonds – died of an apparently self-inflicted gunshot wound. His death was a little too convenient for newspapers on both sides of the political spectrum not to suggest that he had been murdered as part of a political cover up. By mid January the scandalized French government was in turmoil. Prime Minister Chautemps was replaced by Edouard Daladier, who fired the chief of police. The ultra-right political parties took to the streets: Action Française, Croix-de-feu, the Jeunnesses Patriotes and the Mouvement Franciste among other groups clashed with police during a massive demonstration at the Palais Bourdon on 6 February. Fifteen people died; 2,000 were wounded. Daladier dropped out of office. The Communist Party and the other groups on the left did not initially know how to respond. The moment seemed ripe for a fascist or other ultra-right takeover of the broken French government. By the 12th, however, the left did manage to call and organize a general strike, which lasted for three days. The far right, of course, struck back, with violence: riots ensued.

At the time Georges Bataille was confined to his bed by acute rheumatism. He nevertheless rose from his convalescence to walk the streets, in a crippled fashion, and participate in the riots with Michel Leiris and Roland Tual. On 14 January a similar socialist demonstration in Vienna was crushed by Austrian Nazis.

Bataille kept a detailed diary of the events happening around him and recounted in the newspapers, perhaps as an anticipated part of his planned book on fascism in France. 'Restlessness and effervescence have remained extreme everywhere', he began, in terms testifying to the sociological frame through which he read what was happening. Here again his interpretations were only as extreme as the times. For Bataille, the success of the Austrian Nazis on 14 February was a 'catastrophe' that signalled the inevitable and complete takeover of that country by Hitler's party four years and a month later. 'From every quarter, in a world that will quickly cease to be breathable, the fascist constriction tightens.'[2]

This political diary is remarkable in several ways. In it we see one of the most astute political thinkers of the era trying to make sense of events as they are taking place. Yet technical terms like 'effervescence' function less as analytic tools than as descriptive devices, as in a novel. And where Bataille's articles for *La Critique Sociale* had each been the product of a great deal of reflection, the diary was of necessity written in the thick of the events themselves. The articles were each to have been part of a larger work, as well argued, balanced and complete as such things should be. But the diary was part of a life; written too close to the events to bear the burden of objective distance. Bataille would return to the form again five years later, at the beginning of the Second World War.

On 14 February, exhausted from the riots and back in bed, Bataille sent a flurry of letters to other members of the Democratic Communist Circle. The fascists and the conservatives on the far right had revealed themselves: how would the Communists and independents on the left respond? Bataille, who could barely stumble around his room, felt isolated but hungry for action. To Pierre Kaan he lamented feeling 'almost impotent' before the events and said he wasn't sure that the Circle and more generally the left could find a 'new' political position quickly enough. He did however suggest something about the means by which that new position should be developed and disseminated.

> I have no doubt about the level on which we will have to place ourselves: it can only be that of fascism itself, which is to say the mythological level. It is therefore a question of posing values participating in a living nihilism, equal to the fascist imperatives. These values have not yet been posed, it is possible to pose them, but it is perhaps still impossible to know how to do it. To pose these values with their subversive impact, to give them a straightforward meaning, is to deprive them of every possible way of circulating where fascism has already has established itself.[3]

For Bataille, in February 1934, radical politics had already become indistinct from a search for new myths, a search that would have to be conducted in secret if it was to have any effect. In Bataille's reading fascism was capable of infusing politics with the affective appeal of myth and with the psychological lure of hero worship, where the hero was indistinct from the state. Like the fascists Bataille understood the power of myth (and this would lead some to suggest that he was himself a fascist). But Bataille's project would put myth in the service of the community of individuals rather than in the service of their oppressive leaders, political, religious, economic or otherwise.

Laure visited Bataille several times during the spring of 1934 at his home in the Paris suburb Issy-les-Moulineaux. Bataille was still convalescing and Sylvia and Laurence were undoubtedly present, at least occasionally. With Laure Georges talked about politics. The second half of 'The Psychological Structure of Fascism' appeared in March in what was to be – unbeknown to them – the final issue of *La Critique Sociale*. They must have discussed the article, Simone Weil's objections to Bataille's thought, and the direction of the Democratic Communist Circle, which was by then sputtering in inconsequence.

Georges and Laure had known each other since 1931. They met at the Brasserie Lipp, Bataille was there with Sylvia, Laure with Boris Souvarine. Laure and Boris had only known each other a short time, though they were already living together. In the years since then, Georges and Laure encountered one another regularly in the Circle and in connection with *La Critique Sociale*. Laure participated in the Circle, though not assiduously, but she shared the editorial tasks for *La Critique Sociale* with Boris. It is likely that she and Georges would have seen one another from time to time without necessarily spending a great deal of time together. Her visits to his home during the spring of 1934 thus mark a new phase in their relationship: one in which they would pursue one another's company out of interest and respect rather than as a function of shared activities. Bataille later wrote: 'From the first day I felt a complete clarity between she and I. From the beginning she inspired unreserved trust in me.' Yet he also later recognized that he misunderstood her in those days: he perceived her as solid and capable when in fact she was consumed by fragility and distraction.[4]

In April, though still weak, Bataille travelled alone to Rome to enjoy the sun and to do research on comparative history at the Biblioteca Nazionale. It rained but that didn't affect his research. He wrote to Raymond Queneau about his work while attending the 'Mostra della Rivoluzione fascista' exhibition. He hoped to enlist Queneau in his historical research but he also took the opportunity to report on the fascist exhibit. If Bataille believed that politics would have to take the mythological form that the fascists had given it, Rome offered him a privileged vantage point from which to study the phenomenon. Whatever conclusions he reached would be filtered through his writing and activities over the next few years.

On his way back to France, Bataille visited the lake at Nemi and Diana's sacred grove, described in Frazer's *Golden Bough*. The place became a crucial reference for him. A decade later, having taken on the persona of Frazer's madman in flight, he would end *Guilty* with the affirmation: 'I am the King of the Wood, Zeus, a criminal . . .'[5]

A few days later, in Stresa, his health still faltering, he stumbled out onto a pontoon bridge over the Lago Maggiore one morning to sit in the sun. At that moment,

> voices of an infinite majesty, at the same time very lively and sure of themselves, crying up to the sky, were raised in a chorus of incredible strength . . . a loudspeaker was broadcasting mass . . . The voices were raised as though in successive and varied waves, slowly reaching intensity, precipitousness, mad richness, but what arose from the miracle was the bursting forth, as of a crystal which breaks, which they attained at the very instant when everything seemed to give out . . . the choir cried out with superhuman force.[6]

For Bataille, the music of the mass, in that spectacular setting, revealed the power of human yearning, a yearning that forever goes unsatisfied. He was in ecstasy.

In June, after Georges's return to Paris and to health, he and
Sylvia spent a few days at a friend's country house with Laure and
Boris Souvarine. Georges and Laure managed to spend much of
it alone together. It was clear to Georges that Laure's relationship
with Boris was strained, and Boris snapped at him in conversation.
While walking alone together, Georges and Laure spoke of life
beyond politics for the first time. They understood one another
completely. If affairs can be said to have a moment of beginning,
theirs began that weekend, with that conversation.[7]

By all accounts, Colette Laure Lucienne Peignot was a
remarkable person, indeed among the most remarkable of her era.[8]
She was born into an upper-middle-class, fervently Catholic family
on 8 October 1903. Her family's wealth derived from the type
foundry they owned and operated rather than from investments
or some more distant source. Though wealthy enough to have a
summer home on the Seine with tennis courts, they were not so
wealthy as to avoid a connection to the source of their wealth.
Laure was the youngest of four children; she had been preceded
by Charles, Madeleine and Genevieve.

The First World War changed everything in the Peignot
household. Laure's father and three uncles died during the war,
plunging the family into an almost endless mourning process. The
last to die, Lucien, died in the family home of tuberculosis rather
than from injuries. He may have passed the disease on to Laure,
who fell ill for the first time the following year. Her life – like that
of Georges Bataille – would thereafter be one of repeated illness
and convalescence. Death became an omnipresent concern.

The French government and the Catholic Church in France
sponsored a programme that placed priests in the homes of
families, like Laure's, which had suffered greatly in the war. The
priest placed in the Peignot household was Abbé Pératé. He arrived
in 1916 and used his position to initiate a sexual relationship with
Laure's then seventeen-year-old sister Madeleine. Laure herself –

then thirteen – fled his groping hands and other advances but could not speak of what she had seen. Her faith was, understandably, shattered, as was her relationship with her family, who could not face the truth about the Abbé.

Laure's brother Charles travelled in artistic and intellectual circles and introduced her to René Crevel and Louis Aragon, Picasso and Jean Cocteau, Drieu La Rochelle and other similarly famous figures in the mid 1920s. Among them was Jean Bernier, a journalist who was instrumental in bringing together the Surrealist group and the writers associated with *Clarté* in 1925. Jean was eight years older than Laure, a successful author and a militant revolutionary: she fell in love with him.[9] Her family did not support the liaison and Bernier didn't treat her well. Despite this she fled to Corsica with him, persisting. The relationship was doomed and came to its end when Laure checked into a hotel and shot herself in the chest. Fortunately, the bullet missed her heart. She insisted that her suicide attempt had nothing to do with Bernier, rather that it was an attempt to correct the mistake of her birth into an economic and social milieu in which she did not belong. She spent another year convalescing in rest homes in France and Switzerland, a privilege of her wealth.

A year later she was living with a doctor in Berlin, Eduard Trautner, who had written a book entitled *God, The Present, and Cocaine*. About her life with Trautner she wrote:

I flung myself on a bed the way one flings oneself into the sea. Sensuality seemed separate from my real being, I had invented a hell, a climate in which everything was as far away as possible from what I have been able to foresee for myself. No one in the world could ever contact me, look for me, find me. The next day, the man said to me: You worry too much, my dear, your role is that of a product of a rotting society . . . a choice product, of course. Live this out to the end, you will serve the future by hastening society's disintegration . . . You remain within the schema that is dear to you; you serve your ideas in a way, with your vices – there are not many women who like to be beaten like this – you could earn a lot of money, you know.[10]

Trautner clothed her in expensive dresses, black stockings and dog collars; he put her on a leash and whipped her. Once he fed her a sandwich that he had smeared with his shit. She did not go out, she never saw anyone. She gave herself up, completely, at least for a while. 'One night I ran away,' she wrote, without offering further explanation.

She ran far away. In 1930 Laure went to Moscow, hoping to participate in the ongoing adventure of the Communist revolution. She met Victor Serge and had an affair with the novelist Boris Pilniak (who was later executed in the purges). Like the other men, Pilniak treated her badly and life in Leningrad and Moscow did not satisfy her yearning for participation. She went to live in an isolated village, on a small farm, but the weather was too harsh and her health too fragile. Broken, she was hospitalized once again and sent for her brother. On the train home from Moscow with Charles, in an exhausted delirium, she tried to seduce him.

Back in Paris after this series of failed involvements, in a state of disgust, she would 'seduce vulgar men and make love to them, even in the bathroom of a train. But she did not take pleasure in it'.[11] Or so she reported to Bataille. She admitted that, in sexual matters, she was able to transform repulsion into attraction – a capacity for reversal that Bataille would have admired. 'One must *throw* oneself into life and embrace it with all one's might,' she wrote early in life, though later she shared Rimbaud's sentiment that 'true life is absent', perhaps absent from everywhere in the world.[12]

The pattern that emerges in her passionate and contradictory life is one of desperate over-commitment, throwing herself into often hopeless and even senseless situations, followed by an equally vigorous and destructive flight from those situations, before repeating the cycle once again. In each round, Laure is present, offering herself fully, but she is also and simultaneously absent, underappreciated, ignored, even abused. Her flight is thus a flight that is simultaneously toward and away from herself. When she began her affair with Bataille she confessed, 'Until now, it was in my power to break all past ties, so that no human being who had known me would be able to recognize me.'[13] She wrote, 'I want and I need to remain silent and unnoticed.'[14] Her boldness, again in Bataille's recounting, was consumed by terror, by a fundamental and over-whelming fear of death. Her goal, again following Rimbaud, was to have the courage to love death, to love life enough to love *all* of life, even death.[15] The most commonly repeated quotation in her letters and writings comes from William Blake's *The Marriage of Heaven and Hell*: 'Drive your cart and your plough over the bones of the dead.' In recounting her life Bataille praised her simply by saying: 'Never has anyone seemed to me as uncompromising and pure as she nor more decidedly "sovereign", and yet everything in her was devoted to darkness.'[16] Laure was a creature of contrasts.

Laure met Boris Souvarine in Paris in 1930, perhaps through Jean Bernier, certainly within the militant circles that both Bernier and Souvarine frequented. Boris was the kind of independent Communist militant that Laure longed to be. She moved in with him and funded his *Bulletin* with her inheritance. Boris viewed her as a passionate but broken figure, someone in need of his help and protection, the way a parent protects a child. He nurtured her and she him. By 1934, however, Laure felt trapped within the relationship. She had ceased to find Souvarine sexually attractive and her close friendship with Simone Weil, among other things, convinced her that she could have a more independent life while still contributing to the cause. It was in this context that she became close to Bataille.

Bataille's own marriage was in a similar state of crisis. Georges and Sylvia had been married for six years at this point and had a three-year-old daughter. Georges had never been faithful in the traditional sense of this term, but we do not really know how Sylvia responded to his actions. By 1934 she was in her mid-twenties and having some success securing roles in films through her friendships with Jacques Prévert and Pierre Braunberger, who was in love with her. Sylvia was, in short, an increasingly independent woman, who had little reason to tolerate Georges's excesses. Describing the events of that summer, twenty years after the fact, Bataille wrote, in the third person: 'At that time, after several months of illness, Bataille underwent a serious psychological crisis. He separated from his wife.'[17] He casts no blame other than on himself and he does not mention Laure.

On 4 July 1934, only a week after Georges and Laure began their affair, she went to Italy with Souvarine. She stayed in touch with Georges through the mail. He was supposed to embark on a vacation of his own that month with Sylvia and Laurence, but changed his plans. He chose instead to pursue Laure through northern Italy.

Laure, meanwhile, had begun to discuss separating from Boris, who would not hear of it. She however argued that she needed to separate from him, or at least to live independently from him, in order to regain a sense of herself. She described him as strong and herself as weak. Perhaps in keeping with this proposal, she was able to slip away from Souvarine and spend time with Bataille. At the end of the month she slipped entirely away, to Trento, where Bataille was waiting. The town became a talisman in his work, one source of his pseudonym Louis XXX (thirty being 'trente' in French). They returned to Paris together at the beginning of August.

But they did not stay together. Laure returned to Boris and Georges returned to the home he shared with Sylvia. Laure returned to Boris in order to leave him, not to leave him so that she might be with Bataille, but to leave him so that she might be independent and stand on her own. Her plans, however, did not proceed smoothly. Boris was needy, intransigent and spiteful, and in the course of their conversation Laure confessed her affair with Bataille. The resulting argument reduced Laure to a state of psychological collapse. Boris called Simone Weil, whose father was a doctor, and who was able to have Laure admitted to the Saint-Mandé clinic on 5 August. She would stay there for the next few months, in alternating states of extreme nervous tension and chemically sedated calm. 'Life has me by the throat,' Laure wrote to Simone.[18] Boris summarized the crisis for Laure's friends Pierre and Jenny Pascal, 'The psychic life of Laure is a hell that no one has any idea about.'[19]

Georges was able to visit Laure on occasion and to intervene to some extent on her behalf, but in the eyes of the clinic Boris filled the role of immediate family even though he and Laure were not married. Georges enlisted the help of his old psychoanalyst Dr Borel, who examined and treated Laure for several months thereafter. From his conversations with Dr Borel, and from his own rather extensive understanding of psychological and medical diagnosis, Bataille reported to Laure's brother Charles that the crisis was not of an 'extreme gravity'.[20] But Boris and Laure had nevertheless entered into a struggle in which her mental health, and eventually his, served as additional weapons. Laure viewed her current crisis as proof that she should end her relationship with Boris and that he should permit her to do so. Boris, on the other hand, viewed the crisis as proof that she needed him and saw it as a field of activity in which he could prove his value to her. As the months passed, Boris ceased being able to function as he once had. The Circle had broken up, he faltered over finishing his biography of Stalin and over submitting it to Gallimard, and he allowed himself to become distraught to such a degree that Laure, though still at the clinic, took on the role of the level-headed protector in the relationship. The letters they exchanged during this period present a harrowing record of need, projection and misunderstanding.

Laure described her relationship with Georges to Boris in the following terms:

> He loves me and I love him, integrally, which means strongly and healthily . . . I am incapable of telling him and of telling anyone that 'I love him', I only know that he is for me *in the first place* like a brother understanding certain miseries and with whom I can exchange something valuable despite very marked divergences in many points of view, divergences that he recognizes and which are perhaps at the basis of our 'intellectual' relations. In the second place, it is, yes – it is true to say – I can have a sexual exchange with him – I think that not only can I – I would like to again – I should not permit myself to but it is like a closed door and air passes under it.[21]

Laure and Boris had long ceased to have a sexual relationship, if they ever truly had one, so this second point must have stung him all the more. Laure's first point, however, is more significant and telling as it echoes and extends Bataille's own understanding of the 'complete clarity' between them. The relationship between Georges Bataille and Laure was rooted in a fundamental understanding, a clarity that did not require speech or agreement; it was rooted in the communication that precedes and exceeds these things.

Sylvia meanwhile had taken Laurence to Biarritz at the end of July and from there to Tossa de Mar, where André Masson was then living with Sylvia's sister Rose. Georges did not hide anything from her, having perhaps confessed all prior to his departure for Italy. 'I'm suffering frightfully,' he wrote, 'Colette is in a clinic. I have no way of seeing her. I am going mad myself. Tell me when you think you will return.'[22] But Sylvia did not return. Georges's letters to her are precise and brutally honest, but also imploring and testament to his emotional fatigue. 'I want you to understand the degree to which I am close to you and also the degree to which what is now happening to me has not distanced me from you, on the contrary.'[23] At the end of August the estranged couple met in Biarritz. They talked until three in the morning, and Georges at least felt much better. He claimed his obsession with death was dissipating: 'It's life that I love,' he wrote.[24] And he implored her to return: 'You are now the only being in the world near whom I would like to live . . . When I dream of you the sunlight returns to my head.'[25] But she did not return. She apparently accepted some degree of responsibility for the failure of their marriage, even attacking herself in her letters to Georges. He defended her: 'Don't say that you are a monster Sylvia, you are the most charming and pure being that I have ever met. I wish I were an entirely different man.'[26] Their marriage nevertheless ended in the new year, though they did not divorce until 1946. They stayed close for the rest of Bataille's life, close enough for Bataille to spend summer vacations with Sylvia and her second husband, Bataille's friend Jacques Lacan, at his country home.

Bataille moved back into Paris, to 76 bis rue de Rennes, and Laure, once she was ready to leave the clinic, returned to Neuilly, where she had lived with Boris Souvarine. She regained her independence and left Bataille to his own. He saw several other women during these years, the photographer Dora Maar being the only one who is well known. The others pass as names in the diary he kept during these months: Edith Dupont, Denise, Simone, Madeleine, Florence, Janine, Pauline. Edith in particular was a recurrent companion. In November, he travelled with her to Germany, the trip that the narrator of *Blue of Noon* takes with the heroine, Dirty.

Bataille's life during this year of political and psychological crisis passed through phases of sickness and health, riot and isolation, emotional exhaustion and ecstatic epiphany. His marriage ended, his political organization collapsed, his journal halted publication, and he passed through a profound psychological crisis, a crisis which struck to the quick of his ability to love life even under the shadow of death.

10

Counter Attack

Georges Bataille wrote almost nothing during the year of crisis, 1934. The Democratic Communist Circle had broken up; *La Critique Sociale* ceased publication. Boris Souvarine was so hostile to Bataille – and undoubtedly humiliated – that even fifty years later, when he prefaced a re-edition of *La Critique Sociale*, he did not mention Bataille's role in Colette's separation from him: he referred only to a 'friend'.[1] Raymond Queneau, too, took his distance from Bataille's political pessimism and from the chaos of his personal life during 1934. Bataille felt that Queneau 'abandoned' him. Bataille's book on Fascism in France was derived explicitly from these friendships, from his work in the Circle and *La Critique Sociale* and, in the absence of these stimulants, the project seems to have been overtaken by the events.

With André Masson Bataille continued to pursue the publication of 'Sacrifices'. He hoped that André Malraux might take it at Gallimard or that the Galerie Jeanne Bucher, where Masson had exhibited his illustrations the previous year, might publish it. Neither of these hopes was fulfilled. His work and friendship with Masson did, however, provide the impetus for his next project, and indeed for several initiatives over the next few years.

In 1933 Masson had collaborated with the choreographer Léonide Massine to stage a ballet entitled 'Omens' while he was developing the drawings in 'Sacrifices'. A year later Bataille borrowed the title, applying it to a series of his own pieces: a diary of his visit to

Masson's house in Tossa de Mar in May 1935, a collection of essays that would never cohere and, most significantly, a novel that would only be published twenty-two years later, and then under a different title, *Blue of Noon*.

Bataille described *Blue of Noon* as a novel which did not narrate his psychological crisis of 1934 but which reflected it.[2] It had been seven years since the publication of *Story of the Eye*, seven years during which Bataille wrote no fiction, unless one counts his essays in mythological anthropology. Perhaps his renewed acquaintance with Dr Borel, who was treating Laure, spurred him to return to the form, as it had crystallized his writing of *Story of the Eye* years earlier. The two books, however, could not be more different. Where *Story* is abstract and schematic, disinterested in and even mocking of, the potential 'facts' it relates, *Blue of Noon* is a book which is distinctly historical and distinctly political. It is also distinctly personal. *Fascism in France* was to have been a book of historical and political facts and interpretations, but it was a book beyond Bataille's capacities in the thick of the events. *Blue of Noon* on the other hand was possible for him to write: it was a book of myth. In it Bataille transposed the political and personal atmosphere of his year of crisis into the language of myth or, more precisely, the language of a tragic recounting of myth. *Blue of Noon* is a tragedy set in the present, and it says so: 'Several days ago (not in a nightmare, but in fact), I came to a city that looked like the setting for a tragedy . . .'[3] The narrator's insistence that his story is not a nightmare neatly distinguishes it from Surrealist narratives which aspire to represent dreams.

The characters in *Blue of Noon* were drawn, directly and indirectly, from among Bataille's friends and acquaintances. Simone Weil provided the basis of Lazare, the ugly 'Christian' revolutionary. (Simone Petrémont, Weil's friend and biographer, who worked with Bataille at the Bibliothèque Nationale, swears to the resemblance.[4]) Sylvia became Edith (taking the name of the character she played in *Le Crime de Monsieur Lange*, but also that of one of Bataille's girlfriends at the time). Laure certainly suggests some of the characteristics of the anti-heroine Dorothea, or Dirty, as she is called, though several other women in Bataille's life at this point do as well. He took the trip the anti-hero takes with Dirty with Edith, for example. It is, in short, a profound misunderstanding of Bataille's thought and work to equate any figure from life completely with a figure from his fiction. Xénie, with her uninformed openness and good intentions, her foolish overreaching, surely stands in for a member of the literary avant-garde, but it is impossible to be more specific than that.

The settings too reflect real places about which Bataille had either first or second-hand knowledge. The introduction is set in London, which he visited in 1920 and 1927. Part One takes place in Trento, though this is hardly evident from the text. Part Two is set mostly in Paris and Barcelona, the latter of which Bataille visited on numerous occasions while staying with André Masson. He also heard about the riots that took place there in October 1934 from friends who had taken part in them. The novel ends with the trip Bataille and Edith took to Germany in November 1934.

None of these references however fully explains *Blue of Noon*. For one thing, though the book is set in recognizable places, it has a hallucinatory sense of time. The narrative jumps backward and forward; moments are both telescoped and condensed; the narrator loses consciousness in some moments but dwells intently on the details of others. Stories are serially repeated in slightly altered forms. Dreams are recounted as if filled with portent, only to be later dismissed as meaningless. Perspectives shift, words come unhinged. *Blue of Noon* proposes every form of challenge to causal relations and explanations, to psychoanalytic insight, even to psychological depth, and ultimately to political means, motivations and results.

The book aspires to be, as its original title indicated, a book of 'omens', of signs portending the future. But omens are unclear; and they may or may not be meaningful. As a fiction grounded in the facts of the present, *Blue of Noon* runes destiny. These runes appear in the text as elements in a collage: for *Blue of Noon* is in fact a collage of fragments assembled for rumination. The Introduction reprints the first chapter of Bataille's early aborted novel, *W.C.*, Part One reprints an autobiographical piece about him and Laure written during the thick of their affair in August 1934. Part Two, or at least a large part of it, and hence the main bulk of the novel, was written in Tossa at Masson's house in May 1935. (Bataille's diary of the month, itself entitled 'Omens', charts his progress on the book.) Part Two, frequently retells stories from the first two sections as well as other stories. The text enfolds these stories in obsessive comment, interpretation and rumination. As he later explained, 'the freakish anomalies of *Blue of Noon* originated entirely in the anguish to which I was prey.'[5] The obsessive and repetitive disorder of the text reflects its author's anguished and obsessed state of mind. Fact and fiction coincide and collide, amplifying and undermining one another in hermeneutic delirium.

Churning in rumination, *Blue of Noon* plays with time, which is to say with history and with genealogy as well, this last in both the direct sense of parent–child relations and in the larger Nietzschean sense of the genealogy of values. The two senses are related in the question as to whether or not the child will inherit the laws or values of the father. In the Introduction to *Blue of Noon*, Dirty recounts a story about her mother, equating herself with her mother's earlier wayward behaviour. In Part One, Henri, the narrator, encounters the ghost of the Commendatore, the father figure from the legend of Don Juan: Henri hopes his 'blind anger' will exorcise the 'old man's corpse'.[6] In the long Part Two, references to these relations are too numerous to recount. Among the most significant, however, are Henri's two narratives about his necrophilia – narratives in which he masturbates in front of his mother's corpse – and an encounter with Hitler youth at the end of the book. In a book filled with impotent men and indecisive revolutionaries, the adolescent Nazis stand out as vigorously, even obscenely virile and decisive.[7] Henri on the other hand is impotent unless stimulated by evocations, images or thoughts of death. He asks various women to dress the part of a corpse, or to simply play dead, and he masturbates before his mother's corpse. Henri's necrophilia is related to his debauchery. Prostitutes excite him because they are debauched. But Dirty paralyses him – like Medusa – because she is so completely debauched. The thought of death excites him, but death itself – the spectre of the Commendatore – threatens to drive him utterly mad, to bring about his own death. The genealogical and historical problem proposed by the book is one in which children follow their elders to their deaths, one in which death itself provides the lure which leads culture. Thanatos will out.

The dramatic tension of the novel derives from each character's changing place between the poles of this paradox. Edith turns away from Henri's cowardly betrayals, his inability to curb his excesses. Xénie will do almost anything to belong to the world of revolutionary or artistic excess, but she doesn't fully understand that world or its costs. Lazare wants revolution but not revolutionary destruction, at least not at first. Henri plunges ever deeper into excess, ever further into delirium until, at the end of the novel, he makes love to Dirty in a graveyard. Though based on real people, the characters articulate a schematic of all the possible positions on the problem.

Bataille summarized his theoretical debate with Simone Weil about the nature of revolution, and about revolutionary destruction, in a conversation between the narrator and Lazare, Weil's fictional avatar:

Henri: 'Even if there had been a war, it would have mirrored
   what was going on in my head.'
'But how could war mirror anything inside your head? A war
   would have made you happy?'
'Why not?'
'So you think war could lead to revolution?'
'I'm talking about war, not about what it could lead to.'[8]

By the time war finally did come, four years later, Bataille's position
had changed. But in the mid-1930s, he revelled in it, at least in
fiction.

After he completed the book, Bataille lent the manuscript to
close friends like Leiris, Masson, and the art dealer Daniel-Henry
Kahnweiler.[9] They were enthusiastic and Kahnweiler in particular
lobbied André Malraux to publish the book at Gallimard. Nothing
came of it, however, and Bataille didn't press the matter. Within a
year, he dropped it and moved on. 'Confronted with the tragedy
itself, why pay any attention to its portents?', Bataille later wrote
of his failure to publish the text during the decade in which it was
written.[10] But he didn't abandon it entirely. In 1936 he published
Part One under the title the novel would eventually take in
Minotaure, alongside a painting and a poem by André Masson. In
1943 he included the same text in *Inner Experience*. Two years later
Editions Fontaine published the Introduction to *Blue of Noon*, in a
slightly altered form, as *Dirty*. *Blue of Noon* lingered in Bataille's
mounting backlog of unpublished manuscripts and book projects,
but it also dribbled out in spurts, its author apparently obsessed
with the obsessive text.

Blue of Noon uses the language of tragic myth to rethink the
political landscape of its era. This gesture was at the heart of
Bataille's February 1934 proposal to Pierre Kaan for the direction
leftist political action would have to take if it intended to compete
with fascism. While writing his novel Bataille initiated a movement

that he hoped would bring the language and energy of myth out of the realm of fiction and into that of political fact. The movement would eventually be called Counter Attack.[11]

In April 1935, a year after Bataille's proposal to Pierre Kaan, he, Kaan and Jean Dautry sent a card to various friends and comrades which asked simply: 'What to do?/ About Fascism/ Given the insufficiency of Communism.'[12] The card proposed an initial meeting a few days later in the same café where the Democratic Communist Circle held some of its meetings. Counter Attack grew out of this initial impetus and therefore should be viewed as a direct continuation of Bataille's work in the Democratic Communist Circle. Pierre Kaan and Laure's former lover Jean Bernier were both active in various phases of Counter Attack, as they had been in the Circle. But Counter Attack was also very different from the Circle, not only in its expanded and shifted ranks, but in its foundational insight: Counter Attack began where Bataille's debate with Simone Weil left off.

As the primary animator of Counter Attack Bataille expanded its ranks by seeking input from several friends from the Circle and also from new acquaintances. Michel Leiris turned away from the project believing it was 'too literary'.[13] But other friends did not. Through Kojève's seminar Bataille had befriended Jacques Lacan and through Lacan the young Roger Caillois. Caillois was twenty-two at the time and a precocious student of Marcel Mauss and Georges Dumézil. Like Bataille, he was from Reims. Bataille had also recently befriended Pierre Klossowski, whose essays on Sade had begun to appear in Koyré's *Recherches Philosophiques*. Among this group of new collaborators Roger Caillois was the most enthusiastic about the project, at least initially. He proposed calling it an Association of Revolutionary Intellectuals.

In Souvarine's Circle Bataille participated in café discussions that never really went anywhere, and he contributed essays and reviews to *La Critique Sociale*. In Counter Attack, he endeavoured to write collaboratively and to transform the group into a nexus of revolutionary activity. Having written a draft document declaring the principles of the movement over the summer, he submitted it to Kaan, Caillois and others for comment and revision.

As Bataille's plans solidified, both Kaan and Caillois distanced themselves from the movement. It nevertheless also gained significant new adherents. That summer the Surrealist group had participated in the First International Congress of Writers for the Defence of Culture. The event was sponsored by the Communists as a forum for anti-fascist intellectuals. René Crevel was on the organizing committee of the Congress, as was Louis Aragon. Both Crevel and Aragon had split with the Surrealists over questions of political allegiance. Crevel, however, was still loyal enough to find a moment for Breton to present at the Congress. Ilya Ehrenburg understood Breton's objections to Soviet politics and would not hear of him speaking at the Congress. Ehrenburg managed to block the Surrealist place in the schedule and Crevel was so frustrated, and conflicted in his loyalties, that he killed himself. The Surrealists were eventually permitted a chance to speak, but it was very late at night and almost no one was present to hear Eluard read Breton's speech. Only Louis Aragon bothered to rebut the remarks. By the end of the Congress and the end of the summer of 1935 the Surrealist group had effectively ostracized itself from the field of leftist politics in France.

Despite Breton's misgivings about Bataille – and the attacks launched against one another in the previous five years – Counter Attack offered the Surrealists a vehicle for political activism that was revolutionary and on the left but which was also harshly critical of Communism in its then current forms. By the time Bataille organized public meetings of Counter Attack in November 1935 the Surrealists were part of the movement. The Surrealists also brought the Sade scholar Maurice Heine to the group. Heine had been a militant Communist during the early 1920s, before devoting himself to the task of publishing the works of the divine Marquis.

Counter Attack's programme piece begins with a bang:

> Violently hostile to every tendency, whatever form it takes, yoking the Revolution to the benefit of nationalistic or patrimonial ideas, we address ourselves to all of those who, by every means and without reserve, are resolved to demolish capitalist authority and its political institutions.[14]

Counter Attack proposed an anti-capitalist, anti-parliamentarian, anti-democratic, anti-clerical and anti-Communist front against fascism. It proposed a political return to the will of the people and a return of the people to their political will. This in distinction to the rule of the bourgeoisie but also to that of the Communist or revolutionary intelligentsia. Counter Attack took the side of the workers rather than that of the revolutionaries. 'What will decide the destiny of society today is the organic creation of a vast composition of disciplined, fanatic forces capable of exerting a pitiless authority in the coming days.'[15] In continuance of his seemingly now settled debate with Simone Weil, Bataille wrote: 'We are convinced that force results less from strategy than from collective exaltation and exaltation can only come from words that do not touch reason but rather the passions of the masses.'[16]

Where fascism had been able to utilize the 'fundamental aspiration of men to affective exaltation and fanaticism', Counter Attack intended to place that affective exaltation in the service of the 'universal interest of men'.[17] Fascism had its toehold in France through the oppressive triumvirate, 'Father, Country, Boss' – patriarchy, nationalism and capitalism. In its pursuit of universal interests, Counter Attack rejected all three. Instead, it proposed an entirely new social order, which is to say an entirely new moral order. This intention shifted the ground of revolutionary activity from the infrastructure to the superstructure, as Bataille suggested in both 'The Notion of Expenditure' and 'The Psychological Structure of Fascism'. The tutelary thinkers of the new moral order were Sade, Fourier and Nietzsche: Sade for his atheism, Fourier for his insistence on human pleasure as a determinate value in human labour, and Nietzsche for his willingness to 'liquidate *all* moral servitude'.[18]

In November and December 1935 and January 1936 Counter Attack held public meetings on the rue des Grands Augustins, where Picasso had this studio, and in cafés near St Sulpice. The January meeting was held on the 21st in commemoration of the beheading of Louis XVI. Bataille, Breton and Maurice Heine spoke on various topics, as did others in these loosely structured meetings. Tensions and conflicts were nevertheless already beginning to tear at the group. Not all of them were political: Breton's daughter Aube was born in December, for example, and he was excited about and distracted by his new role as a father. More seriously, in an interview published in *Le Figaro* that same month, Breton took complete credit for Counter Attack, which understandably irritated Bataille and undermined the ethos of the movement. In March, the group published a broadside written by Jean Dautry, 'Sous le feu des canons Français . . .' ('Under French Cannon Fire'), which claimed that the members of Counter Attack preferred Hitler's style of 'anti-diplomatic brutality' to the 'drooling agitation of diplomats and politicians', a claim that neither Breton nor Bataille could support.[19] A month later, Bataille penned a text for the group and appended Breton's signature without having asked or even told him that he was doing so. By May 1936, when the first and only issue of the *Cahiers de Contre Attaque* finally appeared, the alliance had dissolved. The Surrealists disavowed the group and the *Cahiers* in a collective note to the press which accused Counter Attack of 'surfascist tendencies'.[20] Jean Dautry had coined the phrase 'surfascism' as a positive one to describe

Counter Attack's intention of surpassing the nationalistic limitations of fascism with the mythic tools of fascism itself. The label however and the stigma it inadvertently carried would be hard for Bataille to live down.

11

Acéphale

By April 1936 Bataille had begun to envision a new form of community, oriented more by religious concerns than by strictly political ones. On 4 April he drafted a programme note, ostensibly for Counter Attack, that constitutes in embryonic form an outline for what would become Acéphale. The word itself appears in the text as a description of the universe, a universe characterized by risk rather than responsibility; the opposite of a 'state'.[1]

Bataille resigned his position as General Secretary of Counter Attack and went to Spain to spend April with André Masson in Tossa de Mar. He spent the month writing. He wrote programme pieces for *Acéphale*: 'The Sacred Conspiracy' and the notes beginning 'In My Own Eyes Existence'. Masson talked with him and sketched a figure whose description emerged from their conversations: a headless figure, neither man nor god, his feet firmly rooted on the earth, a death's head in place of his sex, a labyrinth in his belly, stars on his chest, a knife in one hand, a flaming heart in the other: Acéphale.

> Beyond what I am, I meet a being who makes me laugh because he is headless; this fills me with dread because he is made of innocence and crime; he holds a steel weapon in his left hand, flames like those of a Sacred Heart in his right. He reunites in the same eruption Birth and Death. He is not a man. He is not a god either. He is not me but he is more than me; his stomach is

the labyrinth in which he has lost himself, loses me with him, and in which I discover myself as him, in other words as a monster.[2]

Acéphale recalls the headless god and the braying ass of the Gnostics. But it also recalls Nietzsche's *übermensch*, his super- or over-man; the being beyond human being that a human might become through self-overcoming. For both Acéphale and Nietzsche's superman 'time has become an object of ecstasy'.[3] Acéphale is also a monster: Acéphalic man is utterly unique and uniqueness is monstrous for Bataille as it was for Sade. In French Acéphale is also a pun containing the words assez, meaning 'enough', and phallus.

When Bataille published 'The Sacred Conspiracy' in June, as the inaugural essay in the journal *Acéphale*, the piece was accompanied by Masson's drawings and by a short essay by Pierre Klossowski on the concept of monstrosity in Sade. The sacred conspiracy would be a communal conspiracy or it would not be. 'What I have thought or represented,' Bataille wrote, 'I have not thought or represented alone.'[4] Bataille's descriptions inform Masson's images, which in turn inspire Bataille's writing and meditation. Bataille's writing and conversation in turn infects Klossowski, and on and on.

I am writing in a little cold house in a village of fishermen; a dog has just barked in the night. My room is next to the kitchen where André Masson is happily moving around and singing; at this moment, as I write, he has just put a recording of the overture to *Don Giovanni* on the phonograph; more than anything else, the overture to *Don Giovanni* ties my lot in life to a challenge that opens me to a rapturous escape from self. At this very moment, I am watching this acéphalic being, this intruder composed of two equally excited obsessions, become the 'Tomb of Don Giovanni'.[5]

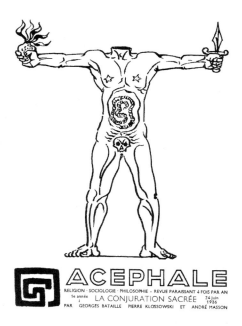

Cover by André Masson for the first issue of *Acéphale*, 1936.

The image of Acéphale – born of two obsessions, Bataille's and Masson's, or perhaps sex and death – becomes a field of meditation and a tomb torn from the pages of *Story of the Eye* and *Blue of Noon*. Here Bataille's writing again returns to the form of a journal, recording daily events, passing moments as they slip beyond the everyday into the realm of the sacred.

Upon his return to Paris in May Bataille proposed the Acéphalic agenda to his friends from Counter Attack. Guy Lévis-Mano published the first issue of the journal in June and Bataille and Masson's *Sacrifices* in December. Bataille held the first meeting of the nascent group in July in the basement of the café La Bonne Étoile. That first meeting was organized around plans for a second issue of the journal: an issue devoted to the reclamation of Nietzsche from the Nazis. When it appeared six months later, the issue included essays by Bataille, Klossowski, Jean Rollin, Jean Wahl and

Nietzsche himself (on Heraclitus), as well as new drawings by Masson. The third issue of the journal, on Dionysus and published a year after the first, added Roger Caillois and Jules Monnerot to the list of contributors. Still later, Michel Leiris and Maurice Heine anticipated contributing to an issue on eroticism that never appeared. In 1938 Leiris's *Miroir de la tauromachie* was published in the Acéphale collection of books edited by Bataille for Guy Lévis-Mano. Masson illustrated the essay, which was dedicated to Colette Peignot after her death. *Miroir* was the only book in the abortive series, though Bataille anticipated writing a 'phenomenology of eroticism' for it as well.

Just as *La Critique Sociale* was not simply the house journal of Souvarine's Democratic Communist Circle, *Acéphale* was not the house journal of the group that Bataille organized alongside it. The two were almost unrelated. Acéphale in fact conceived itself as a secret society, less in the sense that its activities were kept secret from those who were not participants than in the strict sense that it was a society *of secrets*, a group founded on mysteries about which *one could not speak*. The group had its own 'inner journal': a record of its activities and of texts written by its members.[6] *Acéphale* stood apart, as a collection of related texts and images, stimulants for the eponymous group though not necessarily generated by its members.

Other than Bataille, only Pierre Klossowski and Georges Ambrosino both contributed to *Acéphale* and participated in the group. Ever independent André Masson, who lived full time in Tossa, needed no other excuse to retain his autonomy: he contributed to the journal but did not participate in the group. Roger Caillois scoffed at Bataille's project of creating a virulent and destructive creative myth: he too contributed to the journal without participating in the group. Michel Leiris was in the process of writing his thesis in ethnography, on the secret language of the Dogon, and, like Caillois, was hardly disposed to participate in an exercise in creative mythology. Leiris had himself also become an initiate in Dogon rituals during the early 1930s. While Bataille dreamed of becoming an initiate in the sacred rites of a secret society, Leiris already was one and Bataille was intimidated.[7] Though documents related to Acéphale reference Leiris occasionally, one can imagine Bataille's reluctance to push or coerce him into joining the group. A group of would-be initiates hardly needs an initiate in its midst.

The core members of the Acéphale group came from Counter Attack and hence from the Democratic Communist Circle: Georges Ambrosino, Jacques Chavy, René Chenon, Jean Dautry, Pierre Dugan (alias Pierre Andler), Henri Dussat, Imre Kelemen, Pierre Klossowski and Jean Rollin. Later Patrick Waldberg and Isabelle Waldberg (née Farner), Michel Koch and Toro Okamoto joined or considered joining. Patrick and Isabelle Waldberg in particular were integral members of the group during its final year: they lived with Bataille in Saint-Germain-en-Laye, near the Marly forest where the group held its meetings. In the first instalment of the 'inner journal' of Acéphale that Bataille wrote in February 1937, he traced the roots of the group back to April 1935, when he, Jean Dautry and Pierre Kaan initiated what became Counter Attack and even further back to 1925, when he, Leiris, André Masson and Nicolai Bakhtine considered forming a Nietzschean 'orphic' secret society under the name Judas.

In October 1936, as the Acéphale group was preparing to hold the first of its regular meetings, Bataille visited Masson in Tossa once again. This time Laure joined him. Laure's protracted separation from Boris Souvaine had continued from the time of her initial affair with Bataille in July 1934 through her hospitalization and throughout 1935, when she and Souvarine visited Spain together: a show of solidarity with Spanish Communists and probably with each other. By September 1936, however, she had definitively separated from Souvarine and was in Bataille's company when the two of them – as well as Gaston Ferdière (who would later be Antonin

Artaud's physician), Georges Hugnet and Léo Malet – were arrested at a political demonstration supporting young women who had escaped from a reform school.[8] Georges and Laure had obviously and finally become a couple sometime during the year.

Laure did not, however, become a central or even regular participant in Acéphale. At the time of her death her papers did include several pages of material related to Acéphale, and her initials do appear alongside those of several other individuals Bataille undoubtedly asked to join the group in December 1937.[9] But her name does not regularly appear in other archival materials pertaining to the group.[10] It is perhaps most accurate to see her as a shadow figure, located on the fringe of the group, as she had been in the Democratic Communist Circle years earlier.

The first four issues of the journal *Acéphale* carried the subtitle 'religion, sociology, philosophy' (the fifth and final issue had no subtitle). Though illustrated by André Masson, *Acéphale* went beyond the arts. In a letter to Bataille Masson observed with enthusiasm that *Acéphale* was a thing apart: apart from art, literature, politics and science.[11] 'The traditional forms of poetry and mythology are dead,' Bataille wrote summarily: new forms would have to be invented.[12] Bataille's long-standing objection to Surrealism, as an inconsequential movement confined to the arts, furthers the point.

Quotations from Sade, Kierkegaard, and Nietzsche opened the first issue, Kierkegaard having replaced Fourier in the tutelary spirits guiding Counter Attack. Bataille quoted: 'What looks like politics, and imagines itself to be political, will one day unmask itself as a religious movement.'[13] Political agitation was already a thing of the past for the members of Counter Attack. In *Acéphale*, Bataille wrote: 'We are ferociously religious . . . What we are starting is a war.'[14]

An avant-garde, pre-emptive strike on a world bristling with militarization, Acéphale follows Heraclitus, conflating conflict with cosmos. From Nietzsche Acéphale borrows the notion that war, along with political revolution and erotic ecstasy, constitutes the era's 'strongest stimulant to the imagination'.[15] In 'The Practice of Joy Before Death', Bataille offers a Heraclitian meditation: 'I myself am war.'[16]

> In the excessive and lacerating character of the pointless catastrophe that the present war is, it is nevertheless possible for us to recognize the unrestrained immensity of time which remains the mother of men and, plummeting in the chaos, with an unequalled disorder, the limitless annihilation of God.[17]

In the Acéphalic vision, cosmos is conflict, chaos and catastrophe without god, a cause for celebration.

In notes he wrote years later for a preface to *Guilty*, Bataille admitted that he had been drawn, in the years prior to the Second World War, 'to found a religion'. He recognized the project as having been a 'monstrous error', in particular because it testified to the impossibility of any such project.[18] The sacred cannot be provoked, not deliberately: it lies beyond the realm of intentionality. But in the years before the war, Bataille struggled to overcome this limitation: he struggled to found a paradoxical religion: a religion of the death of god.

Acéphale met every month on the full moon in the Marly forest, beyond Saint-Germain-en-Laye. Members were instructed by short notes when and how to arrive, which trains to take at what times. They arrived in silence. New initiates – 'larvae' Bataille called them – were guided in silence by Georges Ambrosino. The meeting took place in the forest beside a tree felled by lightning. Bataille played the role of the priest, the oak was his altar, adorned with the skull of a horse. Blood oaths were sworn, using a knife resembling the one in the image of Acéphale. Adepts were not to speak of what they had seen or undergone, not with anyone. Seasonal meetings, in the spring and autumn, were moments for discussion and

The Egyptian obelisk in the Place de la Concorde, Paris.

elaboration. Additional meetings could be called by two or more members in a time of need.

In late 1936, under the auspices of the group, Bataille planned to pour a pool of blood at the foot of the obelisk of Luxor on the Place de la Concorde and to notify the press that Louis XVIth's skull had been discovered. He intended to sign the note de Sade. The obelisk stands at the centre of the Place de la Concorde, flanked by the Marly horses at the entrance to the Champs Elysées. The point triangulated between the horses and the obelisk marks the location of the guillotine, the public face and focus of the French Revolution, the criminal origins of the Republic, a location that is now an 'empty space, open to the rapid flow of traffic'.[19] The obelisk, for Bataille, was the 'purest image of the head and of the heavens', the 'calmest negation' of the death of god, the negation of time itself.[20] In the figure of the obelisk revolutionary destruction gave way to the ossified politics of empire. Acéphale intended to undermine that empire by accepting the death of god and the catastrophe of time.

In the forest lit by torches and moonlight, in a scene drawn from *The Golden Bough*, Bataille led the group in meditation on the notion of joy before death. In 'Sacrifices', Bataille proposed an image of human being as fragile contingency, as a self-that-dies. In Acéphale, that image assumed the character of a founding myth. To embrace life as utter contingency is to embrace the utter uniqueness of each individual human being. To seek, in meditation, the sense of one's own contingency is to seek the limits of one's potential, the limits of one's unique possibility. A meditation on the limits of one's possibility is ultimately indistinct from a meditation on one's impossibility, one's death. This is not the same as a simple meditation on abstract or disembodied death. Meditating on one's own death remains painful, personal and unique.

The goal of Acéphale was to 'find and rediscover *the totality of being*'. to seek, in other words, the integral or total being that one might be, as an individual body and as a body in the cosmos.[21] The project derives from Heraclitus and Nietzsche but also from the Marquis de Sade. Sade's heroes became monstrous in their search for unique pleasures. They knew themselves to be contingent in their relationship to and place within nature. When Nietzsche's madman proclaimed the death of god, he simultaneously proclaimed the death of god's creation, man, the death of the Christian conception of the cosmos and the death of the Christian community. In fulfilment of these proclamations Acéphale proposed a new community founded on the uniqueness of its members, a community, in other words, of difference.

In the Acéphalic pursuit of joy before death, it was 'necessary to refuse boredom and live only for fascination'.[22] As a celebration of the totality of life, joy before death proposed the 'only intellectually honest route in the search for ecstasy'.[23] 'When we link an extreme joy to the dreadful consideration of death, when we link irony to anguish, we fulfill a liberation greater than any other.'[24] The experience of reversal inaugurated in Bataille's youth by his father's mad speech is fulfilled nowhere so completely as in the Acéphalic agenda.

Over the next two years, through discussions and writings circulated between its members, the Acéphale group slowly formulated 'eleven attacks', the basic tenets of the group:

1. CHANCE
   against mass
2. COMMUNAL UNITY
   against the imposture of the individual
3. AN ELECTIVE COMMUNITY
   distinct from the community of blood, earth and interests
4. THE RELIGIOUS POWER OF TRAGIC SELF-OFFERING
   against military power founded on greed and constraint
5. THE FUTURE IN MOTION, DESTROYING LIMITS
   against the past will to immobility
6. THE TRAGIC LAWBREAKER
   against humble victims
7. THE INEXORABLE CRUELTY OF NATURE
   against the degrading image of a good god
8. FREE AND LIMITLESS LAUGHTER
   against every form of hypocritical piety
9. 'LOVE OF FATE', EVEN THE MOST HARSH
   against the abdications of pessimists and of the anguished
10. THE ABSENCE OF GROUND AND OF EVERY FOUNDATION
    against the appearance of stability
11. JOY BEFORE DEATH
    against all immortality[25]

12

The College of Sociology

In 1937, alongside Acéphale and the eponymous journal, Bataille helped found two other work groups outside the university system: the College of Sociology and the Society for Collective Psychology. Both stand in a direct, if oblique, relationship to Acéphale and to one another.

Bataille later described the College of Sociology as the 'external activity' of Acéphale.[1] The extent to which this was true remains difficult to ascertain. The College was not a degree-granting institution. Rather it was a lecture series and gathering place for researchers in sociology. The College concerned itself with topics that were central to Acéphale – the sacred, myth, Hegel, tragedy, shamanism, revolution – and *Acéphale* ceased publication while the College was in session, perhaps signalling that the journal was not necessary alongside the bi-weekly meetings of the College. After all, most of the contributors to *Acéphale* also spoke at the College. The members of Acéphale however did not. Bataille himself continued writing, not only lectures for the College and documents for the 'inner journal' of Acéphale, but essays published in *Mesures*, *Verve* and the *Nouvelle Revue Française*.

The Society for Collective Psychology was less directly related to either of the other two groups. Founding members of the Society included René Allendy, Adrien Borel, Paul Schiff, Pierre Janet, Michel Leiris and Bataille, though by the following year the group had grown to some forty members. Pierre Janet was by far the most widely known and he served as president. Bataille was vice-president and Allendy secretary-treasurer. The Society was conceived, in April 1937, to study 'the role, in social events, of psychological factors, particularly unconscious factors, and to bring together research undertaken until now in isolated diverse disciplines'.[2] Michel Leiris and Georges Duthuit were the only members, other than Bataille, who spoke at both the Society for Collective Psychology and the College of Sociology. Bataille alone represented Acéphale within the Society. The Society for Collective Psychology chose 'Attitudes Toward Death' as the topic of its inaugural lecture series. Bataille delivered the first lecture on 17 January 1938, perhaps indicating the importance of his role in selecting that topic. Lectures followed on a monthly basis thereafter. Documents related to Acéphale do not mention the Society even though they are entirely taken up with fashioning a mysticism based on the notion of joy before death.

The Society dispersed after a single season; the College of Sociology after two; Acéphale itself after three. During the late 1930s Bataille was highly visible and engaged – speaking publicly on an extraordinarily wide range of topics, before an equally wide range of audiences – and simultaneously hidden – because these audiences did not overlap and no piece of Bataille's writing was pertinent to them all. Nor did Bataille produce a book, or even try to, during these years. The single publication which did address the concerns of each of these distinct groups – 'The Practice of Joy Before Death' – was published without its author's name, and after the dissolution of both the Society for Collective Psychology and the College of Sociology. In contrast to Nietzsche, who left his legacy in books which none of his contemporaries read, Bataille catalysed the consciousness of his time through lectures, ephemera and anonymous publications, resources so reticent to fame and exegesis that a philosophical prejudice against biography might cause us to miss his significance altogether.

In July and August 1937 Bataille and Laure travelled to Italy, to Siena and Naples, where they visited Mount Etna. Bataille recounted the experience two years later, after her death. He wrote:

Arriving at dawn at the crest of the immense and bottomless crater – we were exhausted and, in a way, swelling with a too strange, too disastrous solitude: this was the harrowing moment we leaned over the gaping wound, the rupture in the planet where we stood breathing . . . In the middle of our journey, upon entering an infernal region, we saw the crater of the volcano in the distance, at the end of a long valley of lava, and it was impossible to imagine any place where the horrible instability of things was more evident. Laure was suddenly seized by such anguish that she started running madly straight ahead: the terror and desolation we had entered had made her distraught.[3]

The College of Sociology held its first public meeting at the Grand Véfour café in March 1937, but the lecture series proper did not begin until November.[4] At the March meeting, Bataille spoke on the 'apprentice sorcerer' and Roger Caillois delivered 'The Winter Wind'. In July, the third issue of *Acéphale* included a 'Note on the Foundation of a College of Sociology' signed by Bataille, Caillois, Ambrosino, Klossowski, Jules Monnerot and Pierre Libra, Michel Leiris being conspicuously absent from the list. His participation in the group would not begin until January 1938 when he lectured on 'The Sacred in Everyday Life'. Later he would distance himself from both the text and the College as a whole.

The College of Sociology was ostensibly concerned with sacred sociology and found its first task in defining that phrase. The lectures began on 20 November in the back room of the Galeries du Livre bookstore at 15 rue Gay-Lussac. Roger Caillois outlined the basic methodological assumptions of the French school of sociology and Bataille offered an interpretation of society as a 'composite being' in which the sum of the parts equalled more than the whole: a community, in short, of distinctly different individuals. Bataille's ontological approach to sociology referenced Niels Bohr and other research in atomic physics (undoubtedly suggested by Bataille's friend Georges Ambrosino, who was a physicist) and described the 'sacred' as the 'specific event of the communal movement of society'.[5]

Two weeks later, at the second meeting, Alexandre Kojève spoke on Hegel. Bataille and Caillois had become friends through Kojève's seminar and had been following it together for four years at this point. Kojève's presence is therefore unsurprising, given his friendship with and influence on the group. It is surprising however to see the philosopher listed among the speakers at a College of Sociology. Kojève's presence testifies to the extent to which the College intended to rethink the methodological assumptions of the French school of sociology.

In response to the lecture Bataille wrote a letter to Kojève that articulated his own difference from Hegelian thought more succinctly than anything else he ever wrote. He later published a version of the letter in *Guilty*.

> If action ('doing') is – as Hegel says – negativity, the question arises as to whether the negativity of one who has 'nothing more to do' disappears or remains in a state of 'unemployed negativity'. Personally, I can only decide in one way, being myself precisely this 'unemployed negativity' . . . I imagine that my life – or, better yet, its aborting, the open wound that is my life – constitutes all by itself the refutation of Hegel's closed system.[6]

Bataille's response to Kojève contrasted Hegel's system with his experience of his own everyday life. For Bataille, not every action could be recuperated within the meaningful sweep of history, not every action could be or need be useful. In 'The Notion of Expenditure' Bataille proposed the analysis of meaningless expenditure as a means of understanding communal life. In his letter to Kojève he transposed this analysis into the realm of personal experience.

Over the next month Caillois spoke on animal societies and Leiris addressed the group for the first time, with a lecture on the sacred in everyday life. Both lectures mark significant differences in the thought of the three figures most closely associated with the College. For Caillois animal societies evidence the same drama of recognition, expenditure and difference that characterize human societies. For Bataille, human beings become unique and, strictly speaking, human by distinguishing themselves from animals. Man is the animal that is not one. For Leiris the sacred creates unique individuals, which is to say isolated individuals, by animating moments in life with specific and deeply personal meanings. For Bataille the sacred is supra-individual, it is that which ruptures isolation and negates the personal. Leiris's lecture moved Laure to write a series of notes on the sacred over the next several months. She would give them to Bataille only in the final days before her death.

In December 1937 Georges and Laure travelled with de Sade scholar Maurice Heine to the Emancé forest at Malmaison, to visit the place where the Marquis had asked to be buried. They repeated the trip with Michel Leiris and his wife Zette the following March. After this second trip Laure's tuberculosis came back. She was hospitalized and eventually spent time in the Avon sanatorium and later in a Parisian clinic. In July, when she was released, she moved with Bataille into a house with a garden at 59 bis rue de Mareil in Saint-Germain-en-Laye, near the Marly forest where Acéphale held its meetings.

During these months Bataille continued his work with Acéphale and the College of Sociology, and later with the International Anarchist Federation. Acéphale solidified the language of its 'eleven attacks' and planned to publish a selection of Nietzsche's writings pertinent to their needs under the title *Memorandum*. Roger Caillois

Bataille's residence at Saint-Germain-en-Laye.

meanwhile hoped to edit a collection of books for Gallimard under the series title, 'Tyrants and Tyrannies'. Bataille proposed *Tragic Destiny*, an essay in sacred sociology on fascism in Europe. The book would have included his essays from *La Critique Sociale* and notes on fascism in France as well as newer pieces. But Gallimard didn't pursue the series. As an attempt to rework 'The Notion of Expenditure' and 'The Psychological Structure of Fascism', *Tragic Destiny* offers an embryonic outline of *The Accursed Share*.

Caillois' health at this time also faltered, leaving Bataille to carry the College of Sociology through much of its first year more or less on his own. He gave six of the eight lectures during the spring of 1938: on 'attraction and repulsion', on sex, laughter and tears, on power (in place of Caillois), on the function and structure of the army (following Freud's essay on mass psychology), on churches and secret societies, and on the sacred sociology of the contemporary world. Klossowski gave the final lecture of the first series, on Kierkegaard and tragedy.

Jean Paulhan was impressed enough with the activities of the College to solicit a representative selection of essays for the *Nouvelle Revue Française*. Caillois redrafted the 'Declaration' from *Acéphale* and polished up 'The Winter Wind', Leiris submitted 'The Sacred in Everyday Life' and Bataille pulled his notes on the apprentice sorcerer into a publishable piece. Laure's worsening illness frustrated his progress, however, pushing the publication back into the summer.

By autumn, Laure's illness was grave indeed. In September Bataille wrote to Zette and Michel Leiris with false optimism. But by the first week of November it became clear that her tuberculosis had reached its terminal stage. Laure 'referred to her agony as a "florid bullfight"'.[7]

Marcel Moré, a friend of both Bataille and the Peignot family, was given the task of informing Laure's mother and brother that she was dying. The Peignots – Laure's mother in particular – wanted a religious funeral. Bataille threatened to shoot any priest that dared celebrate such a mass. But he and Laure were unmarried and the family had its rights. Bataille placed a copy of William Blake's 'Marriage of Heaven and Hell' in Laure's coffin as it closed.[8]

During the months and days of her decline, Bataille wrote 'The Sacred', a short essay that for him, of all of the essays he had published up to that point, was 'the only one wherein the resoluteness that drives me appears with a certain clarity'.[9] In the essay he described the sacred as nothing but 'a privileged moment of communal unity, a moment of convulsive communication of what is ordinarily stifled'.[10] In the margin of his draft, beside that line, he wrote 'identical to love'. A ray of sunlight pierced the trees beyond his window and he could not continue writing. He went into the next room to check on Laure and discovered that her condition had taken its definitive turn. She was in a delirium. Bataille realized that they would never speak to one another again, that she no longer understood him. He burst into tears.

The couple nevertheless did speak again, during the days of her delirium. At some point, Laure asked Georges to retrieve some notes she had been writing. He couldn't find them at first, but eventually discovered a sheet bearing the title 'The Sacred'. These were her notes on Michel Leiris's January lecture. She had written:

The sacred is the infinitely rare moment in which the 'eternal share' that each being carries within enters life, finds itself carried off in the universal movement, integrated into this movement, realized . . . The bullfight has to do with the sacred because there is the threat of death and real death, but it is felt, experienced by others, with others. Imagine a bullfight for you alone . . . The sacred moment, an infinitely rare state of grace . . . The poetic work is sacred in that it is the creation of a topical event, 'communication' experienced as *nakedness*. It is self-violation, baring, communication to others of a reason for living, and this reason for living 'shifts'.[11]

She and Georges had never truly spoken of these things. She disdained 'intellectual' conversation and he had not formulated his own thoughts on communication until the days immediately prior to her death. Yet they had written very nearly the same thing. The moment Bataille described as one of 'communal unity' and 'convulsive communication', Laure described as a bare event, a self-revelation that was also a self-violation. The communication that she described as a 'reason for living' passed in silence even at the moment of her death. Reading her notes, Bataille recognized all that he had lost.[12] She died on 7 November 1938.

Bataille illustrated 'The Sacred' with photos of a cemetery, a bullfight, a monument to Dionysus and an image of an Aztec human sacrifice. 'Human sacrifice,' he wrote, ' is loftier than any other.' It is 'the only sacrifice without trickery which can only be the ecstatic loss of oneself'.[13] When the essay appeared in *Cahiers d'Art* the following year, its readers could not know of the loss behind the text, Bataille's loss of Laure, of his privileged interlocutor.

> Pain, terror, tears, delirium, orgy, fever, then death were the daily bread that Laure shared with me, and this bread leaves me with the memory of a formidable but immense sweetness; it was a love eager to exceed the limits of things; and yet, how many times did we attain moments of unrealizable happiness together, starry nights, flowing streams; in the forest . . . at nightfall, she walked by my side in silence . . . I saw my destiny move forward in the darkness next to me . . . her imperfect beauty the mobile image of an ardent and uncertain destiny.[14]

One week after the death of Laure Roger Caillois began the College of Sociology's second year with a lecture on the ambiguity of the sacred. The lecture summarized the first year at the College and did so with enough succinct verve for Caillois to reprint it in *Man and the Sacred*. During its second season the College benefited from a wider range of speakers than it had in its first. Denis de Rougemont spoke on love, René Guastalla on literature, Anatole Lewitzky on shamanism, Hans Mayer on German romanticism, Jean Paulhan on sacred speech and Georges Duthuit on the English monarchy. Klossowski returned to speak on de Sade and the French Revolution, Caillois spoke on the sociology of the executioner and festivals and Bataille addressed the group three times: on the Munich crisis, on the Teutonic Order, on Mardi Gras and, finally, on his practice of joy before death. These lectures were decidedly political: attempts to understand the appeal of fascism, the power of monarchy or the role of individual passion in social revolution, all in the direct light of the events of the day. The College of Sociology had taken over the investigation of the political use of myth and affect that Bataille proposed to Pierre Kaan in 1934.

During these months Acéphale underwent a crisis. The group had been active for a year. The adherence of new members required the previous members to rethink the process of initiation and the nature of growth in an elective community. More importantly, Bataille had deepened his own practice of meditation in the months after the death of Laure. He read about and experimented with yoga and devoted himself to the practice of joy before death. As evidenced in 'The Sacred', this practice was doubly personal: the meditation of a self-that-dies living in a world deprived of his privileged companion. Bataille intended to push Acéphale toward a more complex fulfilment of its goals. The other members were conflicted and driven toward more directly political ends.

By the summer of 1939 the 'inner journal' of Acéphale had grown into a projected *Anti-Christian Handbook*, a manual for the practice of joy before death, that was also the ur-text of the final issue of *Acéphale*.[15] That issue appeared in June 1939 – two years after the previous issue – and without the signature of its sole author, Bataille. Jacques Chavy was listed as managing editor, Patrick Waldberg as a contact for subscriptions, but the author was anonymous. The issue was entitled 'Madness, War, and Death' and contained only three pieces: 'The Threat of War', 'Nietzsche's Madness' and 'The Practice of Joy Before Death'. Each of these loosely structured pieces benefited from a long gestation in the 'inner journal'. The meditations offered in 'The Practice of Joy Before Death' had been perfected by Bataille and by the other members of the group for more than a year. The pamphlet was underwritten by the Galeries du Livre, the bookstore where the College of Sociology held its meetings, rather than Guy Levis Mano, the publisher of the previous issues of *Acéphale*. And on 6 June 1939 Bataille spoke on 'Joy Before Death' at the College of Sociology. With this lecture he brought all of his pre-war projects together – Acéphale and *Acéphale*, the Society for Collective Psychology and the College of Sociology.

For the College, at least, it proved too much. Roger Caillois had grown increasingly wary of what he perceived as Bataille's mysticism. Caillois shared Bataille's interests and perspective – he spoke of their 'intellectual osmosis' in *Man and the Sacred* – but not his approach. He contributed to *Acéphale* but never participated in Acéphale. For Caillois the goal of sacred sociology was to speak, for example, of the secrets kept by secret societies; for Bataille, secrets by definition resisted discourse. Less than a month after Bataille's lecture, and with a lecture still planned for him to give, Caillois left Europe for Buenos Aires, where he would end up waiting out the war.

Leiris, too, took his distance from his old friend. Bataille hoped that the concluding lecture of the second year at the College would consist of three short lectures, one by himself, one by Caillois and one slightly longer lecture by Leiris, summarizing the activities of the College during its first two years. The plan was not to be. Caillois left the country and, on the day before the scheduled talk, Leiris wrote to Bataille outlining his reasons for refusing to speak.[16] The letter is odd in that Leiris typed it – he usually did not type his letters to Bataille – and signed it 'Michel Leiris, Member of the College of Sociology'. Leiris knew that his decision put Bataille in an awkward position. Nevertheless he would not be swayed and it was already too late. In attempting to prepare a lecture summarizing the activities of the College, Leiris realized that the group had departed considerably from its self-proclaimed adherence to the methods and purpose of the French school of sociology. Second, while the original 'Declaration' published in *Acéphale* proclaimed the intention of founding a 'moral community', Leiris realized that such a community could hardly be reconciled with the intellectual rigours of sociological science. In the College, in Leiris's view, science had devolved into a kind of 'order' or church, which itself lacked a coherent doctrine. Finally, Leiris felt that the emphasis on sacred sociology betrayed a basic precept of sociology, which was to study society as a 'total phenomenon' in which no single element could be elevated above any other.

Bataille took Leiris's letter as a personal attack. When he stepped to the podium the following night he was on his own and he felt the necessity to address the conflicts that had arisen within the group by defending his own position. The lecture he gave was both a statement and an enactment of that position. Community for Bataille is born of a crisis in communication, a rupture in communicability in which understanding can nevertheless be shared. Identity is discovered only in self-loss. In communication, as Bataille said, 'beings are lost in a convulsion that binds them together. But they communicate only by losing a portion of themselves. Communication binds them only through wounds where their unity, their integrity disperses in fever.'[17] This notion is as applicable in a community of nations as it is in a community of lovers, and of course in the College of Sociology.

The College suspended its lecture series for summer and, come September, found itself interrupted by a still more profound crisis: the Second World War.

13

War

Germany invaded Poland on 1 September 1939. Two days later Britain and France declared war. Political catastrophe no longer threatened Europe, it had descended upon it.

On 5 September Bataille wrote in a notebook:

> The date on which I am starting to write is not a coincidence. I'm starting because of the events, but not so that I can talk about them. I am writing these notes unable to do anything else. Henceforth, I have to let myself go with the motions of freedom, of whimsy. Suddenly, the moment has come for me to speak directly.[1]

Five years later, he would publish the contents of that notebook under the title *Guilty*. He told Jean Paulhan that the book concerned the 'relationship between eroticism and mysticism' – 'Mystical and erotic experience differ in that the former is totally successful'[2] – but the book considers a great deal more than that.[3] Bataille wrote it day by day, more like a journal than like a book, a record of his experiences, his ongoing practice of meditation, his readings, his fears, his fantasies, his boredom and his evolving thought. At once theoretical and practical, personal and political, the book veers wildly between tones and registers, between horror, boredom and delight. It is simultaneously the most moving of Bataille's writings and the most remote; the one in which he is

most hidden. 'Chaos is the condition of this book and it's boundless in every sense.'[4]

War saturates every page, not as an abstract or philosophical
concern nor in the form of political analysis, but as an apocalyptic
atmosphere, an imminent threat and an opportunity for meditation.
Air raid sirens scream. Restrictions apply. The author must flee
approaching armies. The current war also recalls the previous one
and the way that Bataille and his mother abandoned his father. His
absent father thus haunts these pages and Bataille rediscovers him
in his own sense of solitude and abandonment. 'Alone, wounded,
dedicated to his own ruin, a man faces the universe.'[5] In these pages
Bataille reveals himself as a great solitary, like Nietzsche. 'No one
relates to the war madness, I'm the only one who can do this. Others
don't love life with such anguished drunkenness: in the shadow of
bad dreams, they don't recognize *themselves*.'[6]

In Acéphale, as in Heraclitus, war was a metaphysical principle,
and Bataille, in his notebooks, struggled with this principle as a
fact. Experience robs ideas of their abstraction. It feeds on ideas,
which nevertheless lend life value and structure. To capture this
contradiction in prose is a project for a paradoxicalist, and the
uneasy oscillation between instance and idea characterizes
Bataille's best writing. In his notebooks and in his meditation
he struggled to become a lightning rod of his time, a measure
of the moment in all of its tension, chaos and confusion.

> Sitting on the edge of the bed, facing a window and the night,
> I practised, determined to become a war zone myself. The urge
> to sacrifice and the urge to be sacrificed meshed like gears when
> a drive-shaft starts up and the teeth interlock.[7]

With greater circumspection, he observed: 'Wartime reveals the
incompleteness of history . . . Knowledge, like history, is incomplete.'[8] In the war zone, time, knowledge and self pour out in

sacrificial offering. Hegel had discovered the end of history in Napoleonic conquest and the culmination of knowledge in his own *Phenomenology*. Bataille, by contrast, made quite the opposite discovery: that experience slips away in the stream of life.

The first anniversary of Laure's death fell on 7 November. Earlier in the year, and against her family's wishes, Bataille and Leiris had published *The Sacred*, a short collection of her writings, annotated sparingly by its editors, with clarification, wonder and praise.[9]

> Eager for affection and for disaster, oscillating between extreme audacity and the most dreadful anguish, as inconceivable on a scale of real beings as a mythical being, she tore herself on the thorns with which she surrounded herself until becoming nothing but a wound, never allowing herself to be confined by anything or anyone.[10]

Bataille published his own essay on the sacred a few months later. And he braced himself for months in advance of the anniversary. He ruminated on her life, on their experiences, their travels, the things they shared and that separated them. His notebooks are filled with anguished reminiscences. But Bataille also continued living. He said yes to life, and he felt guilty about continuing to live. He participated in orgies and, during the first days of October, met a woman who would share his life for the next three years: Denise Rollin-Le Gentil.

Denise was thirty-four at the time and married (Bataille was forty-two). She had been a model for painters –André Derain among them – and she had an infant son named Jean. 'I have never experienced, other than from Laure, such an easy purity, so silent a simplicity. However, this time it is only sparkles in a void.'[11] Bataille observed to himself: 'She entered into this room a month ago, no other woman could have been silent enough, beautiful enough, silently inviolable enough to enter it: at least without my suffering from it as much as a clear mirror would suffer from being tarnished.'[12] 'Denise came into my room with the blind gentleness of fate . . . She gave herself up to me, not for a night but for months. We never talked about it. She wanted to stay until the final day.'[13] Ultimately, however, it was Bataille himself who came to stay. By 1942 he had more or less moved into Denise's apartment at 3 rue de Lille. Michel Fardoulis-Lagrange, who spent time with the couple during these years, and who later had a relationship with Denise, told Michel Surya that she did not take Bataille very seriously, that she took him for an 'actor' playing a part.[14]

This opinion should not strike us as entirely strange: Roger Caillois and Michel Leiris both refused to participate in Acéphale on similar grounds. Moreover, but from the opposite perspective, it should be remembered that it was during these years that Bataille discovered dramatization as the key to experience: 'If we didn't know who to dramatize, we wouldn't be able to leave ourselves.'[15] This thought too is a precipitate of paradox: the actor finds *real* freedom in his mask. This paradox requires that the wall of representation be torn down, that experience be reinvented beyond representation.

In his notebooks in October 1939, one month into the war, one month prior to the anniversary of Laure's death, Bataille wrote:

Walking through the streets, I discover a truth that won't leave me alone: this kind of painful contradiction of my whole life is associated for me with the death of Laure and with the bare sadness of autumn. It is also the only means of 'crucifying' myself. On September 28th, I wrote: 'I perceive that, in order to renounce my erotic habits, it will be necessary for me to invent a new way of crucifying myself. This way should be as intoxicating as alcohol.' What I sensed in the moment could make me afraid.[16]

The sentences recall the reversal at the centre of Bataille's experience, the reversal occasioned by his father's mad speech, and they associate that reversal with the death of Laure. But they remain opaque. Why should Bataille wish to renounce his erotic habits? And what did he realize that made him afraid? Who is the implied reader of a text whose author keeps secrets?

A few days later, in the Marly forest, at what was destined to be the final meeting of Acéphale, Bataille asked the three members in attendance to take his life. This wilful self-sacrifice would be the culmination of his practice of joy before death. It would seal the myth of Acéphale and serve as the sacred crime originating a new phase in the life of the community. The other members refused to carry out his wishes. Later that month, on the 20th, he wrote to the group, telling them that they were free of their obligations to him. Acéphale ceased to exist.

This story comes to us through a short memoir by Acéphale member Patrick Waldberg, written and published long after the fact.[17] Perhaps Waldberg made it up. No other record of the incident exists, not even in Bataille's private notes or letters. It is surprising that an incident so charged with portent should pass without remark, that the end of an initiative like Acéphale should fail to require more detailed commentary. Perhaps Bataille recognized that he had gone too far, that his request passed beyond the bounds of reason, beyond the ties of friendship, into a region as foolish as it was grave.

Bataille certainly knew that he had been and would continue to be misunderstood, that a gulf indistinct from death separated him from his communicants, isolated him in his solitude. 'I have the impression of writing from the grave,' he wrote.[18] Bataille even considered withholding the publication of his notebooks until after his death. But when Jean Paulhan asked him for a contribution to *Mésures* in 1940, Bataille offered a digest of the writings under the title 'Friendship', with the caveat that the text appear under the pseudonym Dianus, a name borrowed from the King of the Wood in Frazer's *Golden Bough*.[19] Three years later, preparing the book as a whole for publication through Gallimard, Bataille reluctantly changed the title to *Guilty* to avoid confusion with the earlier, partial publication. As he explained in the book itself,

> the friendship I have to contribute belongs to an accomplice . . . The *saint's* friendship quietly assumes that it will be betrayed. This is the sort of friendship you have with *yourself*, when you know you'll die. When you realize maybe death will *intoxicate* you . . . [20]

Bataille also betrayed *Guilty* itself: the book as published makes no reference to Laure, only passing reference to his father's death, only passing and unremarked reference to his relationship with Denise Rollin, no specific reference to any of his friends, and only a few references to specific places: the Place de la Concorde appears but the town where Bataille spent his youth (Riom-ès-Montagnes) goes unnamed when he revisits it, even the initials used to identify people and places are changed. It is the journal of a life under erasure.

On 21 November 1939 Bataille participated in a discussion on war organized by Marcel Moré at his home.[21] Alexandré Koyré, Paul-Louis Landsberg and Jean Wahl were among the participants. Moré, Landsberg and Pierre Klossowski knew one another from *Esprit*. The others were associated with *Volontés* or with the College of Sociology. Bataille described the discussion in a letter to Roger Caillois, who was still in Argentina, as if it were a continuation of the College. Though Bataille did not become a regular in Moré's discussion group, he did continue to pursue both sacred sociology and a communal outlet for his thought during the war years. He considered, for example, founding a journal – *Religio*, *Nemi*, *Dianus* and *Ouranos* were possible titles – but nothing came of it.

Alongside his notebooks on mysticism, Bataille began writing another book in 1939, one that was both long overdue and a long way from completion, *The Accursed Share*. The project originated in Bataille's writings on heterology in the late 1920s. It continued to gestate in his essays for *La Critique Sociale* and lectures at the College of Sociology. *Tragic Destiny*, the volume he proposed to Roger Caillois in 1938, was to have been based on those essays and lectures, and therefore can be seen as another in the series of abortive versions of the book. The draft Bataille began in 1939 – presented in his *Oeuvres complètes* as *La Limite de l'utile* – would also be abandoned after two years.[22] He rewrote it in 1944 and 1945, only to abandon it yet again, and then – finally – to rewrite it once more in articles published in *Critique* and *Mercure de France* from 1946 to 1949. Bataille's obsessive persistence in regard to the ebullient ideas presented in this book is as obvious as his reluctance to speak in the tone of cold calculation demanded by those ideas. Here again Bataille entered into a paralysing paradox:

> Writing this book in which I was saying that energy finally can only be wasted, I myself was using my energy, my time, working; my research answered in a fundamental way the desire to add to the amount of wealth acquired for mankind. Should I say that under those conditions I sometimes could only respond to the truth of my book and could not go on writing it?[23]

'The object of my research,' he wrote, 'cannot be distinguished *from the subject at its boiling point.*'[24] Boiling, how could he be cold and calculating, scientific? The project foundered for years.

In May 1940 the Germans swept through Belgium and into France, ending the Phony War. Bataille fled Paris with Denise and her son, bouncing from Aubrais to the Auvergne, Freluc and Clermont-Ferrand. By the end of June France had fallen and by the end of August Bataille was back in Paris, living with Denise. These were hardly conditions for creative thought let alone cold calculation. The writer might abhor isolation and quiet solitude, but it is the substance of his work.

At the end of the summer Walter Benjamin – who had come to know Bataille through Marxist circles in the mid-1930s and through the College of Sociology – asked Bataille to look after his manuscripts while Benjamin made his escape from occupied Europe. Bataille deposited his friend's papers in the Bibliothèque Nationale, but Benjamin failed to make his escape. He died in detention on the Spanish border of a morphine overdose.

14
Beyond Poetry

Pierre Prévost introduced Georges Bataille and Maurice Blanchot
to one another in December 1940. Despite several friends and
acquaintances in common, the two had never met. During the
1930s Maurice Blanchot was a right-wing, indeed far-right,
journalist, writing for *Journal des Débats*, *Le Rempart*, *Combat*,
L'Insurgé and other reviews. He had been friends with the
philosopher Emmanual Levinas since the two were students
together at Strasbourg during the 1920s and he shared much of
Levinas's intellectual orientation. Yet Blanchot also wrote with
a catastrophic sense of politics, not unlike Bataille's vision of
'revolutionary destruction'. In 1940 Blanchot was thirty-five and
had just finished his first novel, *Thomas the Obscure*, which would
be published by Gallimard the following year. He was at work on
a second, *Aminadab*, and writing critical essays for *Journal des
Débats*, many of which he would collect into the first of a series
of celebrated volumes in literary criticism, *Faux pas*.

During the occupation, Bataille and Blanchot established a
deep and immediate rapport. Bataille said succinctly, 'links of
admiration and agreement [were] immediately formed.'[1] One mark
of the agreement between the two men can be read in their books:
the first six essays in *Faux pas* offer a catalogue of Bataille's
concerns in *Inner Experience* and even include a review of *Inner
Experience*; *Inner Experience* itself quotes *Thomas the Obscure* and
Blanchot, from their conversations.

Bataille's conversations with Blanchot were to be a crucial catalyst in his work. By the middle of 1941 the process and purpose of that work had shifted: it now included poetry, a genre Bataille had previously vehemently rejected as literary and insignificant. In September he abruptly stopped working on *La Limite de l'utile* to write a short fiction, *Madame Edwarda*. Robert and Elisabeth Godet published *Madame Edwarda* in December 1941, listing the publisher as Editions du Solitaire and the author as Pierre Angélique. The pornographic text was certainly scandalous enough for its author to fear censure. Bataille may have derived his pseudonym from Angela of Foligno, whose *Book of Visions* supplies at least one crucial image in *Edwarda*. Or he may have derived it from Laure, who wrote in *The Sacred*, 'Archangel or whore/ I don't mind/ All the roles are lent to me/ The life never recognized.'[2] Madame Edwarda is a whore who reveals herself to be God.

The fiction is simple: an anguished, drunken man visits a brothel, the Mirrors. He selects a girl, Edwarda, who is naked, bored and ravishing. She touches him and he ejaculates there in the main room, amid the swarm of girls and clients. He passes out. When he regains consciousness, she says, 'I guess what you want is to see the old rag and ruin.' Still in the common room, she stands before him, raises one leg on a chair so that he may see clearly, and says, 'You can see for yourself, I'm God.' She smiles with infinite abandon and the client kisses her 'wound'. They move to her room and make love. Afterwards Edwarda dons a white bolero, a domino cloak and a black velvet mask, and rushes out into the night. She goes to the Porte Saint-Denis and disappears in the dark emptiness of the stone arch. She falls into an ecstatic trance, which simultaneously carries the narrator into the 'beyond'. The narrator knows that his tale is absurd: 'God figured as a public whore and gone crazy – that, viewed through the optic of "philosophy" makes no sense at all.' That which was most high had slipped into the position of that which was most low: God has revealed himself in a female whore, castrating in her

power and 'naked as a beast'. Edwarda regains consciousness, at
least partially, enough to throw herself on a brutish taxi driver. Her
eyes float back into her head, becoming entirely white, like the eyes
of Bataille's father pissing.

> Edwarda's bliss – fountain of boiling water, heartburning
> furious tideflow – went on and on, weirdly, unendingly . . . She
> saw me in the depths of my dryness, from the bottom of my
> desolation I sensed her joy's torrent run free . . . Edwarda's
> pain-wrung pleasure filled me with an exhausting impression
> of bearing witness to a miracle.[3]

The narrator admits that he has told his tale poorly but also insists
that it has a secret meaning that is hidden even from him.

As in Bataille's other fictions, this narrative, such as it is, is built
of clichés and contradictions, and broken by delirious discontinuit-
ies. The tale offers a parody of Christian values, and a direct parody
of Angela of Foligno's Christian experience: Christ asks Angela to kiss
his wounds just as Edwarda asks the narrator to kiss hers. This
parody also presents itself as a revelation, a revelation that is both
physical and spiritual: here the spirit is flesh. Significantly however,
and in psychoanalytic terms, both Edwarda and *Madame Edwarda*
reveal nothing: the absence of a phallus. God here hides in the
absence of God. In *Guilty* Bataille admitted that the brothel was
his true church. In *Madame Edwarda*, he constructed a theological
fable on this very premise. The brothel here is called the Mirrors,
reflecting the representational nature of all faith, all idealism. But
for Bataille there is nothing beyond the mirror. As he says in *Inner
Experience*, 'rapture is not a window looking out on the outside,
on the beyond, but a mirror.'[4] The mirror is itself a stand-in for
language, consciousness, and self-image.

Bataille finished *Madame Edwarda* in October and started a new
text immediately thereafter, *'Le Supplice'* ('Torture'). The text would

become the central section of *Inner Experience*, the first book Bataille published under his own name since *Notre Dame de Rheims* in 1918. Were Bataille another writer one might be tempted to make a great deal of this fact. As it is, he had already published substantially – two pseudonymous fictions, two illustrated pamphlets, a significant translation and numerous articles, over more than fifteen years. But *Inner Experience* is different. It is the first book in which its author's thought appears in so clear a relationship to his life. 'Almost every time, if I tried to write a book, fatigue would come before the end. I slowly became a stranger to the project which I had formulated . . . I escape from myself and my book escapes from me.'[5]

Inner Experience is in fact hardly a book at all. It is the record of its author's experience and the text revels in its disorder. Part Two – Torture – presents itself as the direct record of an emerging thought; broken with memory and reference, with conversations and quotations; shifting tones, registers, and even genres: poems disrupt philosophical poetic prose. Part Three traces the experience in question back to the late 1920s through previously published essays and fragments. Italics distinguish passages written in the present from those written in the past. Part Four offers further philosophical excursus on the nature of the experience recounted in Part Two. The first part of the text seeks to separate Bataille's notion of inner experience from religious and philosophical traditions, East and West, while simultaneously illustrating that separation through disruption: Bataille's experience is immanent and unstable rather than transcendent and ideal. Where philosophical theology prizes the bright clarity of knowledge, Bataille throws himself into nonknowledge. 'Nonknowledge communicates ecstasy . . . Ecstasy is first of all *grasped knowledge,* in particular in the extreme destitution and the extreme construction of destitution that I, my life, and my written work represent.'[6]

Inner Experience proposes a theory of experience that is also a poetics and a method of meditation. The theory turns on a notion that Bataille attributes to Blanchot: that experience is the sole value and authority and that it is an authority that 'expiates itself'.[7] Experience – life, in other words – cannot appeal to anything outside of itself for justification, meaning or value, nor can it account for itself based on the same value continuously over time. This principle rejects the discourses and disciplines of art, philosophy, science and religion simultaneously. Beauty, metaphysical knowledge, practical knowledge and theology ultimately fail to account for experience. Bataille rejects every logic that attempts to justify life from the outside. And he rejects every will to maintain life in the conservative limbo of the status quo. Continuity demands repetition and repetition is indistinct from reassertion. Life is new at every moment. Explanations are ultimately just words.

As a critique of science *Inner Experience* is also a critique of all utilitarian thinking. It stands in a very clear relation to *The Accursed Share*: both reject utilitarian reductionism, *The Accursed Share* with the temper of dispassionate calculation, *Inner Experience* that of the tempest itself: the subject at its boiling point. Inner experience is the opposite of (Hegelian) *useful* activity.[8] It uses intentional activity – project – as a means to escape from the realm of projects.[9] The formulation derives from Pascal and from William Blake: 'Striving with Systems to deliver Individuals from those Systems'.[10]

Surpassing intentionality, Bataille also surpassed his own previous modes of thought and action. During the 1930s Bataille had devoted himself to the politics of agitation, to communal 'activities' in the Hegelian sense. But sacred experience cannot be provoked (the gods, in short, remain indifferent). The 'monstrous error' of Acéphale had been its reliance on intentionality, on project.[11] Then the war put an end to his activities and, as he says, his life became 'less separated from the object of its search'.[12]

The deliverance inner experience proposes is ecstatic but limited, bound by the possible. 'I teach the art of turning anguish into delight,' Bataille writes, 'But anguish which turns into delight is still anguish: it is not delight, not hope; it's anguish, which hurts and perhaps decomposes.'[13] The self-that-dies cannot escape its mortal bonds.

Poetics and meditation are one in *Inner Experience*. In both activities Bataille's method consists in mentally dramatizing relationships that reveal the slippage at the basis of all reality, the way objects slip from identity, words slip from meaning. 'Breath' is a substance that is insubstantial; 'silence' is a word spoken in its own violation.[14] This 'dramatic' method derives from Ignatius de Loyola's Christian meditations, with which Bataille undoubtedly became familiar during adolescence. But it also undoubtedly derives from Arthur Rimbaud's proposal that the poet must transform himself into a visionary through a long, slow derangement of the senses. 'I mimic absolute knowledge,' Bataille writes, in defiance of the Hegelian dream.[15] Forcing the absurd collapse of all knowledge, consciousness slips into the ecstatic release of absolute nonknowledge.

Inner Experience ends with a startling repetition of § 125 of Nietzsche's *Gay Science*, the parable of the madman. Bataille dramatically reinscribes Nietzsche's text within his own and then interprets it in light of Marcel Mauss's theory of sacrifice. The parable describes a sacrifice in which the victim and the executioner meet in mutual destruction. 'We' have killed our highest values and thereby killed ourselves. It is the megalomania and madness of the murderer to wish – like Dianus, the King of the Wood – to take the place of the God and to throw himself at the throat of god.[16] Here hermeneutics functions as dramatic meditation.

In December 1941 Bataille and Blanchot organized an informal discussion group to create a community around the ideas they were exploring in their conversations at that time. They chose to call the group the Socratic College. For Bataille Socrates' two maxims – 'know thyself' and 'I know but one thing, that I know nothing' – constituted, however ironically, the principles of inner experience and nonknowledge.[17] In a programme lecture that Bataille undoubtedly delivered to the group, he established an agenda: to elaborate 'coordinated propositions' leading to inner experience, defining its nature, the methods one might use to attain it, and the conditions – physical, social, political – that supported it.[18] These propositions might touch on various philosophical, religious, or poetic traditions, but the group would not link itself to any given tradition, at least not intentionally. 'A college of philosophers? Surely not. A life preserver thrown to philosophy in peril? Aren't those who fight for the dead already dead themselves?'[19]

Each meeting would begin with a short presentation by one of the members, most often, it seems, by Bataille himself. He was writing *Inner Experience* at the time and used the Socratic College as a communal forum in which to develop his ideas. The first meetings were held in a restaurant on the rue de Ponthieu. Later they moved to the offices of Jeune France, a Vichy supported cultural association, on rue Jean-Mermoz, and finally to Denise Rollin's apartment on the rue de Lille. Most of the members of the group knew one another from Jeune France or related activities: Pierre Prévost, Xavier de Lignac, Romain Petitot, Georges Pelorson, Louis Ollivier and others.

In early 1942 Bataille organized a second group under the same name and purpose, effectively doubling the first though drawing members from among his own close friends rather than Blanchot's. This second group included Michel Leiris, Raymond Queneau, Raoul Ubac, Jean Lescure and Michel Fardoulis-Lagrange. Jean Lescure edited the journal *Messages*, an important outlet for Bataille's writing during these years. Raymond Queneau had only recently re-entered Bataille's life. At this point, he was working at Gallimard and found himself in a position to accept *Inner Experience* for publication there.

In April Bataille's health again failed him. He was diagnosed with pulmonary tuberculosis and his condition was serious enough for him to take a leave of absence from the Bibliothèque Nationale. He would not return to work until 1946. He stayed in Paris through the spring and midsummer, then travelled to Marcel Moré's mother's house in Boussy-Saint-Antoine, where he finished *Inner Experience* in July. Thereafter he moved on again, to Panilleuse, near Tilly: a setting he used for the short fiction, *The Dead Man*, written at the time. He returned to Paris for the winter but moved again in the spring, this time to the hilltop village of Vézelay in Burgundy. Denise and Jean went with him, settling in at 59 rue Saint-Etienne.

Vézelay is a tiny village that has played a large part in the history of Christianity, France, and indeed Europe. The twelfth-century Basilica Sainte Madeleine houses relics of Mary Magdalene and, amid hilltop fortifications, is among the best preserved Romanesque Basilicas. For a millennium the village has been one of the four principal points of origin for the annual pilgrimage of St James, which ends on the Spanish coast at Santiago de Campostela. St Bernard preached the second crusade from Vézelay in 1146; Thomas Beckett excommunicated the followers of Henry II in a sermon delivered at Vézelay in 1166; and Richard the Lionheart and Philippe Auguste assembled their troups in Vézelay for the third crusade in 1190.

When Bataille moved to Vézelay in 1943 the Nobel prize-winning novelist Romain Rolland was among its residents. Bataille rented a small house on the square where the single road splits in two on its way to the Basilica and welcomed a series of guests. Georges Ambrosino visited on several occasions. Michel Fardoulis-Lagrange hid from the occupying authorities in Vézelay for a short time. Paul Eluard and Nusch passed through – during months when Bataille was also writing poetry.

Bataille suggested that Sylvia come for the summer with Jacques Lacan, Laurence and Judith, Sylvia and Jacques's daughter. As a Jew, Sylvia feared that she might be deported from occupied France. She and Georges, however, were still married and marriage to a Gentile offered her some measure of protection. She could not therefore comfortably seek a divorce. Lacan was also still married but, like Sylvia, he too had separated from his spouse. Lacan and Sylvia lived together at 5 rue de Lille, next door to the apartment Georges had shared with Denise Rollin, at number 3. Georges had in fact recommended the neighbouring apartment to Jacques when it became available. This strange ménage became ever more strange on 3 July 1941, when Judith was born. As Sylvia and Georges were still married, Judith took Bataille's name, even though she was the child of Lacan. During the summer of 1943 Laurence came to visit Bataille, but Sylvia, Jacques and Judith did not.

It was just as well. The house Bataille had rented for Sylvia and Lacan was rented by a young woman, then twenty-three, and her four-year-old daughter. Diana Joséphine Eugénie Kotchoubey de Beauharnois, known as Diane, was the daughter of a Russian prince and an English woman. She was married at the time and had also recently been released from an internment camp near Besançon. Ill from her experience, she had retired to Vézelay with her daughter Catherine to recover. Her husband, Georges Snopko, visited from time to time. On one visit he befriended a passing stranger and invited the stranger and his pretty female companion to dinner. Bataille was that stranger. Friends had recently given Diane *Inner Experience* and she had devoured the book prior to meeting its author. When she did meet him, it seemed that fate had once again intervened in his life. Georges and Diane entered into a passionate relationship which did not exclude Denise Rollin but rather included her, at least for a while. By the time the sojourn in Vézelay ended, and all parties had returned to Paris – Diane in September, Georges and Denise in October – things had changed. Georges and Denise split definitively, he to pursue his relationship with Diane.

Denise moved out of her apartment on the rue de Lille, permitting Lacan to take it over, giving him two apartments next to one another. Lacan received his patients and began his seminar in the apartment Bataille had shared with Denise Rollin. Shortly thereafter Denise began a relationship with Maurice Blanchot that would last for the rest of both of their lives. Intimate and alike – the two bound by their silences – Denise and Maurice did not often live together nor often even in the same town. Their relationship did however constitute the major intimate bond of each of their lives.[20]

When Gallimard published *Inner Experience* in 1943 the band wrapping the book read 'Beyond Poetry'. By situating his book beyond poetry Bataille was situating it beyond the inconsequential literature of the Surrealists. He was also indicating that poetry could only be a tool – and one tool among others – in a process in which experience itself was the sole value. As Bataille explained in a letter to Jean Lescure, 'Poetry contents itself with evoking Orestes, one must be Orestes . . . become the man who questions nature, the pure questioning of everything as a completion of man.'[21]

Despite this apparent condemnation of the form, Bataille began writing poetry in 1942, as part of *Inner Experience*, in the notebooks that would become *Guilty*, and separately. Once he had finished those two books, in the summers of 1942 and 1943 respectively, he turned even more intently to poetry and poetic fictions as a means of exploring his ideas and provoking experience. He planned a book entitled *Being Orestes or the Exercise of Meditation*, later changing it to *Becoming Orestes or the Exercise of Meditation*, and still later simply *The Oresteia*. Notes and drafts gestated from the autumn of 1942 to that of 1944, with selections published in Lescure's *Messages*. The book as a whole did not appear until December 1945. Orestes – the murderous errant son – was of course another incarnation of the King of the Wood. Bataille found his story in Frazer, Racine and Aeschylus. A year into his writing, he discovered that Sartre had written his own version of Orestes' story in *The Flies*.

Other poetry and meditational prose fictions followed. *The Little One* can be read as a digest of *Guilty* and a formal analogue to *The Oresteia*. It was published under the pseudonym Louis Trente in 1943. *Archangelical* – written in 1943, published in 1944 – echoed once more Angela of Foligno. *The Dead Man* and *Julie* constitute a fictional suite describing erotic life as a flight both from and toward death. Neither of these last two pieces were published during Bataille's lifetime, nor were many of his poems. But he persisted nevertheless, filling folder after folder with unfinished projects.

On leave from the Bibliothèque Nationale, Bataille needed money badly. Some of his writing during the final years of the war was undoubtedly motivated by financial concerns. In 1944, for example, working with Henri-François Rey, Bataille wrote screenplays, *The Burning House* among them. Once again nothing came of it. He also proposed what he hoped might be some commercial fiction to Gallimard, a novel entitled *Costume d'un cure mort*. Nothing came of that project either, though *Scissiparity* is undoubtedly a residue of the unfinished text. Alongside all of this, Bataille also continued to work on *The Accursed Share*.

Inner Experience meanwhile excited some measure of controversy, even during the war. A group of Surrealists in Belgium – carrying on alone while Breton was in New York – attacked the book in a misguided pamphlet: *Nom de Dieu!* They accused Bataille of idealism of all things and he laughed it off. Jean-Paul Sartre's three-part review of the book, 'Un Nouveau mystique', published in *Cahiers du Sud* from October to December 1943, was harder to dismiss. Sartre was then in ascendancy: the author of *Being and Nothingness* and *The Flies*. His language in the review was both acid and sparkling, humorously dismissive and ironic, yet fuelled by fuming outrage. The two men had yet to meet but Sartre, like Breton before him, felt free to offer a diagnosis of the author under review. While Sartre praised the knotted prose and exquisite pathos of Bataille's book – linking it to precursors from Pascal and Rousseau to Nietzsche and the Surrealists – and praised as well Bataille's critique of Christian theology, Sartre could not abide what he perceived as Bataille's tone of terrified regret for the death of God. For Sartre, it was bad faith to celebrate the ecstasies of inner experience and regret the conditions that created them. For him the death of God announced the ascent of man: an uninhibited opening for human freedom and responsibility. Divine providence had given way to human rationality, will and project. Bataille, of course, had no more faith in human will than he had in God.

Bataille was undoubtedly wounded by Sartre's remarks. Sartre immediately joined André Breton as one of his favoured foes. From this point forward Bataille would often review Sartre's books, sharply if not necessarily always negatively and, in his notebooks, ruminate on differences in their thought. Philosophy itself hereafter wore a Sartrean mask for Bataille.

His first response to Sartre was very direct. He asked Marcel Moré to organize a discussion at his home – as Moré often did during the war – and to invite a host of distinguished guests: friends and colleagues like Blanchot, Pierre Prevost, Jean Paulhan and Jean Bruno, Klossowski, Leiris and Lescure, and privileged interlocutors like Sartre, Camus and Simone de Beauvoir, Jean Hyppolite, Maurice Merleau-Ponty, Maurice de Gandillac and Gabriel Marcel. Arthur Adamov, Louis Massignon, Michel Carrouges and a number of others, including several priests, rounded out a Who's Who of the Parisian intelligentsia. The date was set for 5 March 1944. Moré arranged a banquet lunch despite the wartime rationing and Bataille delivered a prepared lecture on the topic of sin. Bataille's friend Father Jean Daniélou offered a prepared response and Maurice de Gandillac moderated the ensuing discussion.

Guilty had been published in February, but rather than speak from that book or from *Inner Experience*, Bataille delivered a lecture that would constitute the second part of his next book, *Sur Nietzsche* (*On Nietzsche*). Bataille spoke of sin as a means of communication between beings. As a violation of normality, sin could open beings to others. He interpreted the crucifixion as both the greatest sin and the greatest good, the most violent and most communicative image in Christianity. Bataille's auditors struggled with his unorthodox use of Christian terms, his attempt to bridge Mauss's language of sacrificial transgression and Christian language.

The Christians struggled with his concept of sin. Jean Hyppolite objected to Bataille's vitalist language and to his use of Hegel, suggesting that negation should be located within the individual rather than beyond the individual as Bataille believed. Sartre proposed an alternate vision wherein sin would vanish whenever an individual chose to create a new moral order. Bataille's thought did not propose a new order, however, it proposed the violation of and freedom from order. It proposed a freedom that Sartre's thought could not comprehend. Arthur Adamov, Maurice de Gandillac and Louis Massignon admitted that they had been struck by the absolutely authentic, confessional tone of Bataille's voice. Only a few years previously, Roger Caillois and Michel Leiris had scoffed at Bataille's pretense to sorcery, and Denise Rollin viewed him as an 'actor' pretending to a role. Now his voice struck his listeners as absolutely authentic, even as it rejected the foundation of authenticity. While his thought may have been imprecise, and insufficiently both philosophical and Christian, his delivery was ultimately persuasive. Marcel Moré published a summary of the lecture and the full discussion in his journal *Dieu Vivant* in 1945.[22]

Bataille responded to Sartre's criticism in two other ways, both in *On Nietzsche*. He included a direct response as an appendix, admitting that he agreed with Sartre's criticism by and large but noting that Sartre had not understood the *movement* of his thought. Then, in the diary that constitutes the main bulk of *On Nietzsche*, Bataille recounted a party held at Michel Leiris's apartment at which he and Sartre – the philosopher! – got drunk and danced with one another 'in a potlatch of absurdity'.[23]

In April, still suffering from the tuberculosis that had forced him into medical leave two years before, Bataille moved to Samois-sur-Seine. Diane was nearby in Bois-le-Roi and he rode his bicycle there to see her. He also travelled to Fontainebleau every two weeks for lung treatment. These were the final months of the war in France and *On Nietzsche* records the sweep of the armies across the land, the roar of the artillery, the sound of the machine guns, the paranoid instability of the Germans in retreat, and Bataille's loneliness in the absence of Diane. They saw one another only clandestinely at this point, as they had since the previous summer in Vézelay. They also exchanged remarkably tender letters. Bataille: 'You ask me why I love you, I have said why, but it is also because around you I breath the most pure air that I have ever breathed. Naturally, it is also because you make me suffer in the most ungraspable way.'[24] 'You are that which all the others turn away from . . . You are what breathes in the regions of death.'[25] *L'Alleluiah: catéchisme de Dianus* (*Alleluia: the Catachism of Dianus*) derives from letters written to Diane, each section a response to her and to her questions.

> You must know in the first place that everything with a manifest face also has a secret one . . . Lovers discover each other only in mutual laceration. Each of the two craves suffering. Desire desires in them what's impossible . . . The pleasure in fact hardly matters. It's received as an extra. The pleasure or joy, the demented *allehuia* of fear, is a sign you've reached the point of making your heart vulnerable.[26]

In September, just after Paris and Samois were liberated, Bataille's doctor inserted a needle into his patient's lung, searching for infection. He found only that Bataille was cured.

15

Between Surrealism and Existentialism

Bataille returned to Paris in October 1944. It was only a few months after the liberation, and life in the French capital was far from normal. Collaborators like Pierre Laval and the writer Robert Brasillach would soon be executed, others like Louis Ferdinand Céline sent into exile. Charles de Gaulle had returned to head a provisional government, but the economy was ruined with shortages and soon almost run by black marketeers. In the coming years the politics of the post-war era would catch France in the middle of the Cold War, with sympathies and needs both East and West. A stable government would not emerge until 1947, and even that would not last. The fifteen years immediately following the war would also be years of rapid modernization in France. Institutions and intellectuals would struggle to remain relevant. The pre-war dominance of Surrealism would be challenged by new trends like Existentialism; while Communism, in various incarnations – each struggling with the legacy of Stalin – would remain a consistent foil to American-style liberal democracy. In these years Bataille situated himself on the margins of every debate as an infinite source of counterpoint, and he was increasingly appreciated. In a letter to Bataille, René Char wrote: 'An entire and important region of human life *today depends on you*. Yesterday I said this to André Breton who shared my opinion. In a time in which treasures fail . . . it seems almost miraculous to me that you should exist.'[1]

Censorship and paper shortages during the war had restricted publishing. So the liberation launched a pent-up deluge of literary talent: a new generation of publishers sprang up to service a new generation of writers, while also seeking to benefit from the prestige of pre-war voices. During the 1930s Bataille wrote for only a few journals, often working with only one or two at a time. A decade later he was in such demand that he often could not write fast enough to satisfy them all. Still on leave from the Bibliothèque Nationale, his writing was also a financial necessity that was far from sufficient to his needs, which remained simultaneously meagre and complicated by extravagance.

For the first few months Bataille stayed with friends like the painter Gaston-Louis Roux and the composer René Leibowitz, but eventually – once Diane had definitively separated from her husband – he and she were able to live together. In June 1945 they chose to return to Vézelay, moving back into the house at 59 rue Saint-Etienne where Bataille had been living two years previously, when they first met.

In February 1945 Bataille proposed a book series to Pierre Calmann-Lévy under the title *Actualité*. The series would publish collections of essays on various topics, edited by Bataille, Pierre Prévost, Jean Cassou and Maurice Blanchot, at irregular but timely intervals. The first volume – entitled *Free Spain* – would revisit the political situation in Spain a decade after the civil war. A second volume would bring an international perspective to questions in economics and social science. A third would consider the current relationship between politics and literature in France. Calmann supported the project but only the first volume appeared. Albert Camus prefaced the collection, which included writings by Bataille, Blanchot, Albert Ollivier, Roger Grenier, García-Lorca and W. H. Auden among others. Bataille's essay on Hemingway was followed by a text by its subject translated by Diane. Over the next few years Georges and Diane would collaborate on a number of translations from English: Diane doing the actual translation, Georges transforming the piece into accurate and readable French. One of these was a translation of Margaret Mead's *From the South Seas* for Gallimard, another was a collection of poems by William Blake for a Swiss publisher. Neither project came to fruition, nor did the other volumes of *Actualité*. The second collection suffered from the slowness of its contributors before finally losing its funding in 1947. Calmann-Lévy felt that the project had lost its timeliness, and Bataille and the other editors had moved on to different things.

In February and April 1945 respectively Gallimard published *On Nietszche* and *Memorandum*, the second being a selection of Nietzsche's writings edited and introduced by Bataille, a book he had planned since the days of Acéphale. To Bataille's consternation these two books just missed coincidence with the centenary of Nietzsche's birth. In 1945 Bataille also published *The Oresteia*, through Editions Quatre Vents; *Dirty*, through Editions Fontaine; and a new edition of *Madame Edwarda*, through Le Solitaire, illustrated by Jean Fautrier under the pseudonym Jean Perdu. This frenzy of publications – the texts old, new or simply reedited – testifies to the vitality of intellectual life in post-war Paris, to Bataille's significance in the new intellectual order and to his pressing need for money. With his cousin Marie-Louise he wrote a radio play based on Dostoevsky's *Notes from Underground*. Such was the headlong diversity of his activity.

Around this same time, during the autumn of 1945, Pierre Prévost introduced Bataille to Maurice Girodias, a publisher whose father – Jack Kahane – had been Henry Miller's first publisher in Paris. The young Girodias had taken over his father's business in 1939 and was now publishing books in French through his Editions du Chêne. Within a few years Girodias would found The Olympia Press to publish pornographic and literary works in English. Beckett's *Watt*, Nabokov's *Lolita* and Burroughs's *Naked Lunch* were all originally Olympia Press titles. Girodias agreed to fund a journal that Bataille proposed to edit under the title *Critique*.[2]

Models for *Critique* could be found in the seventeenth-century *Journal des savants* and more recently and directly in Souvarine's *La*

Critique Sociale. The journal was to be an international review of publications across arts and letters, the social sciences and even the hard sciences. The disciplinary heterogeneity of its contents recalls *Documents* without recalling the combativeness of that journal. Every article in the monthly would be a review, some long, others short. Encyclopaedic in scope, *Critique* would nevertheless also strive to be timely in relevance and impact. Bataille was to edit the journal with Prévost serving as managing editor. Blanchot, Pierre Josserand, a friend from the Bibliothèque Nationale, Albert Ollivier, from *Combat*, Jules Monnerot and Eric Weil constituted the first editorial advisory board, with friends like Georges Ambrosino and Alexandre Kojève – among many others – contributing articles. The first issue appeared in July 1946, asserting itself in defence of Henry Miller, whose recently translated writings – one of which was published by Girodias – had been banned.

Critique entered an arena crowded with competition. Journals like *Combat* and the Catholic *Esprit* were well established, but the field was dominated by another new publication: Jean-Paul Sartre's *Les Temps Modernes*. Published by Gallimard, beginning in October 1945, with Raymond Aron, Simone de Beauvoir, Maurice Merleau-Ponty, Albert Ollivier, Jean Paulhan and Michel Leiris on the editorial board, *Les Temps Modernes* was Sartre's journal. It preached his doctrine of committed literature: a writing striving to be the measure of its moment and to assert the autonomy of an individual bound by historical contingency. Freedom and responsibility, subject and socius (society) bound together in a political, journalistic prose. Poetry – exemplified in Sartre's reading by Surrealism – takes words for objects and contents itself with pushing pieces around in a literary puzzle. Journalistic prose, on the other hand, commits itself to the world: its words are tools not trinkets. Speaking to the day, and boasting a celebrated roster of recently and increasingly famous writers, the circulation of *Les Temps Modernes* soared.

Critique was never unified in the way that *Les Temps Modernes* was. Even during its planning stages disagreements over the political orientation of the journal threatened to capsize the project. Pierre Prévost and Albert Ollivier rejected Communism, Eric Weil supported it, Blanchot was in the middle, claiming that the anti-Communist position was 'untenable'.[3] Bataille agreed with Blanchot, but argued that the editorial policy and practice should bring together a diversity of perspectives rather than simply assuming an ideologically motivated position. Other frustrations and disagreements would dog the journal over the next few years: Bataille, for example, discussed and supported the publication of works by the Marquis de Sade far too often for Eric Weil's taste. Bataille, for his part, was thinking of writing a book about the Divine Marquis, *Sade and the Essence of Eroticism*.

Despite the diversity of its contents and contributors, *Critique* can be read as representing the range of Bataille's thought and friendships in the era. He and his few closest friends penned a substantial portion of the journal themselves in its early years, whether under their own names or under pseudonyms. Bataille selected the contents – sending Prevost copious lists of books to obtain and of corresponding reviewers – and he sought to be timely. In an era of intense political and artistic debate and upheaval, *Critique* steered a course critical of Communism and bourgeois capitalism, as well as of Existentialism and Surrealism, all of the major ideologies and agendas of its day.

With *Critique* as a reliable and indeed relentless vehicle for his writing, Bataille wrote a great deal, on literature and philosophy, art and economics, psychology, sociology, sexuality, religion, racism, politics and mass death; a thousand pages filling two volumes of his complete works, written between 1945 and 1949.[4] He assembled some of these pieces into longer works – and in fact wrote them with the longer work in mind – *The Accursed Share*, for example. Others were topical and tied to their moment. Still others could be read as fragments of books that Bataille proposed to publishers and hoped in vain to complete: *Maurice Blanchot and Existentialism* and *Surrealist Religion and Philosophy*, for example, both proposed to Gallimard in December 1948.[5] Both titles reflect major topics in Bataille's writing at the time.

With Existentialism in ascendancy, and still smarting from Sartre's negative review of *Inner Experience*, Bataille often situated himself on the side of his old enemy André Breton. Breton had spent the war years in New York, only returning to Paris in May 1946. By this time, Sartrean Existentialism was well established as the reigning trend in thought. Writing in defence of the Surrealists was one way that Bataille could counter the Existentialists. He did not do so naïvely, however, and he was hardly uncritical of his old adversaries. But he nevertheless described himself now – more than a little disingenuously – as Surrealism's 'old enemy *from within*'.[6] In *Method of Meditation*, he described his work more accurately as 'beyond but alongside Surrealism'.[7] While he admitted the intellectual value of the Existentialist endeavour, 'in terms of mankind's interrogation of itself', he wrote, 'there is Surrealism and nothing.'[8]

Bataille's primary criticism of Sartre concerned his interpretation of human freedom as bound by both reason and contingency. Where Sartre saw contingency, the Surrealists – or rather Bataille on their behalf – proposed a will to chance and a limitless revolt. Bataille's support of Surrealism was not unconditional, however. He stood by his previous criticism of Surrealist idealism and of the inconsequentiality of its artistic endeavours. He supported only the Surrealist *demand* for limitless revolt and the Surrealist *style* of aesthetic provocation. And he did so at a moment of transition in the movement. In Breton's absence new leaders and new agendas had arisen. Bataille's friend Michel Fardoulis-Lagrange, for example, founded *Troisième Convoi* in 1945 with the explicit intention of surpassing pre-war Surrealism.[9] Bataille contributed several brief but significant position pieces to the short-lived review, whose other contributors included Jean Maquet, Francis Picabia, Antonin Artaud, Arthur Adamov and

René Char, who had recently become a close friend of Bataille's.

In 1947 *Critique* changed publishers: dropped by Girodias, it was picked up by Calmann-Lévy, the publisher of the abortive *Actualité* series. And Bataille released another raft of short publications and re-editions: *Method of Meditation* through Editions Fontaine; a much revised *Story of the Eye* through Editions K.; *Alleluia: The Catechism of Dianus* illustrated by Fautrier through Auguste Blaizot and, without the illustrations, through Editions K.; *The Story of Rats (Dianus' Journal)* illustrated by Alberto Giacometti and *La Haine de la poésie* (*The Hatred of Poetry*) both through Editions de Minuit. He published so many short books in so short a time that he and his editors feared that he was undercutting his own sales by publishing too much. The texts and editions were each, however, quite different. Some of these publications were deluxe, limited and illustrated editions; others small runs of short pieces that Bataille would later republish in longer collections with larger print runs. Still others were published only under the table – as in the cases of *Madame Edwarda* and *Story of the Eye* – their original editions long out of print.[10] Nor were all of these pieces even published under the same name: Pierre Angélique and Lord Auch signed the pornographic pieces, Dianus was the fictional author of several others.

One may wonder why Bataille did not include *Blue of Noon* in this spate of publications. He proposed a shelf of unwritten volumes to various publishers but released only a short section – *Dirty* – of a novel that was already complete. That book would wait another decade before finding its public. His concern with keeping his writings in print may be read as financially motivated, but it also and simultaneously testifies to an intention to advance both a corpus of constellated texts and a singular thought.

In July 1947 Editions de Minuit contracted Bataille to edit a book series initially titled 'The Drunken Man', later 'The Use of Wealth'. The projected series was to develop the principles of the still embryonic *The Accursed Share* through a number of studies, six per year, including works by Alexandre Kojève on Hegel, Mircea Eliade on Tantrism, Claude Lévi-Strauss on Potlatch and Max Weber on the Protestant ethic and the spirit of capitalism; as well as works by Georges Dumézil, Bronislaw Malinowski, Alfred Métraux, François Perroux, Jean Piel, Georges Ambrosino and Bataille himself. When Bataille read the Kinsey report in 1948 he leapt – without success – to secure its translation rights for the series, ultimately contenting himself with a long review in *Critique* (later reprinted in *Eroticism*). Ultimately the series only published two volumes, Jean Piel's *La Fortune Américaine et son destin* and Bataille's *The Accursed Share*, both in 1949.

The Accursed Share had finally come together – after almost two decades of preliminary articles, outlines and drafts – in pieces written for *Critique* between 1947 and 1949. While Bataille's style in the book is deliberate and assured, his faith in the project often faltered in hesitancy. One measure of this hesitancy is found in the fact that, throughout 1947 and 1948, Bataille attempted to enlist Georges Ambrosino – a physicist friend who had followed him from the Democratic Communist Circle to Counter Attack, Acéphale and now *Critique* – in writing the book collaboratively. Bataille's first proposal was that they simply write the book together. If that was unworkable, they could each write one volume of a multi-volume work, silently correcting one another's work: Bataille covering various forms of sacrificial expenditure in one volume, Ambrosino the physics of expenditure in another. Ambrosino was unresponsive and ultimately demurred, to Bataille's great frustration. Bataille accused him of lacking confidence not only in himself but in others. He nevertheless thanked him with deep sincerity in the second footnote to *The Accursed Share* when it was finally published. 'This book is in large part the work of Ambrosino,' he wrote.[11] The statement offers only yet another testament to the complicity Bataille sought to enact in his writing and life.

Working without Ambrosino, Bataille wrote the book himself, mostly in 1948. He chose books he could review in *Critique* that were related to the topics he wanted to address: expenditure in Aztec sacrifice and in potlatch, in Buddhism, Islam and Protestant Christianity, in modern capitalism, Soviet Communism and the Marshall Plan. A 'theoretical introduction' reiterated the notion of expenditure: that organisms – from single cells to societies, to the cosmic order – ingest or create more energy than they need; while some of this energy can be consumed in a useful manner, the remainder must be wasted, either 'gloriously or catastrophically', though not necessarily within the economic order that originally collected it: cattle can be slaughtered in religious sacrifice, calories can be spent in laughter. The book proposed a Copernican revolution in religious and economic thought and Bataille was simultaneously circumspect and hopeful about its reception. The problem it addressed fell outside the scope of any given discipline though it touched on aesthetics, economics, history, physics, psychology and religion. Like Nietzsche's *Zarathustra*, it was a book written for everyone and no one. Bataille secretly thought it might win him a Nobel Prize.

In February, on hiatus from *The Accursed Share*, Bataille travelled to Paris to give a series of lectures. On the 24th he spoke on 'surrealist religion' at Club Maintenant and on the 26th and 27th he outlined a history of religious experience at the Collège Philosophique. Marc Beigbeder and Jacques Calmy organized Club Maintenant in 1945. Lectures on philosophical and cultural topics were given under its aegis at the Salle de la Géographie at 184 Boulevard Saint-Germain. Sartre gave his 'Existentialism is a Humanism' speech there. The Collège Philosophique, at 44 rue de Rennes, had been founded by Jean Wahl the previous year as a forum for contemporary philosophical thought outside the university system.[12] These were only two of the venues in post-war Paris that continued the legacy of the College of Sociology and other forums for intellectual debate.

From March to May Bataille rewrote his philosophical history of the religious experience as *Theory of Religion*, but his primary concern at the time was still *The Accursed Share*. Though the *Theory* was almost complete and was accepted and even announced for publication by Editions au Masque d'Or, it slipped from the forefront of Bataille's attention and was not published during his lifetime. It became the first of a series of books that Bataille would complete in draft but fail to publish over the next few years.

In Geneva, on 1 December 1948, Diane gave birth to a daughter, Julie, and the family's financial concerns became correspondingly more acute. At 51, living in Vézelay, Georges Bataille had been unable to keep up with his contract as a series editor at Minuit and unable to deliver any of the projects he had recently proposed to Gallimard. He was broke and something had to give.

In February 1949 *The Accursed Share* was finally released. Bataille promoted the book and his work in general with a series of lectures in London – at the Institut Français and at Cambridge – and Paris – at Club Maintenant and at the Collège Philosophique. But the book sold only fifty or so copies in its first year. Needless to say Bataille was not nominated for the Nobel Prize.

Even though *Critique* had been judged the 'best journal of the year' by a jury of journalists in 1948, it too was not selling. Dissension among the members of the editorial board – between Bataille and Eric Weil primarily – and steep financial deficits contributed to its decline. In September 1949 Calmann-Lévy withdrew its funding.

Bataille at the time had his own worries and his hands full. Seeking a reprieve from poverty, he was employed in May by the Bibliothèque Inguimbertine in the Provençal city of Carpentras. By 1 July he had moved his family into a small apartment on a rather dreary little alley running along the rear of the library.

16

Summa

Located a few kilometres from the papal city of Avignon, in the
shadow of Petrarch's Mount Ventoux, Carpentras was itself small,
drab and rather uninteresting, famous only for its strawberries.
The Bibliothèque Inguimbertine, where Bataille now worked, was
founded in 1745 by Monsignor Malachie d'Inguimbert, the former
librarian to Pope Clement XII. Discharged from his duties in Rome,
the Monsignor returned to his native Carpentras and opened his
own private library and art collection to the public. This donation
established the municipal library with a gift of some five thousand
rare books and manuscripts. For an archivist like Bataille the
collection must have been at least initially diverting, if hardly that
of the Bibliothèque Nationale.

Living in an apartment attached to the rear of the library, in
an uninspiring city a full day's travel from Paris, Bataille and Diane
were soon bored. Bullfights in Nîmes provided some diversion.
They attended them with Picasso and his entourage when they
could. But on the whole they would not be happy in Carpentras.
Within two years Bataille would apply for a transfer.

When Bataille arrived in Carpentras he was engaged in a
number of activities, aside from his work at the library. The
cover of *The Accursed Share* announced *From Sexual Anguish to the
Catastrophe of Hiroshima* as the second volume in the series, and
Bataille was intent on writing it. The anticipated volume had
evolved out of the essays on Sade and other topics that he

The library at Carpentras.

published in *Critique* over the previous four years. But this was not his only project.

In March 1949 Bataille had written to Albert Camus from Vézelay to tell him that he planned to bring together a series of essays on morality based on Camus's position. Bataille had been writing reviews of Camus's work in *Critique* and saw those reviews as the basis of a book entitled *Albert Camus: Morality and Politics*. The book would situate Camus in relation to Nietzsche and Sade, Surrealism and Existentialism, and to the political options of the Cold War: Stalinism and the Marshall Plan. Several essays from 1950 – the fiftieth anniversary of Nietzsche's death – commingled the projected book on Camus with one treating Nietzsche and Communism more exclusively. Bataille saw Camus's position as being shared by most people, excluding as he put it 'those who cling to their servitude'.[1] Fearing that Camus viewed him as someone who supported cruelty, Bataille attempted to reassure him that 'only horror of all condemnation, punishment, judgment, leads me to seek a morality beyond justice'. He closed his letter with the hope that Camus would see it as a sign of true friendship. Bataille's tone was one of humble and complete sincerity toward Camus who, at thirty-six, was sixteen years younger than himself.

In December 1949, settled in Carpentras, Bataille entrusted Jean Piel with the task of finding a new publisher for *Critique*. Piel approached a number of likely outlets not only in Paris but also abroad. Albin Michel, Nagel, Macrès, Charles Mayer and Waldemar Gurian were considered in turn, though in the end – in March 1950 – Editions de Minuit assumed responsibility for the publication, undoubtedly thanks to Jêrome Lindon's faith in Bataille himself. Eric Weil and Jean Piel would share the duties of managing editor, leaving Bataille final editorial control. Weil wanted to share the editorial responsibilities with Bataille, but Bataille rejected his proposal. Through the 1950s, however, Bataille would permit Piel to assume ever more responsibility for the direction of the journal. During these years, while Weil made sure *Critique* maintained its ties to the university system, Piel would keep it current: bringing in new writers – like Roland Barthes and, later, Michel Foucault – and new topics, like the New Novel, as they emerged. The first issue of the Minuit series would not appear until October 1950, at which point the journal had been out of circulation for thirteen months.

Bataille was busy during the hiatus working on a novel. In 1944 he had proposed a book entitled *Costume d'un curé mort* to Gallimard but had been unable to finish it. Five years later, he published a few pages derived from the project under the title *Scissiparity* in Jean Paulhan's *Cahiers de la Pléiade* and another related short fiction, 'Eponine', through Editions de Minuit. Inspired by James Hogg's *The Private Memoirs and Confessions of a Justified Sinner* (1824) – 'a monstrous novel' that Bataille reviewed in *Critique* in June 1949 – he expanded 'Eponine' into a full-length novel during the summer and autumn of 1949. These were days of nervous depression for Bataille, anxious and relatively isolated in Carpentras. *L'Abbé C.*, as the novel was called, reflects that state of mind.

The book resembles *Inner Experience* in its use of a complex, in this case *faux*, editorial apparatus to organize a hall of mirrors through which the disordered narrative passes. An 'editor' introduces and concludes the book as a whole; one twin, Charles, introduces and concludes his own account of the events, as well as introducing his brother Robert's 'notes'. Robert C. is a priest and the eponymous subject of *L'Abbé C.* The novel charts his fall from a state of naïve innocence into ecstatic debauchery. This fall is effected by Eponine, an anti-heroine like Madame Edwarda, who reveals her own proximity to God when she bares her ass to Robert in a church tower.

The novel is at once Hegelian and tragic: Hegelian because it proposes a struggle for recognition – and thus domination – and tragic because the characters continually slip from their identities: recognition here consistently proves to be misrecognition. Though twins and hence identical, the brothers are also opposites: Charles being as debauched as Robert is pious. As the story proceeds it becomes clear however that Robert is *acting* the part of a priest rather than fulfilling the dictates of actual faith and, further, that his swooning responses to Eponine's advances are also false or at least exaggerated. Though Eponine – a childhood playmate of Robert's – is the village whore and hence a pariah, her easy virtue is hardly a sin compared to Robert's masquerade. Robert refuses to recognize Eponine in the street. Eponine, for her part, wants to lure Robert into recognizing his desire for her – and thereby to dominate him and regain her identity. But Robert, in his fraudulent soul, has already moved beyond such matters, and he continually slips beyond her grasp and comprehension.

Robert has in fact only recently returned to the small mountain parish, taking the place of a priest who recently passed away. As the story proceeds, Robert himself slips closer to death and eventually dies, not from his repeated illnesses, which are fake, but at the hands of the Gestapo, who torture him for his resistance activities.

These resistance activities are a relative secret throughout the novel: though central to the era, they are not central to the plot. Here again the novel is Hegelian and tragic: the characters are out of step with their time. Tortured, Robert betrayed 'those whom he loved the most' – Eponine and Charles – rather than the actual members of the Resistance. Eponine and Charles – both 'fallen' libertines and hence guilty – were nevertheless innocent, of resistance activity. This final betrayal was Robert's last and greatest crime.

Minuit published the book under Bataille's own name in May 1950. It was the first novel he signed and it was immediately and violently attacked in *Les Lettres Françaises*.[2] The substance of the complaint was itself the result of misrecognition. The reviewer at *Les Lettres Françaises* – who signed her article 'La Dame de Pique' – believed Bataille's book to be the fictionalized biography of a real priest who truly betrayed members of his resistance cell. The reviewer simply failed to read the novel attentively: Robert betrayed only those he loved, he did not betray any members of the resistance. Minuit demanded a retraction of the review and when *Les Lettres Françaises* refused Lindon sued them. Minuit won the suit and *Les Lettres Françaises* retracted their remarks in December. The drama undoubtedly contributed to Bataille's discomfort in Carpentras.

Fortunately René Char lived very close by – just outside Isle-sur-la-Sorgue – and he and Bataille saw one another fairly often. Char had at this point distanced himself from the Surrealists and developed an oracular aphoristic style under the influence of Rimbaud and Heraclitus. He was involved with a number of literary magazines, among them the international *Botteghe Oscure*, edited by Princess Marguerite de Bassaiano in Rome. Bataille would contribute several important articles and poetic writings to the journal over the next few years. Like *Troisième Convoi* before it, *Botteghe Oscure* offered an alternative to *Critique* where Bataille could publish writings that were not reviews.

In 1950, Char published an open letter in *Empédocle*, asking his 'adversaries and sympathizers', whether or not there were any true 'incompatibilities', spheres of activity or concern that simply cannot be reconciled with one another. Bataille responded with an open letter of his own, published in *Botteghe Oscure* in May. Bataille addressed his letter to his 'dear friend', and spoke in an intimate tone, testifying not only to the importance of Char's friendship but of all friendship for him. 'I say we, but I am thinking of you, of myself, of those who resemble us.'[3] The letter provided Bataille with yet another opportunity to distinguish his thought from that of Sartre and the Surrealists and to forge a new community with writers like Char and Blanchot. 'For us, for whom in fact literature was the privileged concern, nothing counts more than books, – books that we read or that we write –, except perhaps what they risk.'[4] 'You know me to be as far from dejection as from hope. I have chosen simply to *live*. I am always astonished by men who, fired-up and eager to act, look down on the pleasure of living.'[5]

On 29 March 1950 Bataille wrote to Queneau in the latter's guise as his editor at Gallimard, to propose the reissue of his first three Gallimard books under a new general title, *La Somme athéologique*. Each of the three books would anchor a volume of the *Summa*, augmented by additional essays and short pieces. *Inner Experience* would be joined by *Method of Meditation* and several studies in atheology. *Guilty* would be retitled *Friendship*, joined by *Alleluia* and a history of a secret society, Acéphale undoubtedly. *On Nietzsche* would be joined by *Memorandum* and other pieces under the new title *The Nietzschean World of Hiroshima*. A fourth volume of essays, mostly from *Critique*, was projected to follow under the title *The Sanctity of Evil*. An outline for this volume included several of the essays Bataille later published as *Literature and Evil*.

On the back of the letter, he presented the proposal in outline form, changing some of the titles a little: volume one would be *The Sovereign Moment*, volume two, *Friendship*, volume three, *The Death*

of Nietzsche. Over the next decade the projected *Summa* – its name
a parody of St Thomas Aquinas' scholastic *Summa theologica* –
would exist primarily as an editorial phantasm, a gathering place
for all of Bataille's aphorisms and essays on theology and experience. Where *The Accursed Share* proposed a systematic survey
of expenditure in economics, religion, eroticism, and politics,
La Somme athéologique proposed the informal record of experiences
studied through their effects.

Gallimard accepted the proposal and Bataille set to work editing
and writing new materials for the first volume. As he worked he
sketched new outlines for each volume, assembling phantom collections of essays and lectures whether he had written them yet or
not. Over the next eight years he would map the *Summa* again and
again – proposing three volumes, four volumes, even five: *Dying of
Laughter, Laughing at Death*, *Pure Happiness*, *The Unfinished System
of Nonknowledge*. With each new outline, the editor experienced the
Summa becoming formless, slipping out of his hands; and this was
the *joy* of it.[6]

The second volume of *The Accursed Share* – now titled *The History
of Eroticism* –also began to take shape in 1950. As with *The Accursed
Share*, Bataille used his essays from *Critique* and other journals as a
way to gather material for the book, which had by now endured a
long gestation. Bataille's writings in mythical anthropology from
the late 1920s already associated the name Sade with a heterological
interpretation of erotic expenditure. In the late 1930s Bataille's
friendship with Sade scholar Maurice Heine encouraged him to
elaborate a phenomenology of eroticism. A decade later, as we
have seen, he anticipated a collection of essays on Sade – and on
the literature about Sade – under the titles *Sade and the Essence of
Eroticism*, *Sade and Sexual Rebellion*, and later *From Sexual Anguish
to the Catastrophe of Hiroshima*. Hiroshima figured in this title – as it
did in *The Nietzschean World of Hiroshima* – as an avatar of expenditure on a vast scale, where human lives could be wasted in heretofore

unimaginable numbers. This vision is linked to eroticism in that, for Bataille, eroticism can be defined as acceding to life even to the point of death.

Thus while the *History of Eroticism* had long been among Bataille's concerns, it was also very much a product of its era, of the Second World War, Hiroshima, Auschwitz and the atomic politics of the Cold War. In extension of this thought, Bataille reviewed John Hersey's accounts of Hiroshima and its aftermath, as well as a number of books on the Nazi concentration and death camps, racism, the excesses of Stalinism and war in general.[7] Bataille, in short, praised eroticism as acceding to life even to the point of death against the horizon of man-made mass death and the potential extinction of the human race in nuclear holocaust. Eroticism, for him, offered a form of consumption that was opposed to the bourgeois accumulation of wealth and to the wars that have historically proven the only outlet for that wealth. 'If we do not make *consumption* the *sovereign* principle of activity,' he wrote, 'we cannot help but succumb to those monstrous disorders without which we do not know how to *consume* the energy we have at our disposal.'[8]

Bataille draws a sharp distinction between eroticism and sexuality, the latter of which is utilitarian in its mechanical pursuit of pro-creation. Eroticism on the other hand is expenditure, perhaps the most *immediate* form of expenditure. It has no goal beyond the immediate expression of desire. Bataille's understanding of desire confounds Hegel with Sade, the Hegelian quest for identity through recognition with Sade's interplay of animality and indifference. Where the Hegelian consciousness acts, desiring recognition, Sade's libertine submits to his or her animal desires while remaining simultaneously indifferent to those desires. Sade's sovereign questions his or her animality and hence also his or her humanity. Where the Hegelian hero masters himself by enslaving others, Sade's sovereign sacrifices herself and others in a potlatch of desire.[9] As a question posed to both animality and to others, eroticism proposes a means by which human beings can rupture their isolation from one another and from the natural continuum of the world.

Eroticism is the privileged field for this inquiry because it is the privileged field of desire. A *history* of eroticism proposes a history of desire and hence, for Bataille, a history of the inner life of human beings. Where the first volume of *The Accursed Share, Consumption* provided a history of expenditure in economic and religious terms, the second volume, *The History of Eroticism*, would provide a history of expenditure in the inner life of humanity. It is a history of inner experience and this is a *necessary* history. Human beings have lost touch with their inner lives, with their desires, not only through repressive denial but also through easy satisfaction (which lacks both recognition and conscious self-sacrifice). *The History of Eroticism* proposes a way out: it proposes a conscientious description of activities that elude consciousness.

In keeping with this purpose, the first draft of *The History of Eroticism* shared the abstract, philosophical approach of Bataille's 1948 'Outline of a History of Religions',[10] and it didn't satisfy him. Several sections of the draft remain incomplete, not only as fragments of prose, but also as fragments of the text his substantial notes anticipated. In May 1951 he submitted the draft to Lindon at Minuit, who found it too rough for publication.[11] Bataille would draft a third, more explicitly political volume to the series – *Sovereignty* – following his thought to the end, at least in draft, before finalizing the *History*.

In January 1951, while he was working on *The History of Eroticism*, Georges and Diane were married in Nantua, where their friends the Costas lived. On the topic of marriage, he had written in the *History*:

> Habit is not necessarily inimical to the intensity of sexual activity. It is favorable to the harmony, to the secret under-standing of one by the other, without which the embrace would be superficial. It is even possible to think that only habit sometimes has the value of deep exploration, in opposition to the misunderstandings that turn continual change into a life of renewed frustration.[12]

Georges finally obtained a transfer in July. Named director of the municipal library in Orléans, he, Diane and Julie moved in time for him to assume the new position in September. They lived at 1 rue Dupanloup, an apartment adjacent to the library and its garden, both under the looming shadow of the Orléans cathedral. The building had once been the palace of the archbishop. Bataille's office opened onto the garden, providing a wonderful place to write. Orléans was also close enough to Paris for Bataille to resume his habit of lecturing there, and for friends like Michel and Zette Leiris to visit often. When male friends visited he shared an Orléans brothel with them. His life, in short, resumed something of its Parisian character, and both he and Diane were much happier there than they had been in Carpentras.

Bataille was close enough to Paris to take part in the latest intellectual feud: the controversy surrounding Albert Camus's *The Rebel*. Camus's book harshly but honestly attacked Stalinism and Surrealism, among other trends, and it was duly savaged in the press, in particular by Francis Jeanson in *Les Temps Modernes*. Bataille rose to the defence of both Camus and the Surrealists in a series of articles published in *Critique* over the following year.[13] These articles built on the reviews of Camus's work that he had published over the previous four years and served to situate not only Camus, Sartre and Breton, but also Bataille's own thought on the fundamental importance of sovereign expenditure.

He also pursued this thought in non-review articles like 'The Sovereign'[14] and in a series of lectures given at Jean Wahl's Collège Philosophique between January 1951 and February 1953. Later, he would publish these talks as 'Lectures on Nonknowledge'.[15] Each of these lectures – 'The Consequences of Nonknowledge', 'The Teaching of Death', 'Nonknowledge and Rebellion' and 'Nonknowledge, Laughter, and Tears' – took up an essential aspect of the problem of sovereignty and hence too of inner experience. Bataille was using the Collège Philosophique in much the same way he used the Socratic College a decade earlier, during the war. All of these texts and lectures – and a great many notes – were preparatory to the new edition of *Inner Experience* as the first volume of *La Somme athéologique*.[16]

In February 1953, the month he delivered the last of the lectures on nonknowledge, he wrote a post-scriptum to *Inner Experience* and abandoned his plans to include a more substantial selection of 'studies in atheology' in this volume of the *Summa*. He now saw the other articles and lectures as constituting an entirely new volume in the series and contented himself with reprinting *Method of Meditation* and the post-script in the new edition of his first book.

In the Post-Scriptum, he neatly summarized what he perceived to be his contribution to the history of thought:

> having discerned the effects, in our human life, of the 'disappearance of the discursive real', and having drawn a senseless light from the description of these effects: this light is blinding, perhaps, but it announces the opacity of the *night*; it announces night alone.[17]

This estimation should be read as a riposte to Gabriel Marcel's criticism of *Inner Experience* as being the work of a failed mystic. Marcel suggested that Bataille had simply failed to travel completely through the dark night of the soul, failed to reach the comforting consolation of dawn's rising faith.[18] For Bataille the collapse of the discursive real, which is to say of language – and hence consciousness, which for Bataille, as for Hegel, begins with language – reveals night alone. *Nothing* is beyond language. To perceive the truth of Bataille's self-estimation is to perceive his corpus as oriented by both analysis and experience, the will to know and the will to be, where discursive knowledge is nonknowledge and being is sovereign, that of the self that dies.

While working through these notions, Bataille began to shift the ground of his thought away from philosophical abstraction back onto anthropological facts. Bataille had never been a philosopher – by either training or inclination – and he had long utilized the methods of anthropology and historical example to ground his research. In 1952 he renewed this emphasis by turning to the study of prehistoric painting, religion and culture. This study would provide a new foundation for his *History of Eroticism*. As before, he began with a series of lectures, review articles and speculative pieces published in *Critique* and other journals.[19] He focused on the cave at Lascaux but ranged widely: considering prehistoric representations of animality, femininity and masculinity, the nature and role of the sacred in prehistoric culture and, crucially, the place of prehistory in contemporary life.

During the spring of 1953, having finished preparing the re-edition of *Inner Experience*, Bataille resumed work on the third volume of *The Accursed Share*, *Sovereignty*. As with the other two volumes, he began by re-editing essays published in *Critique*; these were essays originally written with his projected book on Albert Camus, Nietzsche and Communism in mind.[20] Thereafter he wrote new pieces and published them in *Critique* as well; these over the summer of 1953.[21] By January of the following year, he had nearly completed drafts of both *Sovereignty* and *The History of Eroticism*, or so he wrote to Minuit.

Where *The Accursed Share* considered economic and religious forms of expenditure, and *The History of Eroticism* proposed a history of the inner life of human desire, *Sovereignty* focused on the politics of the self that dies. It traced the history of sovereignty from feudalism through rise of the bourgeois to the present day, and located its discussion of contemporary forms of sovereignty between the two poles of Nietzsche and Communism. 'Sovereign life', in Bataille's schema, 'begins when, with the necessities ensured, the possibility of life opens up without limit . . . Life beyond utility is the domain of sovereignty.'[22] This description of sovereignty does not pertain to the stable power of political states, rather it describes the all-consuming life of a monarch.

> The sovereign, epitomizing the *subject*, is the one by whom and for whom the moment, the miraculous *moment*, is the ocean into which the streams of labor disappear. The sovereign spends festively for himself and for others alike that which the labor of all has accumulated.[23]

The capitalist revolution was a revolution in the denial of sovereignty. Under the reign of the bourgeoisie, expenditure hid itself behind closed doors. The public would no longer be treated to the *ancien* spectacles of wealth. The Communist Revolution furthered the retreat of sovereignty through its insistence on the equality of all men and its hyper-rationalization of the means of production, after which all expenditure would be productive expenditure, sanctioned by the state. Bataille countered this vision of Communism with his Nietzschean morality of expenditure, wherein sovereignty could reassert its rights only as a self that dies.

These were notions he first explored twenty years earlier in *La Critique Sociale*, now deepened by experience and tempered by time. *Sovereignty* is intricate, uneven and, like so many other writings by Bataille, unfinished. Rather than rewriting the draft, Bataille eventually carved it up, publishing pieces in *Botteghe Oscure*, *Monde Nouveau–Paru* and *Literature and Evil* over the next few years. This practice of intellectual and literary abandonment, of incompletion, was of course absolutely consistent with Bataille's thought. 'I resolved long ago,' he wrote paradoxically, 'not to seek knowledge, as others do, but to seek its contrary, which is nonknowledge. I no longer anticipated the moment when I would be rewarded for my effort, *when I would know at last*, but rather the moment when *I would no longer know, when my initial anticipation would dissolve into* NOTHING.'[24]

17
Unfinished

In December 1953 Bataille suffered the first real symptoms of
the disease that, over the next nine years, would slowly kill him:
cerebral arteriosclerosis, a thickening and hardening of the arteries
in his brain. Headaches, facial pain and impaired vision are among
its symptoms; vascular dementia, aneurisms and strokes are its
debilitating and ultimately fatal results. In vascular dementia small
symptom-free strokes occur and accrue damage to neurons over
time. Apathy, depressive emotionalism, momentary confusion and
irritability follow, culminating in a state where sudden losses of
consciousness and bodily control are common. Over the years
Bataille's ability to concentrate would slowly fail him. He would be
hospitalized several times and treated with intravenous heparin,
but it didn't help. According to Michel Surya, Bataille's old friend
and doctor, Théodore Fraenkel, explained the disease to Diane but
did not tell Georges, who suffered without knowledge.[1] The most
agile of thinkers fell prey to the literal hardening of his mind.

In January 1954 Gallimard reissued *Inner Experience*, with
Method of Meditation and 'Post-scriptum 1953', as the first volume
of *La Somme athéologique*. Roger Grenier would interview Bataille
about the book on his radio programme 'La Vie des lettres' in July.
Other than that the eleven-year-old book failed to excite much
initial notice.

Also in January Bataille wrote to Jérôme Lindon at Minuit,
notifying the publisher that he had nearly completed his drafts of

The History of Eroticism and *Sovereignty*. But neither book was to be. *The History of Eroticism* would be entirely rewritten and utterly transformed in 1956 and *Sovereignty* published only in fragments. These books were hardly alone in abandonment among Bataille's writings. More than a quarter of Bataille's *Oeuvres complètes* consists of notes and drafts that he did not publish. Another even larger portion consists of articles published only in ephemeral journals and reviews, never reworked into more permanent form. And many of the books that Bataille did publish – from *Story of the Eye* to *Inner Experience* and *The Accursed Share* – were later substantially rewritten or editorially recast, inserted into some imagined series that would never appear. To appreciate his corpus is to revise our understanding of the creative act: he does not write masterpieces, he writes against them. As we have seen, thought ruins.

During the spring of 1954 Bataille visited the painted cave at Lascaux with the Swiss publisher Albert Skira. The two had known one another since the days of *Documents* when Skira asked Bataille and Masson to develop the journal that eventually became *Minotaure*. Now Bataille convinced Skira to publish a volume on prehistoric art to begin Skira's new series 'The Great Centuries of Painting'. Bataille's book would focus almost entirely on Lascaux, which was at the time celebrated as the 'Sistine Chapel' of the prehistoric world. The small town of Montignac, where Lascaux was discovered in September 1940, was close enough to Orléans for Bataille and Diane to drive down to see the cave with obsessive regularity while he was writing his book.

In *Lascaux, or the Birth of Art*, as the finished book was called in April 1955, Bataille did not presume to be doing the work of a prehistorian, an archaeologist or an anthropologist. Rather he relied, as he had always done, on the thought of others, experts like the Abbé Breuil and Johannes Maringer. Bataille's gesture was to activate their thought within a larger conversational frame and to use it as a vehicle of his own and his reader's experience. In *The*

Tears of Eros, for example, he looked back on *Lascaux*, admitting, 'I forbade myself from giving a personal interpretation of the surprising scene' in the cave.[2] This act of self-denial and hermeneutic refusal was the recourse of nonknowledge.

Prehistory had fascinated Bataille since the 1920s: he included essays and images about it in *Documents*. For him Lascaux and prehistoric art in general testified to the birth of a distinctly human consciousness through the non-utilitarian character of the works. Too, prehistoric images and sculptures were often *formless* in their contrasting uses of realism and iconicity as well as in their visual puns – as in a female statuette shaped like a phallus. Prehistoric representations also reveal the sacred – whether they play a role in prehistoric religions or not – because they reveal the dichotomy between human beings and their world, between humans and animals, and between humans and the material spaces of the caves in which they painted. The sacred here is revealed as an irruption of heterogeneity within the natural continuum. Prehistory also fascinated Bataille as an era in which culture was, at least in his imagination, relatively uniform and therefore universal.

In sharp contrast to his investigation of prehistory, Bataille wrote a complementary study of modernity as revealed in the paintings of Edouard Manet at the same time. Skira published this book too, only a few months after *Lascaux, or the Birth of Art*, again in both French and English, as part of a series entitled 'The Taste of Our Time'. Bataille's interest in Manet's work dated back to the late 1920s, when he borrowed several books on the painter from the Bibliothèque Nationale. His cousin, Marie-Louise Bataille, was at that time writing about him, and the book she then co-wrote with Georges Wildenstein and Paul Jamot would serve as a significant source for Bataille's own writing on the painter. André Malraux's massive art historical fantasy, *The Voices of Silence*, published in 1951, provided another significant source and foil.[3] But Bataille's book is nevertheless very much a work apart. As with *Lascaux* it does not endeavour to add to our knowledge of Manet's work: rather, it endeavours to situate that work decisively at the beginning of a new era in representation and to describe the nature of that era – the modern era – through Manet. The book is as concerned with modernity as it is with Manet.

For Bataille the modern era in representation began when Manet emptied painting of its subject matter. Art became the subject of art when Manet deprived his art of content. For one, in Bataille's vision, does not look at a canvas by Manet to see emotion, or tension or vibrant colour, let alone a narrative or a symbol. Manet's works are deprived of detail in the sense of heightened attentiveness and they are unconcerned with observation beyond the observation of *what is*. Manet shocked his viewers by depriving them of the visual armature of Classical style and content. He substituted the everyday, the mundane – and deprived even that of transcendence. Manet's best works capture an essential emptiness, a void of meaning, with perfect – and perfectly silent – indifference. For Bataille Manet's work destroys the rhetoric of representation.[4]

Manet's virulent indifference is visible in Olympia's gaze. For the reader of Bataille, it recalls the indifference of Madame Edwarda and the apathy of Sade's libertines.

In her provocative literalness she is nothing. Her real nudity (not merely that of her body) is the silence that emanates from her, like that from a sunken ship. All we have is the 'sacred horror' of her presence – presence whose sheer simplicity is tantamount to absence.[5]

And Manet's disruption of the rhetoric of representation recalls Bataille's own will to erode grammar, to speak silence.

Despite assuming its place in a long line of Bataille's inquiries into visual art – from prehistory to da Vinci, Goya, Van Gogh and the Surrealists – André Masson above all – Bataille's *Manet* can be read as a veiled biography of his own motives and concerns. Even his description of Manet can be read as reflecting Bataille himself: he is 'vulnerable, temperamental, impulsive . . . impersonal and aloof . . . but driven by inner forces that gave him no rest';[6] or again, 'unstable, hesitant, always on the edge and tortured by doubt . . . a far cry from placid indifference . . . Essentially erratic and trembling.'[7] This suggestion would surely be absurd were Bataille not the author of *On Nietzsche*, a book which commingles author and subject in an infinite play of identities.

Before and after writing *Manet*, Bataille put a great deal of energy into revising *Madame Edwarda* for a new edition. Austryn Wainhouse translated the original version for Olympia Press under the title *The Naked Beast at Heaven's Gate* and Jean-Jacques Pauvert agreed to publish a new version of the French text, augmented by a preface that Bataille would sign with his own name. Bataille reworked *Edwarda* substantially and decided to expand the story, offering a more complete autobiography of its 'author', Pierre Angélique, in a suite of other texts. The new whole was to be collected under the title *Divinus Deus*, but Bataille left it unfinished. *My Mother*, *Charlotte D'Ingerville*, and *Saint* each had their place in the construction, but Bataille did not complete any of them.

My Mother is the most complete of these draft pieces. It concerns the sexual awakening of the adolescent Pierre Angélique, an awakening that occurred with the active encouragement of his mother, Hélène. At the beginning of the narrative, Pierre perceives his debauched father as a menacing figure who has tormented his innocent mother. The father soon dies, however, and Pierre quickly learns that his mother has in fact been the cause of his father's ruin. Pierre's fears and sympathies slip from mother to father in a play of identities – saintly and debauched – common to Bataille's narratives. Each character exceeds his or her identity, reverses any stable role. Inverting the ideal of a good mother, who would protect her son from harm, Hélène presides over Pierre's initiation into a life of debauchery, pairing him with partners Rhea and Hansi, and sealing their partnership in crime with a final incestuous and fatal – for her – embrace. While writing these stories, rewriting *Edwarda*, and writing his preface to that book, Bataille was also working on the new edition of *The History of Eroticism*, now titled simply *Eroticism*, and on a number of review articles on eroticism and erotic literature, pieces on Pauline Réage's *Story of O*, on Pierre Klossowski's novels, and again on Sade.[8]

In November 1956 Dionys Mascolo, Robert Antelme, Marguerite Duras, Edgar Morin and Louis-René des Forêts organized a committee of intellectuals opposed to the French colonial war in Algeria. Most of the founding members were former members of the Communist party, but the committee soon grew to include all manner of French intellectuals from Cocteau to Claude Lévi-Strauss. Breton, Sartre and Bataille all joined and were there on 5 November in the Salle des Horticulteurs in Paris calling for the end of the war and an end to all racial discrimination on the part of the French government, both domestically or abroad.

Bataille had known Dionys Mascolo – who was married to Marguerite Duras – since 1942, when they met at Gallimard, where Mascolo worked negotiating overseas publication rights. They had become particularly close after Bataille read Mascolo's book *Le Communisme* in 1953 and wrote its author a letter in humble and profound admiration.[9] In the 1950s friendships with Mascolo and Kostas Axelos, and around them the *Arguments* group of dissident Marxists, drew Bataille back into political 'activity', something he had abandoned with the failure of Counter Attack in 1936.

Several things conspired to keep Bataille from becoming more involved in this new generation of political militancy than he did. Living in Orléans rather than Paris posed one kind of problem. More serious however was his increasing physical suffering. By late 1956 he was simply too ill to travel regularly. He could not even count on having the energy necessary to write. And he was also simply too depressed to go on, not only about his physical condition, but about the state of the world. In *Sovereignty* he claimed that the world needed a thought that would not recoil from horror. By the late 1950s Bataille could no longer enfold the horror of the world within his thought. In his perception the Cold War had turned the world into an immense atomic powder keg that could only result in a nuclear catastrophe. In an acute state of depression, he explained his absence from an organizational meeting by saying,

> I remain despite all condemned to remain alone. My physical fatigue and my moral depression agree on this. And what's more, how could I forget that my reflection has engaged me in perceiving more and more the difference between men as more real than their equality?[10]

A month later, in December 1956, Jean-Jacques Pauvert stood trial for publishing Sade. Bataille – along with André Breton, Jean Cocteau and others – spoke in Pauvert and Sade's defence. Bataille did not defend Sade on the pretext of free speech, as if Sade were simply another writer. Rather he spoke of Sade as having made a unique contribution to the history of thought. To read Sade is to descend into an abyss of horror, a monstrous world of crime, he said, where human beings find pleasure in contemplating death and suffering. Sade provided us with a document demonstrating why human beings disobey rationality. 'For someone who wants to go to the bottom of what it means to be human, reading Sade is not only recommended, it is perfectly necessary.'[11] Bataille spoke at the trial not only as a writer and friend of Pauvert, but – as he told the judge – as a librarian (he recommended restricting the circulation of Sade's books) and, surprisingly, as a 'philosopher'. This was perhaps the sole moment in Bataille's long public life in which he used this word to describe himself without qualification. It should be noted however that he spoke as a philosopher when defending the Marquis de Sade, hardly an author of armchair abstractions.

Bataille was at the time also working through more traditional philosophical fare. In the mid 1950s, while pursuing his studies of Lascaux and Manet, Bataille wrote a series of articles on Hegel and on the concept of universal history.[12] This was a long-standing interest of Bataille's, dating back to the late 1920s and early 1930s, when he contemplated starting a journal devoted to it. At that time he tried without success to pique Raymond Queneau's interest and aid. Now, more than twenty years later, he ventured again into the same field, this time alone. Bataille's writings on prehistory (Lascaux) and modernity (Manet), his histories of religion, economics and eroticism, and even his insistence that *Critique* be encyclopaedic in scope, should all be read as attempts to sketch a universal history. In his notes he gave the project a working title: *The Bottle at Sea, or Universal History, from Origins to the Day before the Eventual Disaster*.[13] Unsurprisingly, this too was to remain unfinished. As an universal history – a global and encyclopaedic history of civilization – it was all but unimaginable. For a thinker drawn to working at the limits of his imagination such a fantasy offered an inevitable appeal.

In January 1957 Bataille proposed a collection of critical essays to Gallimard through Dionys Mascolo. Robert Gallimard accepted *Literature and Evil* even though all of the essays had previously been published – mostly in *Critique*, and mostly between 1946 and 1952. The book was the final incarnation of a collection Bataille had envisioned for at least a decade, under various titles, *The Sanctity of Evil* having been the most consistent. Pieces on Baudelaire, Brontë, Blake, Michelet, Proust, Sade and Genet were joined by one on Kafka that Bataille had also used as the final chapter of his *Sovereignty* draft.

Only a few months after Gallimard published *Literature and Evil*, Editions de Minuit published *Eroticism* and Jean Jacques Pauvert *Blue of Noon*. Both of these last two works had been substantially revised over the course of the previous year. Of his decision to finally release *Blue of Noon*, twenty-two years after he had written it, Bataille said only that he deferred to the judgement of his friends. On 4 October 1957 the three publishers – Gallimard, Minuit and Pauvert – threw Bataille a party at the bar of the Pont-Royal. Photographs of the event show an elegantly dressed man possessed by an otherworldly serenity. Georges Bataille was sixty years old.

Over the coming months Bataille would be fêted in other ways as well. Marguerite Duras interviewed him for *France-Observateur* in December, and Pierre Dumayet interviewed him on the television show *Lectures pour tous* in May. The first special issue of a journal devoted to his work also appeared in the spring of 1958 – *La Ciguë* (Hemlock), with contributions by Char, Duras, Fautrier, Leiris, Jean Wahl and others. Bataille's work was being recognized not only by his peers but by a new generation of writers and intellectuals at precisely the moment when Bataille himself was most burdened by illness, slipping away.

During the summer of 1957, Maurice Girodias – the original publisher of *Critique*, now famous for his Olympia Press Traveller's Companion series of pornographic fiction – asked Bataille to edit another journal, this one devoted to eroticism and heavily illustrated. The project recalled the *Erotic Almanac* Bataille had planned in 1929 with Pascal Pia. Bataille accepted the new task and enlisted Patrick Waldberg as managing editor and the photographer Roger Parry as coordinator for the illustrations. Over the next year and a half Bataille and Waldberg, in particular, would generate a prospectus for the journal, set up an editorial board – Gaston Bachelard among its members – and solicit articles. They planned for the journal to appear on a quarterly basis, in both French and English. For contributions, Bataille called on old friends like Michel Leiris, Alfred

Métraux, Pascal Pia and René Leibowitz, as well as acquaintances and newer friends, like Man Ray, Gilbert Lély, Robert Lebel.

The publication would span the disciplines and tackle its topic from several angles, some aesthetic, others scientific. It would be a worthy, if late, successor to *Documents* and a catalogue of Bataille's lifelong concerns. Its subtitle was 'Sexology, Psychoanalysis, Philosophy of Sexuality', but the group struggled to find a suitable title: *Genesis, Transgression, Innocence, Confession, The Human Species* (after Robert Antelme's book). Nothing really satisfied everyone. Over its year of gestation, Girodias demanded ever more scandalous imagery and content while Bataille sought to burnish the scandal with the veneer of scientific lucidity, as he had in *Documents*. The two perspectives ultimately could not be resolved: Girodias withdrew his support in December 1958. At this point Bataille was too ill to pursue the project without him. Instead, he shifted his energy and imagination, reorganizing his thoughts on the history of eroticism and on universal history, into a new book, his last, *The Tears of Eros*.

La Somme athéologique foundered in 1958, with notes for a new volume, *Pure Happiness or the Share of Play*, and for a new edition of *Guilty*. The new edition of *Guilty*, augmented by a short preface – first published in the NRF (Nouvelle Revue Française) in 1960 as 'Fear' – and by *Alleluia: The Catechism of Dianus*, would appear after substantial delays in 1961. Delays also held back the second edition of *The Hatred of Poetry*, now retitled *The Impossible*.

At this point, Bataille could work for only a few minutes at a time, so quickly was his mind exhausted. As the editor J. M. Lo Duca reports of the time he spent working with Bataille on *The Tears of Eros*, in the end, his concentration was so shattered that he could not remember what he had written for more than a few minutes. Having written a caption for a photo in the book and taken that caption into the next room to be typed, he would have forgotten his words by the time he returned.[14]

On 10 May 1960 Bataille's daughter Laurence – now aged 30 – was arrested for her work on behalf of the Algerian Front de Libération Nationale. During the 1950s Laurence had been a model for Balthus and had had some success in the theatre before turning to political militancy. She spent six weeks in the Prison de la Roquette where Bataille – despite his illness – visited her in June.

Under circumstances such as these it is not surprising that it took Bataille almost three years to write his introduction to Pierre Klossowski's translation of the trial documents of the late medieval paedophile Gilles de Rais. Nor is it surprising that *The Tears of Eros* would rely so heavily on illustrations to carry its argument along.

Bataille told Lo Duca that he hoped *The Tears of Eros* would be a more remarkable book than any he had previously published, and much of this did have to do with the illustrations.[15] *The Tears of Eros* offers Bataille's final testament. It recapitulates all of his themes and strategies. It offers a history of desire from prehistory to the present, and therefore a history of representation and of the sacred. It takes us from the painted caves to the Dionysian festivals of Classical Greece to the Satanic cults of the Middle Ages and the libertine fantasies of the Classical Age in France, to the mannerist fever of Surrealism in the twentieth century. The text circles its topics in the hermeneutic delirium of nonknowledge offering an inverse of Hegel's *Phenomenology*: where Hegel relayed the history of consciousness, Bataille revelled in all that consciousness cannot capture, that words cannot describe.

The book culminates in the comparison of the image of Aztec sacrifice that Bataille had by now oft repeated and the images of the Leng Tch'e that first set fire to his tortured imagination in 1925. Describing the image of the Leng Tch'e he writes:

I wonder what the Marquis de Sade would have thought of this image . . . In 1938, a friend initiated me in the practice of yoga. It was on this occasion that I discerned in the violence of this image, an infinite capacity for reversal. Through this violence – even today I cannot image a more insane, more shocking form – I was so stunned that I reached the point of ecstasy . . . What I suddenly saw, and what imprisoned me in anguish – but which at the same time delivered me from it – was the identity of these perfect contraries, divine ecstasy and its opposite, extreme horror.[16]

As Bataille's physical condition continued to deteriorate, he could no longer rely on a steady income from his writing, nor could he foresee continuing in his work as a librarian for much longer. In 1959 Marguerite Duras had donated her profits from *Hiroshima, Mon Amour* to Bataille. Two years later, in March 1961, Patrick Waldberg organized a sale of donated art and manuscripts at the Hôtel Drouot on Bataille's behalf. Masson, Picasso, Giacometti, Fautrier, Michaux, Matta, Miro, Max Ernst, Hans Arp, Victor Brauner and Yves Tanguy were among those who contributed. The proceeds from the sale were used to purchase an apartment at 25 rue Saint-Sulpice, one block from the church, not far from Bataille's former Parisian apartments.

The following February Bataille applied for a transfer from the Bibliothèque d'Orléans to the Bibliothèque Nationale. The move was approved, though he was also given two months medical leave. He, Diane and Julie moved into the new apartment in March, in time to be in Paris for the publication of *The Impossible* in April.

A few months later, in July 1962, Diane took Julie to England, leaving Bataille alone, working on a potential film of *Story of the Eye*. On the night of 7 July he slipped into a coma and was taken to a hospital, attended by Dr Fraenkel. He died on the morning of the 9th after briefly regaining consciousness. Nothing remains of his final agony, whether pleasure or pain.

Bataille's grave at Vézelay.

Georges Bataille was buried in the cemetery at Vézelay, below the basilica. His simple stone grave overlooks the same valley as did his house. Diane, Jean Piel, Jacques Pimpaneau and Michel and Zette Leiris attended the simple ceremony.

References

Citations from Georges Bataille, *Oeuvres complètes* (Paris, 1970–88) are listed as *OC* vol. no., page no. Citations from Georges Bataille, *Romans et récits* (Paris, 2004) are listed as *Romans* page no. Citations from Georges Bataille, *Choix de lettres* (Paris, 1997) are listed as *Lettres* page no. English-language editions are the most current editions available in the US, listed by title and page no. See the Bibliography for complete publication information. Where no previous English version exists translations are my own. Translations have occasionally been modified without remark.

Introduction: *Ecce Homo*

1 *OC* 10, 627; *The Tears of Eros* 206.
2 *Critique*, 195–6 (August–September 1963).
3 *OC* 1, 5.
4 *October*, 36 (1985).
5 *OC* 7, 462; *My Mother* 222.
6 Friedrich Nietzsche, *Beyond Good and Evil*, trans. Walter Kaufmann (New York, 1966), § 268.
7 *OC* 5, 483.
8 The currently available translation of *Inner Experience*, for example, is a travesty of small and large errors.

1 Abandonment

1 All readers of Bataille are indebted to Michel Surya's pioneering

Georges Bataille, la mort à l'oeuvre (Paris, 1987) [in English as *Georges Bataille: An Intellectual Biography* (London, 2002)], to Bernd Mattheus's *Georges Bataille, eine Thanatographie* (Munich, 1984–8), and to Marina Galetti's comprehensive chronology of Bataille's life in the Pléiade edition of Bataille's fiction, *Romans et récits* (Paris, 2004). This author recognizes his enormous debt to them here.

2 *OC* 5, 257; *Guilty* 22.
3 *Romans* 364; *Story of the Eye* 99.
4 *Romans* 104; *Story of the Eye* 93.
5 Ibid.
6 *OC* 2, 10; *Visions of Excess* 4.
7 *OC* 5, 555.
8 *OC* 2, 10; *Visions of Excess* 4.
9 *OC* 1, 252; *The Cradle of Humanity* 41.
10 *OC* 5, 210; *The Unfinished System of Nonknowledge* 89.
11 *OC* 7, 459.
12 *OC* 5, 210; *The Unfinished System of Nonknowledge* 89.
13 See Raymond Queneau, 'Premières Confrontations avec Hegel', *Critique*, 195–6 (August–September 1963).
14 *Romans* 105; *Story of the Eye* 94.
15 Ibid.
16 Ibid.
17 *OC* 7, 459.
18 Fyodor Dostoevsky, *Notes from Underground*, trans. Richard Pevear and Larissa Volokhonsky (New York, 1993), p. 130.
19 *OC* 5, 257; *Guilty* 22.
20 *Romans* 364; *Story of the Eye* 99.
21 See *Lettres* 12.
22 *OC* 1, 612.
23 *OC* 7, 459.
24 *OC* 1, 612.
25 See *Lettres* 21.
26 *OC* 5, 291; *Guilty* 53.
27 *OC* 2, 392.
28 *OC* 1, 612.
29 *OC* 1, 613.
30 *Romans* 106; *Story of the Eye* 95.

31 *OC* 5, 301; *Guilty* 61. See also, for example, *Lettres* 15.

32 Blaise Pascal, *Pensées* (London, 1966). § 136.

2 An Attempt at Evasion

1 *Romans* 365; *Story of the Eye* 101.

2 *Lettres* 14.

3 Friedrich Nietzsche, *The Gay Science* (New York, 1974), Preface § 1.

4 *OC* 5, 369; *Guilty* 123.

5 *OC* 7, 524.

6 See Georges Delteil, 'Georges Bataille à Riom-ès-Montagnes', *Critique*, 195–6 (August–September 1963).

7 *OC* 6, 416.

8 *Lettres* 8.

9 See *Lettres* 21. 'Notre Dame des Rheims' (1918) in *OC* 1, 611–16. For an extended discussion of this piece, see Denis Hollier, *Against Architecture* [1974], trans. Betsy Wing (Cambridge, 1989).

10 *Lettres* 10.

11 *Lettres* 8.

12 *Lettres* 19.

13 For 'L'Ordre de chevalerie', see *OC* 1, 99–102.

14 'La Littérature française du Moyen Âge, la morale chevaleresque et la passion', *Critique*, 38 (July 1949), pp. 585–601; reprinted in *OC* 11, 518.

15 *Lettres* 25.

16 *Romans* 365; *Story of the Eye* 100.

17 *Lettres* 55.

18 *OC* 5, 72; *Inner Experience* 58.

19 *OC* 7, 459; *My Mother* 217.

20 *OC* 8, 562; *The Unfinished System of Nonknowledge* 153–4.

21 *OC* 5, 80; *Inner Experience* 66.

22 *OC* 5, 251; *Guilty* 16.

23 *OC* 8, 220; *The Unfinished System of Nonknowledge* 138.

24 *OC* 5, 257; *Guilty* 22.

3 Violence and Sumptuosity

1 *Lettres* 27.
2 *Lettres* 28.
3 Georges Bataille, 'À propos de "Pour qui sonne le glas?" d'Ernest Hemingway' (1945), in *OC* 11, 26. See also *Romans* 35; *Story of the Eye* 64.
4 Bataille, 'À propos de 'Pour qui sonne le glas?' d'Ernest Hemingway', in *OC* 11, 26.
5 Georges Bataille, 'The Sacred' in *OC* 1, 559; *Visions of Excess* 243.
6 *Lettres* 28.
7 *OC* 12, 86.
8 Found among Marie-Louise Bataille's papers, these stories are reprinted in *Romans* 929–43.
9 *Lettres* 36.
10 *Lettres* 32, 34.
11 *Lettres* 43.
12 *Lettres* 33.
13 *Lettres* 32, 34, 35, 39.
14 *Lettres* 34.
15 Ibid.
16 *Lettres* 45.
17 *Lettres* 37, 39, 44, 54.
18 *Lettres* 50.
19 *Lettres* 46.
20 *Lettres* 37.
21 *Lettres* 54.
22 Ibid.
23 *Lettres* 51.
24 *Lettres* 47.
25 *Lettres* 48.
26 *Lettres* 47.
27 Alfred Métraux, 'Rencontre avec les ethnoglogues', *Critique*, 195–6 (August–September 1963), p. 677.
28 *OC* 10, 13; *Erotism* 9.
29 *The Tears of Eros* 201.
30 Métraux, 'Rencontre avec les ethnoglogues', p. 678.

31 The depth and extent of this influence has yet to be adequately explored in the critical literature on Bataille, whose work is now typically read by philosophers and literary critics. Studies include *Écrits d'ailleurs, Georges Bataille et les ethnologues*, ed. Dominique Lecoq and Jean-Luc Lory (Paris, 1987) and two excellent books by Michèle Richman, *Reading Georges Bataille: Beyond the Gift* (Baltimore, 1982) and *Sacred Revolutions: Durkheim and the Collège de Sociologie* (Minneapolis, 2002). Jean Baudrillard furthers this line of inquiry, particularly in *Symbolic Exchange and Death* (London, 1993).

32 *OC* 8, 562; *The Unfinished System of Nonknowledge* 154.

33 François Warin has explored the complex relationship between Nietzsche and Bataille more completely than anyone else. See François Warin, *Nietzsche and Bataille: la parodie à l'infini* (Paris, 1994).

34 *OC* 5, 353; *Guilty* 108.

35 *OC* 8, 562; *The Unfinished System of Nonknowledge* 154.

36 *OC* 8, 563; *The Unfinished System of Nonknowledge* 155.

37 *OC* 8, 563; *The Unfinished System of Nonknowledge* 154.

38 See Michel Surya, *Georges Bataille* (London, 2002) 62.

39 See Lev Shestov, *Dostoevsky, Tolstoy, Nietzsche* (Cleveland, 1969).

40 *OC* 8, 563; *The Unfinished System of Nonknowledge* 154.

4 Underground Man

1 Michel Leiris, 'From the Impossible Bataille to the Impossible *Documents*', in Georges Bataille and Michel Leiris, *Échanges et correspondances* (Paris, 2004), p. 15; Michel Leiris, *Brisées: Broken Branches* (San Francisco, 1989), p. 237.

2 Bataille and Leiris, *Échanges et correspondences*, p. 16; Leiris, *Brisées: Broken Branches*, pp. 237–8.

3 *OC* 8, 172; *The Absence of Myth* 38.

4 *OC* 8, 171; *The Absence of Myth* 36–7.

5 Fyodor Dostoevsky, *Notes from Underground*, trans. Richard Pevear and Larissa Volokhonsky (New York, 1993), p. 130.

6 Bataille and Leiris, *Échanges et correspondences*, p. 17; Leiris, *Brisées: Broken Branches*, p. 238.

7 André Masson, 'Le s*OC* de la charrue', in Masson, *Le Rebelle du sur-*

réalisme, ed. Françoise Levaillant (Paris, 1994), p. 75.

8 Bataille and Leiris, *Échanges et correspondences*, p. 17; Leiris, *Brisées: Broken Branches*, p. 238. See also *OC* 8, 171; *The Absence of Myth* 35.

9 See Fernande Schulmann, 'Une amitié, deux disparus', *Ésprit* (November 1963).

10 *OC* 5, 247; *Guilty* 12.

11 *OC* 8, 179; *The Absence of Myth* 42.

12 *OC* 8, 174; *The Absence of Myth* 38.

13 *OC* 8, 173; *The Absence of Myth* 37. See also *OC* 12, 558 and 561.

14 *OC* 8, 178; *The Absence of Myth* 41.

15 *OC* 7, 459; *My Mother* 218.

16 *Romans* 363; *Story of the Eye* 97.

17 Bataille and Leiris, *Échanges et correspondences*, p. 17; Leiris, *Brisées: Broken Branches*, p. 239.

18 *Romans* 113; *Blue of Noon* 12.

19 *Romans* 363; *Story of the Eye* 97.

20 On Adrien Borel, see Elisabeth Roudinesco, *La Bataille de cents ans: Histoire de la psychoanalyse en France* (Paris, 1982), vol. I.

21 Madeleine Chapsal, 'Georges Bataille', in Chapsal, *Quinze écrivains: entretiens* (Paris, 1963), p. 14.

22 *OC* 7, 459; *My Mother* 218.

23 *OC* 2, 9–10; *Visions of Excess* 3–4.

24 *Romans* 103; *Story of the Eye* 92.

25 He borrowed Jankélévitch's translation from the Bibliothèque Nationale on 10 February 1923. See *OC* 12, 554.

26 See *Lettres* 68; *OC* 12, 565, 588.

5 *Incipit Parodia*

1 Bataille published *Story of the Eye* pseudonymously and never mentioned *Notre Dame de Rheims*.

2 *OC* 1, 81; *Visions of Excess* 5.

3 *OC* 5, 179; *Inner Experience* 155.

4 *OC* 7, 20; *The Accursed Share* 10.

5 *OC* 1, 86; *Visions of Excess* 9.

6 In October and November 1927 Bataille borrowed a series of books by

and about Heraclitus, Greek metaphysics, and Nietzsche and Greek thought from the Bibliothèque Nationale. See *OC* 12, 567.

7 *OC* 1, 84; *Visions of Excess* 7.

8 See 'Sacred Sociology and the Relationships between "Society", "Organism", and "Being"', in Denis Hollier, ed., *Le Collège de sociologie* (Paris, 2005), pp. 31–60; Denis Hollier, ed. *The College of Sociology* (Minneapolis, 1988), pp. 73–84.

9 *OC* 1, 82; *Visions of Excess* 6.

10 *OC* 1, 86; *Visions of Excess* 9.

11 *OC* 2, 25; *Visions of Excess* 82.

12 *OC* 2, 20; *Visions of Excess* 78.

13 *OC* 2, 30; *Visions of Excess* 86.

14 *OC* 2, 29; *Visions of Excess* 85.

15 More has been written about *Story of the Eye* than about any other single text by Bataille. Patrick French's *The Cut: Reading Bataille's Histoire de l'oeil* (Oxford, 2000) is an outstanding summary and extension of the literature.

16 *Romans* 102; *Story of the Eye*. The City Lights Books translation of the text also includes a section about *Story of the Eye* from Bataille's book *Le Petit* (*The Little One*) as well as a note proposing a potential continuation of the text. While informative, these two sections are not part of *Story* in the same way that 'Coincidences' is.

17 *Romans* 365; *Story of the Eye* 98.

18 *Romans* 106; *Story of the Eye* 96.

19 *OC* 1, 82; *Visions of Excess* 7.

20 *Romans* 79; *Story of the Eye* 46.

21 *Romans* 52; *Story of the Eye* 5.

22 *OC* 1, 82; *Visions of Excess* 7.

23 *Romans* 89; *Story of the Eye* 65

24 See Elisabeth Roudinesco, *Jacques Lacan* (New York, 1997), pp. 122–4; Michel Surya, *Georges Bataille* (London, 2002), p. 147.

6 Heterology

1 Alfred Métraux, 'Rencontre avec les ethnoglogues', *Critique*, 195–6 (August–September 1963), p. 628.

2 *OC* 1, 152.

3 *OC* 1, 157.

4 On *Documents*, see in particular Georges Didi-Huberman, *La Ressemblance informe ou le gai savoir visuel selon Georges Bataille* (Paris, 1995); Denis Hollier, 'The Use Value of the Impossible', in Hollier, *Absent Without Leave* (Cambridge, 1993); Michel Leiris, 'From the Impossible Bataille to the Impossible *Documents*', in Leiris, *Brisées: Broken Branches* (San Francisco, 1989); Conor Joyce, *Carl Einstein in Documents* (Philadelphia, 2002); and, for an exploration and extension of its logic, strictly within an art historical domain, see Yve-Alain Bois and Rosalind Krauss, *Formless: A User's Guide* (New York, 1997).

5 Leiris, *Brisées: Broken Branches*, p. 242.

6 Alastair Brotchie, ed., *Encyclopedia Acephalica* (London, 1995) reprints the 'Critical Dictionary' in English translation.

7 See Leiris's notes in *Brisées: Broken Branches*, pp. 3–4, 61–2. The Glossary itself is reprinted in Michel Leiris, *Mots sans mémoire* (Paris, 1969).

8 *OC* 1, 217; *Visions of Excess* 31.

9 Oddly, *Encyclopedia Acephalica* organizes the 'Dictionary' in alphabetical order and thereby subverts the project it intends to celebrate.

10 For Eisenstein's lecture, see Sergei Eisenstein, 'The Principles of the New Russian Cinema', in Eisenstein, *Writings, 1922–1934* (London, 1988), pp. 195–202.

11 *OC* 1, 230; *Visions of Excess* 56.

12 *OC* 1, 179; *Visions of Excess* 15.

13 *OC* 1, 220; *Visions of Excess* 45.

14 *OC* 1, 225; *Visions of Excess* 51.

15 *OC* 1, 225; *Visions of Excess* 50.

16 *OC* 1, 319; *Visions of Excess* 129.

17 *OC* 1, 217; *Visions of Excess* 31.

18 *OC* 1, 230; *Visions of Excess* 55.

19 *Documents*, 4; Brotchie, *Encyclopedia Acephalica*, pp. 99–106.

20 *OC* 1, 221; *Visions of Excess* 46, 48.

21 *OC* 11, 572; *The Absence of Myth* 31.

22 *Romans* 150; *Blue of Noon* 68.

7 Excremental Philosopher

1 See André Breton, *Manifestos of Surrealism* (Ann Arbor, 1969).
2 Michael Richardon's collection of Bataille's 'writings on Surrealism', *The Absence of Myth*, is thus doubly disingenuous. By collecting its disparate pieces into a 'book', Richardson forces a liaison between Bataille and Surrealism that never took place. Second, by isolating those writings from the rest of Bataille's work as 'writings on Surrealism', Richardson draws the rest of Bataille's work away from Surrealism, to which it is surely proximate. Bataille often writes *against* Surrealism but that does not make him a Surrealist. This theme will develop as we proceed.
3 See 'The Castrated Lion' and 'Notes on the Publication of "Un Cadavre"', in *OC* 1, 218 ff.; *The Absence of Myth* 28–33.
4 *OC* 2, 93; *Visions of Excess* 32.
5 *Romans* 364; *Story of the Eye* 99.
6 Georges Bataille, 'Le Cadavre maternel', in *OC* 2, 130.
7 *Romans* 130; *Blue of Noon* 38.
8 *Romans* 156; *Blue of Noon* 76.
9 Bataille reviewed *Psychopathia sexualis* in *La Critique Sociale*, 3 (October 1931). He reports reading the 'extraordinary' book in a letter to Raymond Queneau dated 6 September 1931.

8 The Democratic Communist Circle

1 *Lettres* 62 ff.
2 *Lettres* 68; *OC* 1, 275–6, 291–4, 328.
3 See Marina Galletti, ed., *L'Apprenti Sorcier* (Paris, 1999), p. 86.
4 See Michel Surya, *Georges Bataille* (London, 2002), p. 522.
5 Partially translated as Alexandre Kojève, *Introduction to the Reading of Hegel* (Ithaca, 1980).
6 *OC* 6, 416.
7 Raymond Queneau, 'Premières confrontations avec Hegel', *Critique*, 195–6 (August–September 1963).
8 *OC* 5, 20, 259; *Inner Experience* 8; *Guilty* 24.
9 *OC* 1, 337.

10 *OC* 1, 662.

11 *OC* 1, 339; *Visions of Excess* 160.

12 *OC* 7, 285; *Theory of Religion* 9.

13 *OC* 12, 621; *The Tears of Eros* 149.

14 Marcel Mauss and Henri Hubert, *Sacrifice: Its Nature and Function* (Paris, 1898).

15 *OC* 1, 90–96; *Visions of Excess* 130–36.

16 *OC* 5, 83; *Inner Experience* 69.

17 *OC* 1, 313; *Visions of Excess* 124.

18 *OC* 1, 317; *Visions of Excess* 127.

19 *OC* 1, 309; *Visions of Excess* 121.

20 See Simone Pétrement, *La Vie de Simone Weil* (Fayard, 1973), p. 306.

9 Crisis

1 *OC* 2, 262.

2 *OC* 2, 253–62.

3 Marina Galletti, ed., *L'Apprenti Sorcier* (Paris, 1999), p. 112.

4 Laure, *The Collected Writings* (San Francisco, 1995), p. 238.

5 *OC* 5, 364; *Guilty* 117.

6 *OC* 5, 91; *Inner Experience* 75–6.

7 Laure, *The Collected Writings*, p. 239.

8 See Laure, *The Collected Writings* and Laure, *Une Rupture* (Paris, 1999).

9 See Jean Bernier, *L'Amour de Laure* (Paris, 1978).

10 Laure, *The Collected Writings*, p. 92.

11 Laure, *The Collected Writings*, p. 238.

12 Laure, *The Collected Writings*, pp. 59, 111.

13 Laure, *The Collected Writings*, p. 134.

14 Laure, *The Collected Writings*, p. 133.

15 Laure, *The Collected Writings*, pp. 89, 237.

16 Laure, *The Collected Writings*, p. 237.

17 *OC* 7, 461; *My Mother* 219.

18 Laure, *Une Rupture*, p. 55.

19 Laure, *Une Rupture*, p. 122.

20 Laure, *Une Rupture*, p. 69.

21 Laure, *Une Rupture*, p. 100.

22 *Lettres* 88.

23 *Lettres* 90.

24 *Lettres* 92.

25 *Lettres* 93–4.

26 *Lettres* 98.

10 Counter Attack

1 Boris Souvarine, 'Prologue', *La Critique sociale* (Paris, 1983).

2 *OC* 7, 459; *My Mother* 219.

3 *Romans* 121; *Blue of Noon* 23.

4 Simone Pétremont, *La Vie de Simone Weil* (Paris, 1973), p. 308.

5 *Romans* 112; *Blue of Noon* 154.

6 *Romans* 122; *Blue of Noon* 24.

7 *Romans* 205; *Blue of Noon* 151.

8 *Romans* 133; *Blue of Noon* 42.

9 See *Romans* 1036 ff.

10 *Romans* 112; *Blue of Noon* 154.

11 Marina Galletti, ed., *L'Apprenti Sorcier* (Paris, 1999) is the essential sourcebook on the evolution of Bataille's political thought and involvement during this era. On Counter Attack see pp. 119–298.

12 Galletti, *L'Apprenti Sorcier*, p. 124.

13 Georges Bataille and Michel Leiris, *Échanges et correspondances* (Paris, 2004), p. 210.

14 *OC* 1, 379.

15 *OC* 1, 380.

16 *OC* 1, 411; *Visions of Excess* 167.

17 *OC* 1, 382.

18 *OC* 1, 392.

19 *OC* 1, 398.

20 Reprinted in *OC* 1, 672–3.

11 Acéphale

1 Marina Galletti, ed., *L'Apprenti Sorcier* (Paris, 1999), p. 282.

2 *OC* 1, 446; *Visions of Excess* 181.

3 Galletti, *L'Apprenti Sorcier*, p. 478.

4 *OC* 1, 446; *Visions of Excess* 181.

5 Ibid.

6 See Galletti, *L'Apprenti Sorcier*, p. 336.

7 *OC* 8, 171; *The Absence of Myth* 36.

8 See Michel Surya, *Georges Bataille* (London, 2002), p. 227.

9 Galletti, *L'Apprenti sorcier*, p. 433.

10 Laure, *The Collected Writings* (San Francisco, 1995), pp. 58ff.

11 Galletti, *L'Apprenti Sorcier*, p. 307.

12 Galletti, *L'Apprenti Sorcier*, p. 370.

13 *OC* 1, 443; *Visions of Excess* 178.

14 *OC* 1, 443; *Visions of Excess* 179.

15 *OC* 2, 392ff.

16 *OC* 1, 557; *Visions of Excess* 239.

17 Galletti, *L'Apprenti Sorcier*, p. 480.

18 *OC* 6, 373.

19 *OC* 1, 512; *Visions of Excess* 221.

20 *OC* 1, 504; *Visions of Excess* 215.

21 Galletti, *L'Apprenti Sorcier*, p. 375.

22 *OC* 1, 443; *Visions of Excess* 179.

23 *OC* 1, 554; *Visions of Excess* 236.

24 Galletti, *L'Apprenti Sorcier*, p. 382.

25 Galletti, *L'Apprenti Sorcier*, pp. 464–5; *OC* 2, 385–6.

12 The College of Sociology

1 *OC* 7, 461; *My Mother* 220.

2 *OC* 2, 444.

3 *OC* 5, 499–500; Laure, *The Collected Writings* (San Francisco, 1995), p. 247.

4 See Denis Hollier, ed., *Le Collège de sociologie* (Paris, 1995). An earlier, incomplete, edition of this book is available in English, *The College of Sociology, 1937–1939* (Minneapolis, 1988). See also Georges Bataille, *La Sociologie sacrée du monde contemporain* (Paris, 2004).

5 Hollier, *Le Collège de sociologie*, p. 53; *The College of Sociology, 1937–1939,*

p. 82.

6 Hollier, *Le Collège de sociologie*, p. 75–6; *The College of Sociology, 1937–1939*, p. 90; *Guilty* 123.

7 Laure, *The Collected Writings*, p. 86.

8 See Marcel Moré, 'Georges Bataille and the Death of Laure', in Laure, *The Collected Writings*, pp. 240–45.

9 *OC* 5, 505; Laure, *The Collected Writings*, p. 251.

10 See *OC* 1, 562; *Visions of Excess* 242.

11 Laure, *The Collected Writings*, pp. 41–5.

12 *OC* 5, 505–6; Laure, *The Collected Writings*, pp. 252–4.

13 See *OC* 1, 563; *Visions of Excess* 244.

14 *OC* 5, 501; Laure, *The Collected Writings*, p. 249.

15 *OC* 2, 377–99.

16 Hollier, *Le Collège de sociologie*, p. 819; *The College of Sociology, 1937–1939*, p. 354.

17 Hollier, *Le Collège de sociologie*, p. 806; *The College of Sociology, 1937–1939*, p. 337.

13 War

1 *OC* 5, 246; *Guilty* 11.

2 *OC* 5, 247; *Guilty* 13.

3 *Lettres* 176.

4 *OC* 5, 264; *Guilty* 28.

5 *OC* 5, 267; *Guilty* 31.

6 *OC* 5, 246; *Guilty* 12.

7 *OC* 5, 250; *Guilty* 15.

8 *OC* 5, 262; *Guilty* 26.

9 See Laure, *The Collected Writings* (San Francisco, 1995), pp. 37–94.

10 Laure, *The Collected Writings*, p. 87.

11 *OC* 5, 509.

12 *OC* 5, 515.

13 *OC* 5, 521.

14 See Michel Surya, *Georges Bataille* (London, 2002), p. 282.

15 *OC* 5, 23; *Inner Experience* 11.

16 *OC* 2, 510. The English version of *Guilty* translates '*crucifier*' as 'tor-

ment', see p. 22.

17 Patrick Waldberg, 'Acéphalogramme', *Magazine Littéraire*, 331 (April 1995); reprint in Marina Galletti, ed., *L'Apprenti Sorcier* (Paris, 1999), pp. 584–97.

18 *OC* 5, 251; *Guilty* 17.

19 See James Frazer, *The Golden Bough* (London, 1922), pp. 187ff.

20 *OC* 5, 278; *Guilty* 41.

21 See *Digraphe* 17 (1978), pp. 121–39.

22 *OC* 7, 181–281, 502–98.

23 *OC* 7, 21; *The Accursed Share* 11.

24 *OC* 7, 20; *The Accursed Share* 10.

14 Beyond Poetry

1 *OC* 7, 461; *My Mother* 221.

2 Laure, *The Collected Writings* (San Francisco, 1995), p. 50.

3 *Romans* 338; *Madame Edwarda* in Bataille, *My Mother*, p. 158.

4 *OC* 5, 69; *Inner Experience* 54.

5 *OC* 5, 72; *Inner Experience* 57–8.

6 *OC* 5, 66; *Inner Experience* 52.

7 *OC* 5, 19; *Inner Experience* 7.

8 *OC* 5, 59; *Inner Experience* 46.

9 *OC* 5, 60; *Inner Experience* 46.

10 *The Complete Poetry and Prose of William Blake*, ed. David V. Erdman (New York, 1988), p. 154.

11 *OC* 6, 373.

12 *OC* 5, 109; *Inner Experience* 92.

13 *OC* 5, 47; *Inner Experience* 35.

14 *OC* 5, 28–29; *Inner Experience* 16.

15 *OC* 5, 67; *Inner Experience* 53.

16 *OC* 5, 177; *Inner Experience* 153.

17 *OC* 6, 285; *The Unfinished System of Nonknowledge* 11.

18 *OC* 6, 286; *The Unfinished System of Nonknowledge* 12–13.

19 Ibid.

20 See Christophe Bident, *Maurice Blanchot: Partenaire Invisible* (Paris, 1998), pp. 272ff.

21 *Lettres* 192.
22 See 'Discussion on Sin', *OC* 6, 314–59; *The Unfinished System of Nonknowledge* 26–74.
23 *OC* 6, 90; *On Nietzsche* 75.
24 *Lettres* 230.
25 *Lettres* 231.
26 *OC* 5, 395, 403, 416; *Guilty* 147, 152, 160.

15 Between Surrealism and Existentialism

1 Quoted in *Lettres* 402, footnote.
2 See Sylvie Patron, *Critique, 1946–1996, une encyclopédie de l'esprit moderne* (Paris, 1999).
3 *Lettres* 290.
4 Volumes VII and XI, as well as portions of III, V, IX, and X.
5 *Lettres* 392.
6 *OC* 11, 31; *The Absence of Myth* 49.
7 *OC* 5, 194; *The Unfinished System of Nonknowledge* 77.
8 *OC* 11, 32; *The Absence of Myth* 51.
9 *Troisième Convoi* was reissued in one volume by Editions Farrago in 1998.
10 Bataille also revised *Story of the Eye* thoroughly enough to warrant including both this new version and the older original in his complete works.
11 *OC* 7, 23; *The Accursed Share* 191.
12 See Jean Maquet, 'Les Conférences du "collège philosophique"', *Critique*, 31 (December 1948).

16 *Summa*

1 *Lettres* 394.
2 See 'La Trahison en liberté', *Les Lettres françaises*, 317 (22 June 1950).
3 *OC* 11, 18; 'Letter to René Char on the Incompatibilities of the Writer', in Allan Stoekl, ed., *On Bataille, Yale French Studies*, 78 (1990), p. 33.
4 *OC* 11, 22; 'Letter to René Char on the Incompatibilities of the Writer',

p. 37.

5 *OC* 11, 17; 'Letter to René Char on the Incompatibilities of the Writer',
   p. 32.

6 See my introduction to *The Unfinished System of Nonknowledge* for a
   more detailed discussion of this process.

7 See 'A propos de récits d'habitants d'Hiroshima', *Critique*, 8–9
   (January–February 1947), pp. 126–40 [*OC* 11, 172–88]; 'Sartre', *Critique*,
   12 (May 1947), pp. 471–3 [*OC* 11, 226–8]; 'Réflexions sur le bourreau et
   la victime', *Critique*, 17 (October 1947), pp. 337–42 [*OC* 11, 262–8];
   'Caprice et machinerie d'État à Stalingrad', *Critique*, 36 (May 1949),
   pp. 447–54 [*OC* 11, 472–80]; 'La guerre et la philosophie du sacré',
   Critique, 45 (February 1951), pp. 133–43 [*OC* 12, 47–57]; 'La Civilization
   et la guerre', *Critique*, 47 (April 1951), pp. 363–7 [*OC* 12, 74–8]; and
   'Racisme', *Critique*, 48 (May 1951), pp. 460–63 [*OC* 12, 95–100].

8 *OC* 8, 11; *The Accursed Share II & III* 16.

9 Just as Sade's quintessential sovereign – Justine's sister Juliette – is
   female, the quintessential sovereigns of Bataille's fictions are female:
   Simone, Dirty, Edwarda, Hélène.

10 *OC* 7, 406–42.

11 See *Lettres* 471.

12 *OC* 8, 110; *The Accursed Share II & III* 127.

13 See 'Le Temps de la révolte', *Critique*, 55 (December 1951), pp. 1019–27
   and 56 (January 1952), pp. 29–41 [*OC* 12, 149–56] and 'L'Affaire de
   "L'Homme révolté"' *Critique*, 62 (July 1952), pp. 1077–82 [*OC* 12,
   230–36].

14 *Botteghe Oscure*, 9 (1952), pp. 23–38; *OC* 12, 195–208; *The Unfinished
   System of Nonknowledge* 185–95.

15 See *Tel Quel*, 10 (Summer 1962); *OC* 8, 190–233; *The Unfinished System
   of Nonknowledge* 111–50.

16 See *OC* 8, 563–92; *The Unfinished System of Nonknowledge* 153–82.

17 *OC* 5, 231; *The Unfinished System of Nonknowledge* 206.

18 See Gabriel Marcel, 'The Refusal of Salvation and the Exaltation of the
   Man of Absurdity', in *Homo Viator: Introduction to the Metaphysics of
   Hope*, trans. Emma Craufurd (New York, 1962), pp. 185–212.

19 See Georges Bataille, *The Cradle of Humanity: Prehistoric Art and
   Culture*, ed. Stuart Kendall, (New York, 2005).

20 'Kafka devant la critique communiste', *Critique*, 41 (October 1950);

'Nietzsche et Jésus selon Gide et Jaspers', *Critique*, 42 (November 1950); 'Nietzsche à la lumière du marxisme', *84*, 17 (January–February 1951) and 'Nietzsche et Thomas Mann', *Synthèses*, 60 (May 1951).

21 'Le paradoxe de la mort et la pyramide', *Critique*, 74 (July 1953); 'Le communisme et la stalinisme', *Critique*, 72–3 (May–June 1953).

22 *OC* 8, 248; *The Accursed Share II & III* 198.

23 *OC* 8, 286; *The Accursed Share II & III* 241.

24 *OC* 8, 258; *The Accursed Share II & III* 208.

17 Unfinished

1 Michel Surya, *Georges Bataille* (London, 2002), p. 474.

2 *OC* 10, 588; *The Tears of Eros* 36.

3 See, in particular, André Malraux, *The Voices of Silence* (Princeton, 1978), pp. 99ff.

4 *OC* 9, 130; *Manet* 49.

5 *OC* 9, 142; *Manet* 67.

6 *OC* 9, 119; *Manet* 24.

7 *OC* 9, 159; *Manet* 110.

8 'Sade, 1740–1814', *Critique*, 78 (November 1953), pp. 989–6 [*OC* 12, 295–303]; 'Hors des limites', *Critique*, 81 (February 1954), pp. 99–104 [*OC* 12, 305–11]; 'Le paradoxe de l'érotisme', *La Nouvelle NRF*, 29 (May 1955), pp. 834–9 [*OC* 12, 321–5]; 'L'érotisme ou la mise en question de l'être', *Les Lettres Nouvelles*, 36 (March 1956), pp. 321–30 and 37 (April 1956), pp. 514–24 [*OC* 12, 395–413]; and 'L'érotisme, soutien de la morale', *Arts*, 641 (23–9 October 1957), pp. 1, 3 [*OC* 12, 467–73].

9 See *Lettres* 446–8.

10 *Lettres* 467.

11 *OC* 12, 455.

12 See 'Hemingway à la lumière de Hegel', *Critique*, 70 (March 1953), pp. 195–210 [*OC* 12, 243–58]; 'Hegel, la mort et le sacrifice', *Deucalion*, 5 (October 1955), pp. 21–43 [*OC* 12, 326–47]; 'Hegel, l'homme et l'histoire', *Monde Nouveau–Paru*, 96 (January 1956), pp. 21–3 and 97 (February 1956), pp. 1–14 [*OC* 12, 349–69]; 'Qu'est-ce que l'histoire universelle?', *Critique*, 111–12 (August–September 1956), pp. 748–68 [*OC* 12, 414–36].

13 See *OC* 12, 642–5.

14 *The Tears of Eros* 3.

15 *The Tears of Eros* 11.

16 *OC* 10 627; *The Tears of Eros* 206.

Select Bibliography

Recent editions of Bataille's works in French

Choix de lettres, 1917–1962, ed. Michel Surya (Paris, 1997)
La Sociologie sacrée du monde contemporain (Paris, 2004)
Lettre à René Char (Cognac, 2005)
Lettres à Roger Caillois (Rennes, 1987)
Oeuvres completes, 12 vols (Paris, 1970–88)
Romans et récits, ed. Jean-François Louette (Paris, 2004)
Une Liberté souveraine, ed. Michel Surya (Paris, 2000)

Georges Bataille and Michel Leiris, *Échanges et correspondences*, ed. Louis
   Yvert (Paris, 2004)
Georges Bataille et al., *L'Apprenti Sorcier: textes, lettres, documents,
   1932–1939*, ed. Marina Galletti (Paris, 1999)
Georges Bataille et al., *Le Collège de sociologie*, ed. Denis Hollier
   (Paris, 1995)

Recent editions of Bataille's works in English

L'Abbé C. (London, 1983)
The Absence of Myth, ed. Michael Richardson (London, 1994)
The Accursed Share, vol. 1 (New York, 1988)
The Accursed Share, vols 2 and 3 (New York, 1991)
Blue of Noon (London, 1986)
The College of Sociology, ed. Denis Hollier (Minneapolis, 1988)
The Cradle of Humanity: Prehistoric Art and Culture, ed. Stuart Kendall,
   (New York, 2005)
Encyclopedia Acephalica, ed. Alastair Brotchie (London, 1995)

Eroticism: Death and Sensuality (San Francisco, 1986)
Guilty (Venice, CA, 1988)
The Impossible (San Francisco, 1991)
Inner Experience (Albany, NY, 1988)
Literature and Evil (London, 1985)
My Mother, Madame Edwarda, The Dead Man (London, 1989)
On Nietzsche (New York, 1992)
Story of the Eye (San Francisco, 1987)
The Tears of Eros (San Francisco, 1989)
Theory of Religion (New York, 1989)
The Trial of Gilles de Rais (Los Angeles, 1991)
The Unfinished System of Nonknowledge, ed. Stuart Kendall (Minneapolis, MN, 2001)
Visions of Excess, ed. Allan Stoekl (Minneapolis, MN, 1985)

Journals (*reprint editions*)

La Critique Sociale (Paris, 1983)
Documents (Paris, 1992)
Acéphale (Paris, 1995)
Troisième Convoi (Tours, 1998)

Selected books about Georges Bataille

Peter Tracey Connor, *Georges Bataille and the Mysticism of Sin* (Baltimore, 2000)
Georges Didi-Huberman, *La Ressemblance informe ou le gai savoir visuel selon Georges Bataille* (Paris, 1995)
Patrick Ffrench, *The Cut* (Oxford, 1999)
Denis Hollier, *Against Architecture* (Cambridge, 1989)
Francis Marmande, *Georges Bataille politique* (Lyons, 1985)
Arkady Plotnitsky, *Reconfigurations* (Gainesville, FL, 1993)
Michèle Richman, *Reading Georges Bataille* (Baltimore, 1982)
Michel Surya, *Georges Bataille: An Intellectual Biography* (London, 2002)
François Warin, *Nietzsche et Bataille: la parodie à l'infini* (Paris, 1994)

Acknowledgements

This book was completed with the aid of a grant from Eastern Kentucky University. Andrew Schoolmaster should be recognized for his generosity.

Vivian Constantinopoulos at Reaktion Books should also be recognized, for her understanding and for her instrumental role in the preparation of this book, which took far longer than it should have.

Vanessa Corrêa took several of the photographs included herein. She also read and commented on the manuscript as a whole. Her suggestions, needless to say, improved it immeasurably. For this, and for everything else, this book is dedicated to her.

Photo Acknowledgements

The author and publishers wish to express their thanks to the following sources of illustrative material and/or permission to reproduce it.

Photo © 2007 Artists Rights Society (ARS), New York/ADAGP, Paris: p. 131; photo Édouard Baldus/Library of Congress, Washington, DC (Prints and Photographs Division, LC-USZ62-62429): p. 136; photos André Bonin, © Editions Gallimard: pp. 6, 191; photo Maurice Branget (Roger-Viollet, courtesy of Rex Features, BRA-100671): p. 19; photo Louis Carpeaux/ Vérascope: p. 50; photos Vanessa Corrêa: pp. 144, 166, 185, 210.